Corporate Therapy
and Consulting

Mental Health Practice Under Managed Care
A Brunner/Mazel Book Series

S. Richard Sauber, Ph.D., Series Editor

The Brunner/Mazel Mental Health Practice Under Managed Care Series addresses the major developments and changes resulting from the introduction of managed care. Volumes in the series will enable mental health professionals to provide effective therapy to their patients while conducting and maintaining a successful practice.

Mental Health Practice Under Managed Care, Volume 5

Corporate Therapy
and Consulting

Len Sperry, M.D., Ph.D.

Brunner/Mazel, *Publishers* • New York

Library of Congress Cataloging-in-Publication Data

Sperry, Len.
    Corporate therapy and consulting / Len Sperry.
       p.   cm.–(Mental health practice under managed care ; 5)
    Includes bibliographical references and index.
    ISBN 0-87630-820-5 (paper)
    1. Psychology, Industrial.   2. Employees–Counseling of.
   3. Employees–Mental health services.   4. Psychotherapists–
  –Employment.   I. Title.   II. Series.
    HF5548.8.S6258   1996
    158.7–dc20   96-24807
                                                    CIP

Published by
BRUNNER/MAZEL, INC.
19 Union Square West
New York, New York 10003

Manufactured in the United States of America

10   9   8   7   6   5   4   3   2   1

Contents

Foreword

Psychological sophistication has increased among managers and executives, and since the end of World War II, there has been a parallel increase in the need for and use of psychological consultants. The work of traditional industrial psychologists made significant contributions to the selection and assignment of military personnel, the design of military equipment, and the assessment of morale. In addition, the progressive work of former chief of U.S. Army Psychiatry, General William C. Menninger, moving psychiatric services from the rear echelons to positions behind the front lines, gave rise to the concept of emotional first-aid stations, which, in turn, became the forerunners of what today are called employee assistance programs.

Menninger's work also led to his interest in prevention or keeping psychologically healthy people functioning well. In 1955, he asked me to take on the task of turning his interest in prevention into a functional reality. I spent the better part of the next 18 months reading the then sparse literature on prevention and interviewing all kinds of people who worked in or consulted with business, labor, and government organizations. I discovered to my chagrin that much of what we had to know about the treatment of people who become psychologically ill was almost unknown in management circles. That discovery led to my creating the Division of Industrial Mental Health at The Menninger Foundation, starting seminars for executives and industrial physicians on psychoanalytic aspects of leadership and the management of change and being part of a pioneering study at the Kansas Power and Light (KPL) Company.

When I began my research, I was also dismayed to find that there were so many brief, limited studies in industrial psychology, which provided little information and no way of integrating their findings into an assessment of the psychological issues in an organization. After a two-year study at KPL, the need for such a diagnostic method became apparent. To meet that need I wrote *Organizational Diagnosis* and taught a seminar on that topic for 14 years at Harvard University.

In the mid-1950s, a parallel development was beginning, growing out of social psychology, that resulted in the emergence of T-groups and their variants and ultimately into more systematic teaching of organizational psychology and organizational development. Now Organizational Development (OD) practice and consultation is widespread.

However useful some OD techniques are in helping people work together better, few practitioners in this field have a significant enough depth of understanding about people. Most OD work, therefore, is short-term and limited to relatively simple interventions.

The limits of OD together with the recognition, on the part of psychological clinicians, of organizational problems among their patients and clients and sometimes in the organizations in which they themselves worked, as well as changes in the clinical practice of psychotherapy, led increasing numbers of clinicians into organizational consultation. Many sought guidance and direction in brief seminars since there were no formal training programs for them. Repeatedly they asked the few self-taught pioneers in the field for such training in order to have a systematic way of learning how to undertake organizational consultation as well as for supervision and guidance. These early consultants who were also teaching could offer reading lists and, in some cases, suggest specific methods. But there was no basic text available that could establish a frame of reference for consultants of all clinical orientations.

Now, however, Len Sperry has formulated just such a text. *Corporate Therapy and Consulting* not only delineates steps clinicians should take as they begin as organizational consultants, it also sets those steps in the context of organizational methods and practices. It is, therefore, simultaneously integrative. Thus, it is a "first": a fundamental resource for clinicians who turn their sights on organizations and their insights into organizational and individual advantage. This is the text with which organizational consultants will start and that will guide them in a simple, direct, and systematic way, to an expanding literature that is congenial with their clinical orientation and experience. As they become more experienced, they will return to it repeatedly to broaden their horizons and as a point of departure for their own teaching and writing.

Today, 40 years after my own beginning in this field, I am delighted to write this foreword to a long overdue, basic text. For me *Corporate Therapy and Consulting* is a highly gratifying and significant landmark in the field of consulting.

> *Harry Levinson, Ph.D.*
> *Chairman of the Levinson Institute*
> *Emeritus Clinical Professor of Psychology*
>   *in Psychiatry*
> *Harvard Medical School*

Acknowledgments

This book has been "in process" for several years. My heartfelt thanks to the many "giants" in the field of psychological consultation who have influenced me in untold ways. Intellectual mentors include Harry Levinson, Ph.D., Manfred Kets de Vries, Ph.D., and Alan McLean, M.D. My appreciation to colleagues in the Division of Consulting Psychology of the American Psychological Association, as well as those on the GAP Committee on Occupational Psychiatry. The role modeling of Bill Humber, Ph.D., Peter Brill, M.D., Barrie Greiff, M.D., and Duane Hagen, M.D. has positively impacted my personal and professional life. Finally, I want to acknowledge the encouragement and assistance of Richard Sauber, Ph.D., editor of this series, as well as Natalie Gilman, Anna Nelson, and Maggie Kennedy, along with all those at Brunner/Mazel, for making this book possible.

Introduction

Today, no organization—be it profit or nonprofit, manufacturing, service sector, or health care organization—is immune from the forces of rapid economic and cultural change. We witness the harrowing consequences of this change in the downsizing and demise of once proud and emulated corporations, in the rising tide of workplace violence, and in work teams straining to survive in today's competitive markets. While "planned change" typified organizational life from the 1950s to the early 1980s, crises and instability characterize much of organizational life today. Traditionally trained organizational consultants are facing challenges never before imagined. Because they usually lack a clinical perspective and clinical skills, their ability to respond to a whole range of corporate concerns is limited. On the other hand, clinicians armed with an organizational perspective can address such concerns. This new breed of "clinician-consultants" will not necessarily replace traditionally trained organizational consultants, but rather will provide "clinical-organizational" interventions and services that complement traditional organizational interventions and services.

With an expanded vision of their role in organizational change processes and with additional assessment and intervention strategies and skills, clinician-consultants can readily meet a number of the challenges that modern organizations face today. At a time when many clinicians are seeking alternatives to traditional clinical practice, the prospects of providing consultation services to a variety of corporations and organizations—particularly those not usually serviced by organizational consultants, such as nonprofit organizations, health care organizations, and family-owned businesses—may be an exciting, challenging, and welcome option for clinicians who are willing and prepared to expand their practice options.

Specifically, *Corporate Therapy and Consulting* provides clinicians with an overview of the corporate therapy and consultation process and a basis for extending clinical skills to organizational settings. It illustrates conceptual maps for understanding behavior in organizations—both adaptive and maladaptive—and provides strategies for understanding and mastering the corporate therapy and consulting process: from contracting, assessing, and planning interventions to effecting organizational change and healing. These processes are described and illustrated with case examples.

Two audiences are targeted: (1) clinicians and mental health professionals who are becoming increasingly involved with rendering consultation to various kinds of organizations and who need the conceptual maps and intervention strategies necessary to perform this function; and (2) trainees and graduate students in various clinical and counseling, as well as organizational training programs.

The book consists of nine chapters. The first chapter describes the practice of corporate therapy and consultation and the role of the clinician-consultant. Chapter 2 discusses the process of becoming a clinician-consultant, including the requisite knowledge and skills needed to competently practice this type of consultation. Chapter 3 provides an overview of a strategy for understanding organizations and organizational behavior, while Chapter 4 extends the clinician's diagnostic understanding and skills to organizations and corporate concerns. Chapter 5 provides the reader with an extensive overview of the most common interventions strategies utilized by organizational consultants, while Chapter 6 describes common clinical-organizational interventions consistent with the practice of corporate therapy and consultation. Chapter 7 describes the psychological and organizational dynamics impacting executives and executive functioning. Chapter 8 describes three consultation intervention strategies with executives: coaching, consulting, and work-focused psychotherapy. Extensive case material illustrates these interventions. Finally,

Chapter 9 describes the consultation process in an area of great need: health care organizations. Several case examples of the application of organizational and clinical-organizational interventions are provided.

It is hoped that the book's discussion of the roles of the organizational consultant and the clinician-consultant and the similarities and differences between organizational and clinical-organizational interventions will provide the reader with a useful perspective and language. It is futher hoped that these distinctions will be helpful for those who teach clinicians and consultants, for those striving to practice at the nexus points between the clinical and the consultation realms, and for corporate leaders seeking assistance with the challenges of conducting business in this era of seemingly endless change.

1

The Practice of Corporate Consulting and Therapy

I fondly remember my early years as an organizational consultant. Starting in 1972, I functioned as an external consultant doing executive assessments, executive consulting and coaching, team building, management development training, and stress management workshops. Later, I became an internal consultant, functioning as Director of Staff Development for a large, multinational corporation that had been one of my early clients. In this position I designed and implemented a leadership development program and overhauled the corporation's performance appraisal system. I also supervised a staff of four Ph.D. organizational psychologists who spent most of their time doing executive assessments, career development counseling, training programs, as well as some test validation work.

Consulting to organizations, however, is very different now than when I first began in the field. At that time I had never heard the terms "corporate reengineering" or "downsizing," and while I facilitated the corporation's long-range planning, it was a far cry from the "strategic planning" consultation I do today. In those days, we talked a lot about "planned change" and "organizational development," but our interventions were narrowly focused and rather superficial, when compared with the kinds of changes organizations are undergoing today. So why is organizational consultation so different today?

THE PHENOMENON OF CHANGE

The environments of business and organizational life are radically different, compared to 10 years ago, because of a number of political, economic, and cultural changes. To better appreciate these differences, it is useful to clarify the term "change" itself. If change is thought of as the process of transforming the manner in which an organization acts from one set of behaviors to another, change can be either planned or unplanned. When I first began organizational consulting in the early 1970s, "planned changes," or deliberate and systematic change efforts, were common. These included implementing performance appraisal systems, initiating management development training, and the like. "Unplanned" changes such as a product recall, union strike, or the death of a senior executive were not particularly common crises. More common unplanned changes involved, for example, the turmoil created by an alcoholic or manic-depressive executive.

In the early 1970s I was never asked to consult on such problems as an employee stalking another employee, a hostile takeover, or an unexpected mass layoff of middle managers. In the past, changes were typically incremental or "first-order" changes, while today, changes are just as likely to be fundamental in nature or "second-order" changes. Table 1.1 defines the various terms involving change and the change process.

Twenty years ago, the external environments of organizations tended to be relatively stable. Changes—and even crises—primarily originated from within the organization, and consultants were sought to aid in managing these internal planned and unplanned changes; implementing management development programs and performance appraisal systems were among common consultation requests.

Today, both the internal and external environments of organizations seem to change constantly, with crises further exacerbating the levels of stress experienced by the organization's leaders and members. Needless to say, hostile takeovers, large-scale downsizing, unprovoked violence, and other crises have significantly increased the stressors associated with organizational life. Not surprisingly, consultation requests have likewise changed. Consultation is now

TABLE 1.1

The Terminology of Change

Change	=	Process of transforming the manner in which an organization acts from one set of behaviors to another; can be planned or unplanned, first-order or second-order
Planned Change	=	Deliberate and systematic change; may be policy driven
Unplanned Change	=	Accidental; without a plan or not policy driven
First-Order Change	=	Incremental change (i.e., stress management program)
Second-Order Change	=	Fundamental change (i.e., reengineering)

more likely to involve reestablishing stability between internal and external environments, as well as dealing with the clinical sequelae of change and crises. Instead of being narrowly focused on management development or performance appraisal systems, consultation now may focus on changing the organization's strategy, structure, culture, and team functioning in order to increase productivity and competitive advantage, while also attending to the psychological well-being of its leaders and members—including their clinical needs. While traditionally trained management consultants and industrial/organizational psychologists may be quite adept at effecting planned change efforts in organizations, they do not have the clinical background needed to effectively deal with serious psychological crises.

On the other hand, clinicians are trained to deal with crisis situations and their sequelae. As such, they have much to offer organizations beyond the provision of traditional psychotherapeutic services. With their understanding of organizational change processes and additional assessment and intervention strategies and skills, clinician-consultants can readily meet a number of the challenges that contemporary organizations face today.

I am not suggesting that this new breed of clinician-consultants will replace organizational consultants or that they should. Rather,

I am suggesting that clinician-consultants can complement the work of the organizational consultant. Organizational consultants have tended to consult with larger, for-profit corporations. But there are other segments or "niches" in the consultation market. There are many nonprofit community and professional organizations, as well as health care organizations and family-owned businesses, that have not traditionally been serviced by organizational consultants and that could be well served by clinician-consultants who provide corporate therapy and consultation or even traditional organizational consultation. Clinician-consultants should be able to develop expertise in one or more of the clinical-consulting areas described later in this chapter. Such "niche" consultation services will probably be a growth industry throughout the second half of the 1990s and into the next century.

Furthermore, health care reform will continue to dramatically impact the entire health care industry: insurance carriers, HMOs, PPOs, regional health alliances, provider groups, to name a few. These groups and organizations will need corporate therapy and consultation to survive. Ongoing power struggles and interpersonal conflicts are predictable as providers, case managers, and administrators attempt to coexist in this turbulent environment. It will also be needed for many other issues, including resistance to change.

WHAT IS CORPORATE THERAPY
AND CONSULTING?

The phrase "corporate therapy" was used in a feature story in the *Wall Street Journal* to describe how psychologists are now consulting on issues such as executive personality clashes and failure-prone executives (Naj, 1994). "Corporate psychiatry" was used to describe consultation with executives experiencing emotional distress (Sperry, 1993). Earlier, the phrase "occupational clinical psychology" described the application of clinical-psychological skills in organizational settings to the psychological concerns of employees and executives in order to enhance individual and organizational effectiveness and efficiency (Manuso, 1983). Essentially, occupational clinical psychology was used as a preventive measure or for health maintenance in organizations.

Historically, occupational clinical psychology has emphasized mental health and has focused on the "troubled employee." Harry Levinson, Ph.D., is one of the early pioneers in this field. He championed the role of what he called the "clinician-consultant"(Levinson, 1983) as distinct from the role of the traditional organizational consultant. Levinson believes that the clinician who provides consultation to an organization needs diagnostic and intervention methods for organizational work akin to the diagnostic and intervention methods used in working with individual clients and patients. Accordingly, Levinson's book, *Organizational Diagnosis* (1972), reflects the distinct needs and perspectives of the clinician-consultant. His clinical approach to organizational issues contrasts markedly with the traditional consultation approach of nonclinical consultants, as described in Weisbord's book, *Organizational Diagnosis* (1978).

Who are organizational consultants and how do they practice? Organizational consultants are a varied lot, representing training and development specialists, human resources specialists, management consultants, as well as industrial/organizational(I/O) psychologists. Those who are I/O psychologists practice as internal or external consultants to private and public organizations, including consulting firms. Those in consulting firms tend to serve large corporations with between 5,000 and 50,000 employees. They usually focus their consulting efforts on employee selection, organizational development, performance appraisal, and employee and managerial assessment.

Among I/O psychologists functioning in various settings, only a small percentage of consultant time is spent on personal and career counseling. Howard (1991) found that 73 percent spent no time doing career or vocational counseling, and 81 percent did no personal counseling. Among Ph.D.s who represent themselves as "consulting psychologists," a recent survey showed that they most often provided the following consultation interventions: individual assessment, problem solving, individual process consultation, organizational development, and organizational assessment (Kurpius, Fuqua, Gibson, et al., 1995). It should not be surprising that neither I/O nor consulting psychologists report doing traditional clinical interventions.

While the organizational consultant primarily focuses on organizational troubles, the clinician-consultant focuses on troubled employees. "Corporate therapy and consultation" is simply an extension of occupational clinical psychology in that it focuses on troubled employees and executives as well as on the troubled or troubling organization in which they work.

What do clinician-consultants who practice corporate therapy and consultation do, and what skills and competence are required? Clinician-consultants should already have basic clinical skills applicable to individuals and groups. Some clinician-consultants will have considerable organizational consultation skills applicable to individuals, teams, and whole organizations. Many clinician-consultants will not have such organizational skills, which although desirable, are not required. Nevertheless, clinician-consultants should have sufficient clinical-organizational consultation skills, particularly in the niche in which they choose to practice. It is important to emphasize that those wanting to function as clinician-consultants should not practice outside the scope of their training and licensure.

ORGANIZATIONAL VS. CLINICAL-ORGANIZATIONAL VS. CLINICAL INTERVENTIONS

What are clinical-organizational interventions, and how do they differ from clinical and organizational interventions? In the past it was relatively easy to distinguish clinical work from consultation work: the clinician typically did initial evaluations and individual psychotherapy—and sometimes couples, family, and group therapy—while the consultant typically did executive coaching and consultation, career counseling, and some type of team and/or organizational interventions. These traditional forms of consultation require considerable skill and experience and are usually provided by a variety of management and organizational consultants. With the changes in the nature and type of consultation needs, these traditional organizational interventions will still be necessary and useful, but I believe that the demand for clinical-organizational interventions will increase dramatically. Figure 1.1 illustrates the relationship of clinical, organizational, and clinical-organizational interventions.

Clinical-Organizational Interventions

Essentially, clinical-organizational interventions are clinically focused interventions applied to organizationally related problems in organizational or corporate contexts. They are therapeutic or quasi-therapeutic methods for either dealing with distressing or potentially distressing organizational issues or situations or for preventing them. Traditional organizational interventions, usually referred to as "organizational development" (French & Bell, 1995), are most appropriately utilized in instances where changes in an organization can be planned, that is, designed, implemented, and evaluated. Two organizational interventions that are currently in

FIGURE 1.1

The Interrelationship of Organizational, Clinical-Organizational, and Clinical Interventions

vogue today are strategic planning and culture transformation. Clinical-organizational interventions, on the other hand, are more appropriately utilized when changes are unplanned, such as in crises or to prevent or ameliorate crises. Crisis Intervention Stress Debriefing (CISD) and "merger syndrome" consultation are two examples of clinical-organizational interventions.

In brief, traditional organizational consultants utilize organizational interventions in dealing with planned change in noncrises contexts, while consultants utilizing clinical-organizational interventions are more likely to be dealing with unplanned changes, usually in crisis situations or to prevent crises. Table 1.2 lists a number of organizational and clinical-organizational interventions, as well as traditional clinical interventions. These clinical-organizational interventions were recently described and cataloged (Sperry, 1995b). You will note in Table 1.2 that disability evaluation is listed under both clinical and clinical-organizational interventions. Even though both involve a similar process, they can be quite different. When the disability evaluation is complete, with little or no concomitant investigation of the worker's organizational context, the evaluation is clinical. However, when the evaluating clinician assesses the worker's organizational context for possible determinants of the claimed disability and then assists the organization in reducing other occurrences of the disability, the intervention is clinical-organizational.

In short, today, there is an increasing need for clinical-organizational interventions, largely due to the current unprecedented amount of crises and unplanned changes occurring in the corporate setting. As noted previously, I believe clinician-consultants are particularly well disposed to providing these kinds of consultation services. Figure 1.2 illustrates the context for clinical-organizational interventions.

THE PROCESS OF CONSULTATION

Irrespective of whether one practices organizational consultation or corporate therapy and consultation, there are some basic similarities in approaching the individual, team, or the entire corporation within an organizational context. Like the psychotherapy process,

TABLE 1.2

Taxonomy of Organizational, Clinical-Organizational, and Clinical Interventions by Individual, Team, and Organization

	Organizational Interventions	*Clinical-Organizational Interventions*	*Clinical Interventions*
Individual	• Executive assessment consultation • Executive coaching and consultation • Career development counseling and consultation • Retirement counseling and consultation	• Hiring, discipline, and termination consultation • Work-focused psychotherapy • Outplacement counseling and consultation • Stress disability and fitness for duty evaluation and consultation	• Psychotherapy • Psychiatric evaluation • Psychopharmaco-therapy • Psychiatric disability evaluation
Team/Inter-group	• Team development	• Dual-career couples counseling and consultation • Conflict resolution with work teams • Conflict resolution in family businesses	• Couples therapy • Family therapy • Group therapy
Organization	• Management and leadership development consultation • Strategic planning consultation • Restructuring and transformation consultation • Stress management consultation • Performance appraisal systems consultation	• Crisis intervention consultation • Consulting on resistance to planned change efforts • Merger syndrome consultation • Downsizing syndrome consultation • Treatment outcomes consultation • Mental health policy consultation • Violence prevention consultation	• Milieu therapy

FIGURE 1.2

Intervention Type as a Function of Type of Change

	INTERVENTION	
	Planned	**Unplanned**
CHANGE **Planned**	Organizational	Clinical-Organizational
Unplanned	Clinical-Organizational	Clinical-Organizational

most models of consultation proceed through phases (Dougherty, 1990; Gallessich, 1982; Lippitt & Lippitt, 1978). The seven phases briefly described here represent the typical process of either organizational consultation or corporate therapy and consultation.

1. **Preliminary exploration and contract negotiation.** The consultant and the consultees—that is, the people with whom the consultant works directly in the client organization—explore the consultee's or the organization's needs in relation to the consultant's competencies, interests, and values. The task is to determine whether there is sufficient *fit* to justify working together. If there is sufficient fit, a tentative contract begins to evolve, possibly even resulting in a written contractual agreement.

2. **Entry.** The consultant now officially enters the organization and begins to get acquainted with and to explore the problems and concerns of individuals, work teams, divisions, and so on. Similar to the engagement phase in psychotherapy, the task is to get sufficiently "inside" the organization

to understand its general nature, establish open communication, and develop sufficient rapport and acceptance before continuing further.

3. **Diagnosis and formulation.** Similar to the psychiatric evaluation and formulation process, the task here is to gather and interpret sufficient data from interviews, observations, instruments, and review of appropriate records, so as to formulate a descriptive, explanatory, and prognostic statement of the actual problem (Sperry, Gudeman, Blackwell, & Faulkner, 1992). This diagnostic process includes examining the context of the problem and the organizational systems affecting it.

4. **Feedback, and setting and planning the intervention.** In this phase, the consultant meets with the consultee and provides feedback on the problem formulation and the proposed goals and feasibility of the intervention alternatives. Sometimes it is concluded that there is no realistic solution, that the goals can be reached without further help from the consultant, or that the consultation would require skills and demands outside the consultant's expertise or availability. However, if there is mutual agreement to proceed, the goals and intervention alternatives are discussed and negotiated in terms of time and money, barriers to be anticipated, and roles and responsibilities of consultee and consultant.

5. **Implementation of intervention.** Next, the agreed-on strategy is implemented.

6. **Evaluation of outcomes.** An evaluation of the degree to which goals have been achieved is conducted and discussed. The evaluation provides feedback for further decisions.

7. **Termination of consultation.** Termination may come at any phase in the process. Usually it comes at the end of the process, after sufficient positive change has been noted. Termination plans may include follow-up sessions to reinforce the change and reduce relapse. These include temporary task forces, the engagement of an internal consultant, or on-site visitation or telephone follow-ups by the contracted consultant (Gallessich, 1982).

CONCLUDING NOTE

There is an increasing need for a new breed of consultants to organizations that can provide clinically based interventions in organizational and corporate settings. By translating and extending their clinicial knowledge and skills, clinicians should be able to develop competency in clinical-organizational interventions. Chapter 2 describes the basic knowledge and skills of consultation and the means of translating and extending them in the corporate realm.

2

Preparing to Practice Corporate Therapy and Consultation

Increasing numbers of clinicians have become involved in organizational and clinical-organizational consultation. Even more are expected to enter this exciting and challenging area of practice in the near future for the reasons noted in Chapter 1. These clinicians-turned-consultants will parlay their clinical skills and apply them to organizational dilemmas, aiding troubled executives, work teams, and even entire organizations. Many will find this experience gratifying as they discover how to apply their clinical sensitivity to new environments. Others will find it frustrating, as they discover the many ways in which organizational consultation differs from clinical practice. This chapter addresses the training and experience as well as the knowledge and skills necessary to function as a clinician-consultant.

THE CONSULTANT'S TRAINING AND EXPERIENCE

Becoming a consultant to organizations involves a socialization process whereby the clinician begins to think and act like a consultant and is able to adapt to and find acceptance in the workplace environment. This is not to suggest that the clinician should relinquish his or her identity as a clinician; rather the clinician should extend his

13

or her role and repertoire of knowledge and skills to include both consultative and clinical dimensions. In other words, a clinician-consultant who practices full-time in a workplace context functions as a consultant, while retaining clinical acumen; whereas a clinician who is sensitive to workplace issues, who is involved in a clinical context, functions as a clinician with organizational acumen.

Essentially, the worlds of the clinician and of the consultant are quite different, for example, in the matter of roles and tasks. Consultant roles can be viewed as a continuum, ranging from directive to nondirective (Lippitt & Lippitt, 1978). In directive roles, the consultant acts primarily as an expert; whereas in nondirective roles, the consultant is primarily a process consultant (Schein, 1987) who facilitates the consultee's expertise. The most common role that consultants take on is that of expert or technical adviser (Gallessich, 1982). In this case the consultee needs the knowledge, advice, or service that the consultant can provide on request.

TRAINING IN CONSULTATION

Unfortunately, there is little training in organizational or clinical-organizational interventions in clinical training programs at present. Most clinician-consultants must acquire a knowledge base and skills through actual experience, with little opportunity for training, reflection, or supervision. Given the range of conceptual knowledge and skills that must be acquired, translated, extended, or unlearned to function effectively in the corporate setting, it is not unreasonable to suggest that the clinician seek opportunities to formally learn about and reflect on the transition to the clinician-consultant role.

But what formal opportunities are available? Perhaps the most common training opportunities are found in graduate schools of business administration or management, which offer credit and non-credit courses and seminars in such areas as organizational behavior, human resources management, organizational development, management consultation, and related topics. There are also a number of graduate programs in psychology that offer course work in industrial and organizational psychology. Summer training institutes are offered as well, such as the ones at Cape Cod and Door County, with well-known organizational psychologists like Harry Levinson and Edgar Schein.

As noted earlier, there is a difference between the knowledge and skill acquired through experience, without opportunity for training, reflection, or supervision, and the experience-based learning that has these components. At least one ethicist (Lowman, 1985) questioned whether a clinical psychologist can represent himself or herself as an organizational consultant without prior formal training or expertise and not violate the ethical standards of the American Psychological Association.

ACTING LIKE A CONSULTANT

While the clinician thinks and acts somewhat differently from the organizational consultant about formulating professional issues and concerns, the clinician-consultant combines attributes of both positions. To begin this discussion, it is useful to first compare and contrast clinicians and consultants before more specifically discussing the role of the clinician-consultant. The usual expectations and demeanor for the clinician are to limit contact with clients or patients to the office or clinic and then to act in a fairly focused, therapeutically detached manner. The consultant, on the other hand, is expected to have extensive contact with his "patient" or consultee, both in a professional and a social context. Dinner at an executive's private club, tennis or golf during an exercise break at a seminar, or a weekend visit to a chief executive officer (CEO)'s country home are not uncommon social contexts for the organizational psychiatrist.

Whereas the clinician may have a hard-and-fast rule against personal disclosure with psychotherapy patients in a clinical setting, the issue is more complex in a corporate social setting. There it may be inappropriate *not* to share some of one's personal life. However, to do so without constraint may ultimately be a disservice to the consultee. Still, the consultant must maintain awareness of his or her boundaries and the consultee's need for those boundaries to be maintained since transference dynamics often compel the consultee to want more informal, social, and personal contact with the consultant (Tobias, 1990).

The effective consultant must manifest certain attributes not usually expected of the clinician in private practice. First, organizational consultants should be able to mix comfortably with a wide variety of individuals, from factory workers and clerk-typists to CEOs. They should also be able to tolerate back-to-back meetings and conferences and to be comfortable with and effective at public speaking. Many consultants are expected to do a considerable amount of public speaking as well as formal and informal teaching and will spend considerable time in liaison and other educational efforts. Consultants should also be comfortable around executives who tend to be active, pragmatic, and quick to make decisions since this style contrasts with the more reflective, passive, and theoretical style of many clinicians. Finally, the consultant should be able to quickly size up individuals, groups, and situations because there is seldom the luxury of having one or more evaluation sessions as in a psychotherapy practice.

Regarding consultation styles, Nevis (1987) distinguishes between two very different styles or approaches to consultation, which he calls the "Sherlock Holmes" and the "Lieutenant Columbo" approaches. Holmes-style consultants formulate clear hypotheses and use clues and rigorous deductive logic to arrive at the truth. This style of consultation is particularly useful when clues are clear and unambiguous. But, as many consultants find, clues are often ambiguous, there is frequently no one clear solution, and the deductive logic of the consultant does not match the internal logic of the consultees.

The Columbo style is less formalized and more intuitive and can more easily contend with ambiguity. Frequently, Columbo-style consultants learn more from a wrong guess than from a right one. Whereas Holmes-style consultants tend to err on the side of arrogance, Columbo-style consultants would rather err on the side of humility.

In clinical practice, a similar distinction can be noted between the vigorous, empirical approach of the academic clinician and the relationship-oriented approach of the dynamically oriented private practice clinician. Clearly, the more useful and effective approach can only be determined by a conjunction of the consultant's style, client or consultee preference, and the type of consultation problem.

Ideally, both the Holmes-style and the Columbo-style approaches can be incorporated. For example, even in the most straightforward consultation projects requiring the consultant's expert opinion, it is still important to understand the underlying corporate culture. Likewise, both accountability and results are important, even in the most process-oriented consultations.

LEVELS OF INVOLVEMENT IN CONSULTATION TO ORGANIZATIONS

Now that we have compared the worldviews and practice styles of clinicians and consultants, we can attempt a description of the clinician-consultant's overall view and practice style. Not all clinician-consultants function in the same manner because most do not engage in corporate therapy and consultation activities all of the time. Following are five different levels or degrees of involvement for a clinician-consultant regarding organizations and work issues.

1. Clinical Practice with Sensitivity to Work Issues

At this first level, the clinician-consultant would be involved in a traditional private or mental health clinic practice and would see traditional outpatients but would have an awareness of and sensitivity for work-related issues. Accordingly, this clinician-consultant would take a routine, chronological work history from his or her patients, with particular interest in the present job and its demands, occupational hazards and stressors, relations with peers and superiors, "fit" between the patient as worker and the job, level of job satisfaction and commitment, hours and shifts worked, and level of balance among job demands and family and personal needs. This awareness of and sensitivity for work-related issues would likewise extend to subsequent treatment. At this level, the clinician would probably have some reading or workshop knowledge of the management and organizational behavior literature and would perhaps scan the business section of the local paper or read the *Wall Street Journal.*

2. Clinical Practice with a Specialized Interest in Work Issues

At this second level of involvement, the clinician-consultant would also be situated in a private or general clinic practice but would have occasional referrals from a corporate consultant, from its managed care program, or by word of mouth from executives who have been or currently are clients or patients of the clinician-consultant. The clinician-consultant's specialized practice might involve one or more areas such as work compulsivity with executives or professionals, couples therapy with dual-career couples, or work-focused psycho-therapy (see Chapter 8), and he or she would likely have developed a reputation among peers, and possibly in the business community, for this specialty, much as a clinician develops a reputation for treating, for example, anorexia or agoraphobia. At this level of involvement, the clinician-consultant would still view himself or herself as primarily a clinician. He or she would also include a work history in the psychological evaluation and be attentive to the therapeutic issues involved in work attitudes, authority transferences, and the like. Also at this level, it is expected that the clinician-consultant has developed sufficient working knowledge and skills to treat these particular clients and patients competently.

3. Part-Time External Corporate Consultation

At this third level of involvement, the clinician-consultant becomes more actively involved with the corporate world, either because he or she spends time on the corporate turf or communicates regularly with corporate clients.

This part-time designation means that the clinician-consultant is also involved with a private or clinic practice, academics, and so on. This clinician-consultant may consult primarily to employees and the staff of an employee assistance program (EAP), to a corporate managed care program in a consultation or liaison capacity, to executives or work teams, or even to organizations as an adviser, expert, liaison, or process consultant. Alternatively, the clinician-consultant might specialize in fitness for duty or stress disability evaluations and consultation.

Whatever the specifics, this clinician-consultant will view himself or herself as both clinician and organizational consultant. He or she will have formal or informal training in consultation, a reading knowledge of organizational behavior, and likely belong to one or more professional organizations or networks like the Division of Consulting Psychology of the American Psychological Association. The clinician-consultant functioning at this level should not be confused with the EAP or managed care consultant who does do case consultations but may have little or no knowledge or concern about the employee's work history or context.

4. Full-Time External Corporate Consultation

Whether in individual or group practice, this clinician-consultant spends the majority of his or her time on workplace issues. His/her identity is clearly that of a consultant with clinical sensitivity and competence, but he or she does not see himself or herself primarily as a clinician. This clinician-consultant may have a general practice with several corporate clients on retainer or provide niche consultation in an area such as disability consultation, dual-career couples consultation, or violence prevention consultation and may receive referrals from various businesses and insurance companies. This clinician-consultant will have an in-depth knowledge of the world of work, organizational behavior, and his or her specialty areas and may work in conjunction with a group of clinical psychologists, social workers, and management or technical consultants.

5. Full-Time Internal Corporate Consultation

When employed by the corporation as an internal consultant, this individual may function in specific roles and capacities with either employees, executives, or both, and is probably more a consultant than a clinician-consultant since the ethical issues involved with dual roles make it difficult to function as both clinician and consultant to the same corporation. Nevertheless, there are a number of advantages to being an internal consultant, not the least of which are a regular salary and benefits plan. Also an internal consultant might be hired with little or no formal training or organizational experience and through on-the-job training become a skilled consultant. Another important advantage is that the internal consultant has actual membership in the corporation and is usually seen by the client as "one of us." The external consultant, on the other hand, has only quasi-membership in the corporation and does not have the image of an insider. The internal consultant also knows the organization's history and its typical problems, patterns, and attempted solutions and can identify the key decision makers and the power and politics of the system, without needing to engage in the arduous diagnostic process that the external consultant must engage in.

There are, however, some disadvantages to the internal consultant's role. One is that it is more difficult to have credibility as an expert in the corporation. Steele (1982) referrs to this consultant's lack of credibility as "the prophet without honor in his own land." Similarly, by being viewed as an insider, the consultant may be taken for granted. Also, by being close to one group, the consultant may be perceived as "not objective," which will allow for scapegoating and stereotyping.

STRATEGIES FOR INCREASING INVOLVEMENT IN CONSULTATION TO ORGANIZATIONS

Below are some strategies and tactics that may be helpful for the clinician-consultant to become more involved in corporate consultation.

1. Begin to acquire an elementary knowledge of the world of work by studying a few general books on work stress and organizational behavior and a specialty book or two in your area(s) of interest–be it executive stress and work addiction, organizational change, dual-career marriages, women executives, or psychiatric work disability. Skim the daily *Wall Street Journal* or business section of the local paper; skim the local weekly business newspaper and one of the weekly business magazines like *Business Week* or *Nation's Business*. Carefully read the *Harvard Business Review* and *Fortune*.

2. Because much corporate consultation involves working with

task-oriented groups such as project teams and management teams, use every opportunity to study group dynamics and group process in your clinical practice. This includes becoming acquainted with internships or one or more therapists skilled in family therapy and group therapy. If you had little training or experience in these modalities during residency, volunteer to colead group therapy sessions in your clinic or practice with an experienced group therapist. If functioning as a group co-therapist is not possible, supervision— particularly supervision of group and family therapy—can be accomplished by videotaping your sessions and meetings and reviewing your work weekly or biweekly with an experienced colleague.

3. Take formal courses, workshops, and seminars on organizations, organizational behavior, organizational diagnosis, and so on, as indicated earlier in the section "Training in Consultation." This formal training may be available in schools of business or public health or in graduate programs in psychology. Attend courses and workshops on organizational consulting offered at the annual meetings of professional organizations, such as the American Psychological Association.

4. Become a member of your professional discipline's specialty group in consultation. This includes the Division of Consulting Psychology of the American Psychological Association for psychologists. Some state psychological associations also have divisions of consulting psychology. You might also begin to network with other members of these specialty groups in your geographical area.

5. Besides thinking organizationally, you should begin thinking of how you can sell yourself and how your developing consultative skills can meet felt needs in your community. The term *marketing* may sound somewhat alien to a clinician, but essentially marketing refers to understanding the needs of potential clients, evaluating and developing one's capabilities to meet those needs, and utilizing a variety of methods to bring potential customers (clients) in contact with the supplier (you as consultant). It is essential that you develop a well-thought-out marketing plan. Metzger's *Developing a Consulting Practice* (1993) is a readable and useful resource for developing an effective marketing plan involving both direct and indirect marketing strategies.

Your marketing plan may specify that you spend four to six hours a week in soliciting new business or clients, which may mean writing an occasional article or arranging to have your practice highlighted in a short article in the local business newspaper and offering to give talks at meetings of the local chapter of the American Society for Training and Development (ASTD), the Young Presidents Organization (YPO), or to personnel administrators. It may also mean writing a manuscript for submission to a national business magazine or journal, and if it is published, you can give potential clients reprints to further "validate" your expertise. Professionally, it may mean developing a consulting team composed of other full- and part-time members or subcontracting for technical consultation outside of your expertise, such as health benefits analysis or strategic planning. Finally, it also means that you may narrow or expand the focus of your practice.

THE CONSULTANT'S KNOWLEDGE
AND SKILL BASE

Developing an adequate knowledge base and skill competence in corporate therapy and consultation requires the transfer and translation of existing knowledge and skills, the acquisition of new knowledge and skills, and the unlearning, or at least disengagement, of previous learning.

Transferable Knowledge and Skills

The most obvious transferable knowledge and skills include clinical diagnosis and treatment. These skills have immediate relevance in organizational settings, given that the incidence of psychiatric symptoms is noted in about 25 percent of employees (Dauer, 1989). The abilities to listen, empathize, and respond therapeutically are indispensable skills in the corporate setting. Knowledge of human development and behavior and the ability to formulate individual and group conflicts and problems in psychological terms can also be transferred to the corporate setting. Finally, the ability to perform individual and group therapeutic interventions, or referrals for such interventions, is also transferable.

Translation of Existing Knowledge and Skills

With some effort, clinicians should be able to translate or extend the boundaries of their traditional clinical knowledge to corporate contexts. Considerable translation has occurred from individual and group psychodynamics to organizational psychodynamics, particularly by a small group of prolific psychodynamic writers (Kets de Vries, 1989; Levinson, 1972, 1973, 1981; Zaleznik, 1989, 1990). Some family systems concepts and dynamics have also been translated into organizational terms and contexts. Finally, a number of individual and group interventions have been translated for use with individuals and teams in organizational settings. This chapter describes several of these translations.

New Knowledge and Skills

Knowledge of organizations, organizational behaviors, consulting models, and the consulting process are prerequisites to the development of skill competency (Dougherty, 1990). For that reason, a solid knowledge base is essential. Chapter 3 provides an overview of the organizational dynamics that the clinician-consulant-to-be can extend by reading, taking formal courses or seminars, and having discussions with more experienced consultants.

Again, the clinician-consultant must acquire a body of knowledge and a number of new skills. These include understanding organizational systems and behaviors, the leadership process, and management principles. Numerous specific organizational consultation skills are needed, including entry, contracting, organizational diagnosis, and planning and implementing intervention strategies. These intervention strategies include, but are not limited to, career development, team building, developmental counseling, organizational development, process consultation, and mental health policy formulation. Knowledge of ethical issues unique to organizations is also required.

Unlearning or Disengaging Knowledge and Skills

Several previously learned skills and formulations are less appropriate and less useful in corporate settings. Foremost is the clinician's tendency to focus on intrapsychic dynamics and to diagnose pathology. In organizational settings, it may be more appropriate and useful to frame issues as having interpersonal and organizational determinants rather than only intrapsychic determinants. For example, a worker may be distressed and symptomatic primarily because of role ambiguity or conflict rather than simply because of personal pathology. A major challenge for clinicians in corporate settings is to use conventional everyday language, rather than clinical terminology, in speech and written reports. Finally, the propensity to conduct therapy must be reined. It is proper to engage in therapeutic talk with corporate individuals, but it is usually inappropriate to conduct formal therapy with them while one is engaged as an internal or external consultant. Usually psychotherapy is a matter of outside referral for executives or referral to an employee assistance program (EAP) for employees.

CONSULTATION MODELS

Four models of consultation, relevant to corporate therapy and consultation, are reviewed here: mental health consultation, clinical consultation, organizational consultation, and educational and training consultation.

Mental Health Consultation Model

Caplan (1970) distinguishes four types of mental health consultation. *Client-centered case consultation* is equivalent to the clinical consultation model discussed in the next section. It focuses on cases, and the goal is to diagnose the problem and recommend a solution. Most psychiatric consultation referrals in general hospitals and mental health clinics, as well as in the workplace, are of this type. For instance, the senior vice president for personnel may request a psychological evaluation of a junior executive suspected of substance abuse. In *consultee-centered case consultation,* which Caplan discusses in the most detail, the focus is on the case, yet the primary goal is increasing the competence of the consultee. For example, a psychologist consults with a group of shop foremen to increase their understanding of alcoholism and how its early signs can be recognized.

Program-centered administrative consultation focuses on a corporate program or project. The primary goal is to assist the consultee in planning, implementing, or evaluating a project, such as when the consultant is asked to help the EAP director develop a corporate-wide depression awareness program. Finally, in *consultee-centered administrative consultation,* the focus is on a program; however, the primary goal is to help the administrator function more effectively by increasing his or her expertise.

Clinical Consultation Model

Based largely on the medical model, the clinical consultation model is somewhat familiar to clinicians, especially those who have worked in an inpatient or other medical setting. This model conceives of problems in terms of a patient's disease or dysfunction, whether the "patient" is a corporate executive, a work team, or the entire corporation. Its primary goal is the diagnosis and remediation of the problem, and its success is defined by the remediation of symptoms and the restoration of normal function. A complete and comprehensive diagnostic workup is this model's hallmark. Levinson's diagnostic approach as described in *Organizational Diagnosis* (1972) exemplifies this model.

Levinson's case study outline is a rigorous and time-intensive method of analyzing the "patient." The case study report involves four major sections: (1) genetic data, (2) organizational structural and process data, (3) interpretive data about the current organizational functioning, attitudes and relationships, and (4) an analysis and conclusion section that includes both genetic and dynamic formulations with prognostic conclusions and recommendations. Levinson's approach blends psychoanalytic theory with systems theory. Unlike the mental health consultation model, the liaison function is limited in Levinson's approach.

Organizational Consultation Model

The basic assumption of the organizational consultation model, unlike the previous models, is that problems arise because the corporation's personnel lack the knowledge, skills, or values to function at optimum levels of effectiveness. This model is clearly not based on the medical model. Organizations—either work teams, divisions, or whole organizations—are viewed as "clients" rather than as patients, and the process—the "how"—is considered as important as the context—the "what." The behavior of individuals, teams, and organizations tends to be cyclical or repetitive and often counterproductive (Blake & Mouton, 1976). Thus, the primary goal of consultation is to identify and change ineffective cyclical behavior. Another important goal is to help individuals better deal with the complexities of corporate life in order to enhance their effectiveness.

The organizational consultant is either an internal or an external consultant who applies organizational and behavioral science knowledge to managing change and increasing the organization's effectiveness. The consultant utilizes a variety of interventions, such as organizational diagnosis, team building, executive seminars, strategic planning, and career and developmental counseling to achieve specific goals. Representative writings on this model are by Blake and Mouton (1985), Schein (1987), and Lippitt and Lippitt (1978). Chapter 5 describes several common organizational consultation interventions.

Education and Training Consultation Model

The education and training consultation model may be the most common form of consultation. Prearranged and organized consultant-led seminars, lectures, and workshops that are information centered—rather than diagnostic and treatment focused—exemplify this model. The clinician-consultant who presents a lecture on executive stress to a local Young Presidents Organization (YPO) group is utilizing this model, which conceives of consultee problems in terms of deficits in knowledge or skills. The goal of consultation is to provide the knowledge or skill training needed. Representative of this approach is the *Annual Handbook for Group Facilitators,* edited annually by Jones and Pfeiffer since 1972 and published by University Associates. This publication and *Instrumentation in Human Relations Training,* also edited annually by Jones and Pfeiffer since 1975 and also published by University Associates, provide user-friendly "lecturettes," background theory, training exercises, and short self-scoring instruments for use by consultees in seminars and workshops.

TRANSLATING AND EXTENDING CLINICAL EXPERTISE TO ORGANIZATIONAL SETTINGS

This section presents a number of concepts from the clinical perspective that have been translated and extended to organizational dynamics. Specifically, concept translations and extensions are noted from the psychodynamic, cognitive, behavioral, and family systems literatures.

Psychodynamic Perspective

Psychodynamic insights, particularly psychoanalytic ones, are prominent in the organizational literature. Perhaps the most famous psychoanalytic saying relevant to the workplace is that "the key to mental health consists of balancing love and work." Although this diction is usually attributed to Freud, and although he very well may have believed it, he never actually said it (Fine, 1990, p. 160). A comprehensive discussion of the meaning of work itself from a psychoanalytic perspective is yet to be presented.

However, there is a considerable psychoanalytic literature on work-related issues and concepts. General overviews of psychoanalysis and organizations can be found in Diamond (1993) and Czander (1993). Diamond (1993) offers an up-to-date synthesis of the classical, object relations, self-psychology, and interpersonal theories of organizational behavior. Kets de Vries (1993) offers a penetrating analysis of pathology in corporate leaders from an object relations perspective. Finally, Czander (1993) describes the application of classical, object relations, and self-psychology concepts to the consultation process.

Cognitive Perspective

Little is written from the cognitive therapy perspective on leadership and organizations. Ellis (1972) applies the concepts of rational-emotive therapy in his book *Executive Leadership*. Essentially, Ellis describes *rational sensitivity* as a means of clarifying and focusing one's thinking and emotions to become more tolerant, flexible, and open-minded. Increasing the executive's rational sensitivity can be accomplished through formal rational emotive therapy or through self-therapy using the rational sensitivity method. However, as a general psychotherapeutic treatment intervention, the cognitive therapy literature is replete with information on the treatment of anxiety, depression, marital problems, and personality disorders (Beck, 1977, 1988; Beck, Freeman, & Associates, 1990)—the most common concerns that executives present in psychotherapy. And cognitive therapy tends to be a good therapeutic "fit" for many executives because it tends to be an active, focused, and time-limited approach.

Behavioral Perspective

The behavioral view of work and organizations is primarily focused on the "what" of behavior and has little interest in the "why," in contrast to the psychodynamic and cognitive views. A basic premise of behavioral psychology is *positive reinforcement*. Essentially, work that gets reinforced or rewarded is work that gets done. LeBoeuf (1985) calls this the "greatest management principle in the world"—also the title of his book. If results are not achieved, then the right behaviors are not being reinforced. Rewards such as basic compensation, bonuses, and benefits packages, to name just a few, are based on this understanding. Serious research on the behavioral approach to organizations is regularly funded by the public sector as well as by the private sector. The *Journal of Organizational Behavior Management* is a quarterly publication reflecting this perspective.

Family Systems Understanding

A wealth of concepts from the family systems literature have relevance for understanding organizational behavior. The similarities among structures, roles, and functioning of families and those of organizations have been noted by many.

Structural family therapy as developed by Minuchin (1974) assumes that family members relate according to certain rules. These rules, whether explicit or implicit, provide the family with an operating structure. Applied to organizations (Hirschhorn & Gilmore, 1980; Short, 1985), structural theory emphasizes the structural subsystem of the organizational system and its hierarchical pattern. It also emphasizes the manner in which roles are established and alliances and coalitions are formed. The concepts of boundary, coalition, and homeostasis are central to structural theory and are particularly germane to understanding organizational behavior.

CONCLUDING NOTE

Preparing to function as a clinician-consultant requires a socialization process as well as the translation and extension of previously acquired clinical skills. Compared to organizational consultants, clinician-consultants are more likely to function in the first four of the five levels of corporate involvement described earlier in the chapter. In addition, the psychodynamic and family systems literatures provide a particularly rich resource of theoretical and practical aid for the psychiatric consultant in the workplace. The translation of psychodynamic and systems viewpoints to reflect organizational realities is relatively recent and will continue as more psychodynamic and systemically trained clinician-consultants engage in the practice of corporate therapy and consultation.

3

Organizational Dynamics

This chapter describes organizational dynamics, that is, the composition and functioning of a work organization. Five subsystems of the organization will be described, and the process by which organizations develop, adapt, and decline will be traced. The interface between individual worker, work organization, and family will be described next. This is followed by a brief examination of healthy and "sick" organizations. Finally, three models for understanding organizational dynamics conclude the chapter.

THE SUBSYSTEMS OF AN ORGANIZATION

Imagine an organizational system as a set of five overlapping, concentric circles representing the subsystems of structure, culture, leaders, workers, and strategy within a larger circle representing the suprasystem or the organization's external environment. Figure 3.1 illustrates this configuration, which is greatly adapted from Kast and Rosenzweig (1973).

Structural Subsystem

Structure refers to mechanisms that aid an organization to achieve its intended task and goals. The task is divided into smaller, person-sized jobs or roles and clustered into larger sets labeled teams, departments, or divisions. Structure specifies the reporting relationship of all roles, their span of control and scope of authority, and their

FIGURE 3.1

The Anatomy of an Organization and Its Subsystems

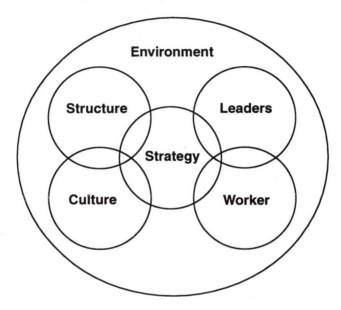

location in a hierarchy of roles–called an organizational chart. It also indicates the expectations of each role along with policies, procedures, and routines for interacting and communicating with others in the performance of tasks (Miller, 1990). Roles prescribe the boundaries of acceptable behavior for a particular job, while norms define group behavior. Norms are shared group expectations about what constitutes appropriate behavior. *Role ambiguity*–meaning the lack of clarity as to how an individual in a role is expected to behave– and *role conflict*–the inconsistency or contradiction in the messages about a role that an individual is to play in the work context–are often major sources of stress in an organization.

Structure also specifies the ways in which the person in a role performs. A formal means of measuring role performance is called performance appraisal. In addition, structure defines decision-making procedures, such as which information will be utilized and how routine decisions are made and reviewed, particularly the degree of control and participation of the person in a specific role or job title (Leavitt & Bahrami, 1987). Another basic function of structure is to control and coordinate information among the other subsystems as well as the suprasystem.

An organization's structure might be thought of as a "snapshot" of an organization's work process "frozen" in time so that it can be viewed. That snapshot could show a structure that is orderly or rigid, organic or chaotic, decentralized or overly bureaucratic, or divisionalized or fractured. Because of the interrelated nature of the subsystems, structure molds culture and strongly influences the decisions of corporate leaders (Miller, 1990). It can greatly account for a worker's job productivity and satisfaction as well as significantly impact health and well-being.

Cultural Subsystem

Culture refers to the constellation of shared experiences, beliefs, assumptions, stories, customs, and actions that characterize an organization. The major determinants of culture are the values held by senior executives, the history of the corporation, and the senior executive's vision of the organization. These translate into culture through the shared experiences, memories, stories, and actions of employees. The corporate culture provides a guide to action for new situations and for new employees. Culture is to the organization what personality and temperament are to the individual. Thus, culture defines an organization's identity both to those inside and outside the organization.

In their classic book, *Corporate Cultures*, Deal and Kennedy (1982) list five aspects of culture: corporate relations or business environment, corporate values, corporate heroes, corporate rules and rituals, and the "secret" network—the rumormongers, spies, cliques, and whisperers that form the "hidden hierarchy of power" in the organization. The culture of a corporation may be difficult to describe in words, but everyone senses it. It gives an organization its unique "flavor" and essentially is "just the way we do things around here."

This subsystem subtly controls the behavior of its members. Accordingly, management can influence its workers by effectively managing the organization's culture. Stable organizations have strong, clear cultures that are consistent with other subsystems. The general character of a corporation's culture tends to remain the same, but its manifestations may be healthy or dysfunctional.

The concept of "core cultures" developed by Schneider (1994), a psychological consultant, is useful in understanding the character or personality of an organization. Core culture refers to the innermost essence of an organization's culture and represents the culture's nucleus. As one moves from the nucleus to the periphery, however, one finds a myriad of different looking organizations.

According to Schneider, there are four core cultures in particular: control, collaboration, competence, and cultivation, and characteristics of all four core cultures can be found in a single organization. Like an individual character, a core culture develops naturally in the course of human events. One core culture in a given organization is not better than another. Each has its own mix of strengths and weaknesses and has its own role to play in the structure and conduct of organizational life. Nevertheless, a particular core culture may be better suited to a particular organization's mission than another.

Core culture is also intimately tied to leadership. How leaders of an organization believe things should be done drives the kind of culture that is established. Finally, the foundation of each core culture is reflected in its focus and in its decision making. In other words, each core culture is uniquely defined by the kind of input that is important to it and by the processes it utilizes to form judgments and make decisions.

Control Culture

The control culture focuses its attention primarily on the tangible, the practical, and the utilitarian. Its decision-making process is analytically detached, formula oriented, and prescriptive. The best occupational counterpart for this culture would be a surgeon. A surgeon has to get control, to stay in command of the situation, and to be very thorough and methodical. Surgeons must stay attentive to the realities of their task, and they must be analytically detached and impersonal when deciding what to do. Essentially it is a no-nonsense and matter-of-fact culture as well as a serious and highly realistic world where considerable emphasis is placed on objective certainty and on having information and methods that can be relied upon, and where discipline and predictability are very important.

Given its content and process nature, this culture is highly task oriented, particularly concerning daily tasks. Getting the job done on a consistent, regular, and current basis is very important, and strong emphasis is placed on rules and adherence to them. While production is clearly important for every culture, it holds center stage in a control culture.

The epistemology, or view of how something becomes known or believed, for this culture is distinct from the other three cultures. In the control culture something is believed when the organization's goals and reality coincide. Furthermore, the well-being of the organization as a system comes first, before customer or employee. Accordingly, the design and framework for information and knowledge in the control culture is built around the goals of the organization and the extent to which those goals are met and objectivity lies at its very center. How decisions get made in a corporate culture hinges on content and methods that exist outside people. In the control culture reality lies outside people. As a result, people are used essentially in the service of externals: what gets worked out and how the work is done.

Collaboration Culture

The collaboration culture focuses a great deal of attention on concrete, tangible reality; actual experience; and matters of practicality and utility. However, its decision-making process is people driven, organic, and informal. While the surgeon best represents the control culture, a nurse best embodies the working person counterpart in a collaboration culture. Nurses are focused on the immediate, real, and physical matters that pertain to their patients. Serving the sick, infirm, or injured has immediacy. Patients need to be treated now, not down the road. In addition, a nurse typically works as part of a medical team. Judgments about what treatment is needed and how to conduct it usually come from the team. The process is dynamic and highly participative and the relationship between the patient and the nurse is extremely important. What the two accomplish together—the synergy created—contributes considerably to the effectiveness of the outcome.

Synergy is the natural definition of success in the collaboration culture. Synergy itself captures the content and process of this culture where involvement and empowerment are important. There is no place for the helpless, or detached, or overly independent employee here. The dynamic process enables people to empower one another and deliver what is within each to the other in order to bring about something more. Interaction and involvement as well as harmony and cooperation are central elements in this "can-do" culture.

This culture probably puts more trust in its people than any of the other three. Because its content is immediate reality and actual experience, and its process is driven by connections between people, the risk of the organization being surprised by problems is higher in this culture than in any other. For instance, while the cultivation culture is also people driven, its focus on the future and on possibilities gives it more time to deal with unforeseen events. Accordingly, the collaboration culture must be more adaptive, ready, and able to make adjustments than the other three.

While the epistemology of a control culture involves the connection between the organization's goals and reality, in a collaboration culture, the connection is between people's experience and reality. The organization moves ahead through the collective experience of people from inside and outside the organization. Collaboration culture people know something when collective experience has been fully utilized.

Competence Culture

The competence culture focuses attention on potentiality, imagined alternatives, creative options, and theoretical concepts. Its decision-making process is analytically detached, formula oriented, scientific, and prescriptive. The best occupational counterpart to the competence culture is the research scientist. A research scientist focuses on what might be and looks at data, information, patterns, and underlying meanings and relationships. Anticipated outcomes or hypotheses drive the scientist's work as he or she investigates insights. The essence of science itself is to go beyond what we already know or have learned and to determine what else is possible, and theoretical development is often at stake. The scientist's process is the scientific method. This means that the scientist must stay analytically detached, objective, and follow prescribed formulas for making judgments. Possibility is determined objectively by the relevant scientific principles.

This culture is a world of external verification and merit in which objective feedback is probably more critical than in any other culture. Feedback provides external verification and tells the competence culture whether its output has merit. Life in a competence culture is intense and high-strung. People in this culture always have standards to reach and go beyond, and their work is rigorous and carries a sense of urgency. The norms are excellence, superiority, and challenge.

In the epistemology of the competence culture people believe something when conceptual system goals and reality connect. As a result, the framework for information and knowledge is built essentially around the conceptual system goals of the organization and the extent to which those goals are met. Also the competence culture has competition at its center. People compete with one another in a highly competitive world that has more stringent standards and problems that stand in the way of getting the job done. The more competent individuals are in this culture, the more effective they are at competing. In contrast to the collaboration culture, this culture is often a win–lose world in which discord is present and less competent people fail. Because superiority is paramount, inferiority stands out and is discredited. An organization whose goal is to create one-of-a-kind products or services instinctively fills the organization with one-of-a-kind people specialists to achieve that goal.

Cultivation Culture

The cultivation culture focuses attention on possibilities, inspirations, and creative options. Its decision-making method is people driven, organic, open minded, and subjective. The best occupation counterpart for this culture would be the religious steward, such as a minister, priest, or rabbi. Religious stewards focus on catalyzing and cultivating growth and development among their people. They strive to help people fulfill their potential, particularly spiritual potential. They also focus on people's inspirations and aspirations and herald ideals and higher level purposes. The content of the steward's philosophy is possibilities and potentialities, and the process he or she uses is highly subjective, organic, and frequently emotional. A religious steward emphasizes empowering people and unleashing that which is internal to them. This occurs both in the steward's own organization and with outside constituents.

The cultivation culture is very much a world of purpose, evolution, and change. Its organizations are magnetic, wherein the magnetism is caused essentially by the level of commitment that its people can attain. The cultivation culture gets results because its people believe in the purposes of the organization, in themselves and their leaders, in enriching their customers or constituents, and especially in their willpower and determination. In addition, this culture is value centered, and it highly encourages, indeed nourishes, self-expression. Employees are given every opportunity to be all that they can become, and they identify strongly with their organization.

The epistemology in the cultivation culture is determined by the values and ideals that are at its center. People understand when there is a connection between what they value and reality—when what is espoused is put into operation. Whereas attaining knowledge in the collaboration culture is based on experience, in the cultivation culture it is based on what people value or hold as ideal. Change is perhaps more automatic and natural in this culture than in any of the other three, since characteristics of this culture, growing, creating, and developing, are essentially matters of change. In clear contrast to the objectivity of control cultures, the cultivation culture is one of subjectivity. Decision making hinges on content and processes that exist within people. Organic, evolutionary, and emotional judgment rest within people. As a result, people within a cultivation culture work in the service of internals: what is worked on and how it is done.

Leader Subsystem

Leadership refers to a process of influence whereby an individual persuades, enables, or empowers others to pursue and achieve the intended goals of the organization. Leadership and management are terms that have been used synonymously until recently. Today, many endeavor to distinguish the two. They contend that while management involves the five functions of planning, organizing, staffing, directing, and controlling, leadership involves only one component of the directing function. They add that an effective leader creates a vision that tells members where the corporation is going and how it will get there, and then galvanizes members' commitment to the vision by being ethical, open, empowering, and inspiring (Bennis & Nanus, 1986). Not all agree with this bifurcation. Jaques and Clement (1991) contend that good leaders must be good managers and vice versa.

There are at least three ways of conceptualizing the leadership process. One way is to assume that effective leaders have the flexibility to shift their style from being "boss-centered"—called the autocratic style—to being "employee-centered"—called the participative style—to accommodate the needs of specific situations (Tannenbaum & Schmidt, 1958).

A second way is to think of leadership as combining two styles simultaneously but in different proportions. One style is task centered, the other being employee or person centered. Blake and Mouton (1964) plotted these two styles on a 2 × 2 chart or grid. This grid is divided into nine assessment points where the vertical axis represents increasing concern for people and the horizontal axis represents increasing concern for the task or production. Leadership style is evaluated by rating the leader's tendency to the "task" and the person" quality from 1 to 9. For instance, a leader who is rated at 1,1 is considered completely ineffective regarding people and production, while a leader at 9,9 is considered maximally effective. A leader rated at 9,1 would be considered as giving too much priority to people but unable to get the job done. Conversely, a leader at 1,9 would be adjudged as inconsiderate and too demanding of production. Leaders at the midpoint (5,5) show balance.

A third way of thinking about leadership, "situational leadership," considers three factors/"situational needs": the personal characteristics of the leaders, the nature of the organization, and worker characteristics. "Task-oriented leadership" is most effective in situations when all three of the situational needs or factors are favorable and least effective in situations wherein the factors are relatively unfavorable. "Relations-oriented leadership," however, is most effective in situations in which the three factors are only moderately favorable and in which only some factors are favorable (Fiedler, 1967).

The leadership subsystems play a critical role in shaping themes that harmonize the subsystems of structure, culture, and strategy (Kets de Vries & Miller, 1984). In Miller's aforementioned research, leadership style is characterized as either "craftsman," "builder," "pioneer," or "salesman" in the successful firms he studied and later as "tinkerer," "imperialist," "escapist," or "drifter" when these same corporations began to decline (Miller, 1990).

Worker Subsystem

Organizational researchers have largely neglected the attitudes of those in the organization who are led–the workers. Since an important key to a leader's success is the behavior of his or her subordinates, this is an unfortunate oversight. Uris (1964) has studied "followership" style and concluded that subordinates have a preference for either the autocratic, democratic, or "free-rein"–participative–leadership style. He found that workers function best with leadership that corresponds with their followership style. For example, a subordinate with an affinity for being firmly led, with little choice or influence, will respond favorably to the autocratic leadership style. The lack of match between leadership and followership styles probably accounts for a great deal of conflict, stress, and decreased worker productivity and performance.

Individuals do not work in isolation; rather they work for memberships in small groups as a way to increase their adaptability within the organizational system. These groups may be a formal part of the structural subsystem, such as work teams, or they may be informal. The informal group, also called the informal organization (Leavitt & Bahrami, 1987), is formed by workers, usually around a workplace issue or an outside activity. Actually, these groups accomplish much of the organization's work. Chance meetings at the coffee machine, impromptu lunch meetings, and informal telephone calls go a long way toward defining and achieving the organization's intended goals. Needless to say, the presence of a "disaffiliative" or hostile informal organization can seriously undermine the organization's objective.

Strategic Subsystem

Strategy refers to the organization's overall plan or course of action for achieving its identified goals (Pfeiffer, Goodstein, & Nolan, 1989). Corporate strategy is based on the organization's vision and mission statements. The vision statement answers the question: "What can the organization become, and why?" while the mission statement answers "What business are we in, and who is our customer?" Strategy answers the "How do we do it?" question. There are three levels of strategy: the corporate strategy, which charts the course for the entire organization; the business strategy, which is charted for each individual business or division within the corporation; and the functional strategy, which deals with the basic functional areas—for example, marketing, finance, and personnel—within the firm.

Strategy takes the form of a strategic plan, and the process of developing and implementing the strategy is called strategic planning and management. This process will be described in some detail later in the chapter. An important consideration in strategic planning is achieving a good fit between the strategic and structural subsystems, since a given strategy can best be carried out by a given structure (Miller, 1990).

Most organizations believe strategic planning is essential for corporate success. A key function of strategic planning is helping the corporation achieve its goals by effectively organizing its people. Yet, many firms struggle to achieve their goals, often because of a failure to link their business strategies with the ways in which people are managed. For that reason, the workplace psychiatric consultant can impact the organization by advocating that the corporate strategy includes both a business plan and a people plan (Sperry, 1991b).

Just as a business plan describes targeted business goals and results in measurable terms, the people plan must also detail "people results" in measurable terms. It is insufficient to just state slogans such as "people are our most important asset" or "our employees make the difference." Targeted people goals must be specified just as targeted business goals are specified. Examples of targeted business goals are: "We will increase our market share by 15 percent," and "We will increase sales by 20 percent." Examples of targeted people goals might be "We will have the highest productivity and cost containment scores in the industry," or "ninety percent of our employees will rate their supervisors as good or excellent on showing respect to subordinates," or "ninety percent of our employees will state that they are proud to work here." Such "people results" can be articulated, quantified, and assessed through surveys, interviews, or formal third-party observations. These results will also be manifested in job productivity, satisfaction, and morale, noted on a daily basis (Busch, 1990).

By attempting to incorporate both a "people plan" and a "business plan" into the corporate strategy, corporate leadership may need to change past management practices that resulted in high levels of stress, distrust, or dissatisfaction. The goal of integrating both plans is to achieve a reasonable balance and synergy between people and production (Sperry, 1991b). An effective integrative corporate strategy should positively impact all the other subsystems and probably will require changes in the structural subsystem.

These five subsystems interact and mutually influence one another. The configuration of these subsystems is also greatly affected by its suprasystem—the outside environment, especially during times of major changes, such as economic recessions, war, drought, and so on.

Environmental Suprasystem

The environmental suprasystem refers to those factors outside an organizational system that influence it and interact with it. The environment includes economic, legal, political, and sociocultural factors. It also includes technological factors, such as competitors, shareholders, customer demands, and standard industrial practices.

THE DESIGN OF AN ORGANIZATION

The design of an organization can be likened to the skeletal subsystem of a person, which provides a framework that supports the other subsystems. Organizational design refers to the overall configuration and interrelationships, particularly among the roles and positions in the structural subsystem, but it also reflects the configuration of all the subsystems and the suprasystem (Morgan, 1986). An organizational chart illustrates these positions and relationships.

The continuum of organizational designs ranges from the hierarchical or bureaucratic at one end to the adaptive at the other end. *The hierarchical design* takes a pyramidal shape, with a clear chain of command, strict division of specialized jobs, and a comprehensive set of rational rules and rigid guidelines. Communication and decision sending proceed from the top—the senior executive level—of the pyramid down through middle management and then to the worker at the bottom of the pyramid. Hierarchical organizations are designed for stable times and conditions and seem particularly suited to a manufacturing or industrial economy.

The *adaptive design,* on the other hand, emphasizes flexibility, horizontal communication, a low level of specialization and standardization, and high levels of cooperation (Forisha-Kovach, 1984). The adaptive design can be likened to a network where managers function much as switchboard operators, coordinating the activities of employees, suppliers, customers, and other stockholders. Large construction firms, like Bechtel, function in ways similar to the adaptive organization. They handpick crews of employees and outside contractors with the skills appropriate for each new dam, refinery, or airport project. In an adaptive organization, a skilled scientist or marketer who is a leader on one project may switch to the role of follower on a subsequent project. Obviously, the adaptive organization design is useful in fast-changing markets like computers, telecommunications, and publishing.

In between these two polar designs are the matrix design and the "flat" organization. The *matrix design* is common in medical schools with major hospital affiliates where the staff and faculty report to both institutions. The *flat organization* refers to a hierarchical design wherein there is a layer of executives and a layer of workers with few, if any, layers of middle managers (Dumaine, 1991).

ORGANIZATIONAL PROCESSES

Describing how organizations work is no small undertaking. The field of organizational behavior is devoted to describing and explaining how organizations work. This section focuses on four processes related to organizations: (1) the concept of "fit"; (2) the stages of growth and decline in organizations; (3) the process of adaptation or strategic planning; and (4) health and pathogenesis in organizations. A brief discussion of the relationship of worker, job, organization, and family dynamics completes this section.

The Concept of "Fit"

Achieving and maintaining a sense of balance and harmony is central to organizational well-being. In the organizational literature, balance is usually described by the concept of "person–environment fit," also called "person–organization fit" (Levinson, 1981).

Achieving balance and a good fit between person and organization is a challenge to corporate leadership and the consultants they engage. A basic assumption is that not all persons are equally suited to all organizations.

A second assumption is that a good fit or balance results in higher job performance, higher job satisfaction, increased self-esteem, and less stress. Similarly, dysfunctional responses to poor fit include increased level of stress, burnout (defined as a syndrome of emotional exhaustion and cynicism among employees who engage in "people work"), role ambiguity, and role conflict (Muchinsky, 1990).

A third assumption is that indications of poor fit do not necessarily reflect deficits within either the person or the organization. Rather, problems usually are functions of the lack of fit between the needs and resources of the person and those of the setting.

This third view is in stark contrast with the more common perception among many in management and leadership who assume that problems experienced by individuals are primarily due to their own constitutional or character deficits. Because an organization can significantly influence an individual's attitudes, behavior, and overall health, this view implies a "blaming the victim" philosophy. Similarly, the view that organizations totally control how a person thinks and behaves is one-sided. The person–organization fit model assumes some measure of joint responsibility. With regard to achieving change, the model involves matching individuals with suitable subsystems, rather than a modification of the individual or the subsystem (French, Rogers, & Cobb, 1974).

A fourth assumption is that fit between a person and an organization is dependent on matching each party's developmental needs. Arthur and Kram (1989) suggest that fit or reciprocity between the two parties is best understood in terms of their developmental stages and the representative needs of those stages. Synthesizing a wide variety of research on individual and organizational development, these authors specify three stages of personal-organizational development: (1) exploring-exuberance (the expansion and entrepreneurial stage), (2) advancing-directedness (the professionalization stage), and (3) protecting-stewardship (the consolidation stage).

A fifth assumption is that person–organization fit can also be improved or enhanced by altering the person–for example, by coaching, training, or even psychotherapy–or by altering the organization–for example, by job redesign–or by some combination of the two. If the environment is assumed to be fixed or balanced, corporate leaders might consider modifying their selection process or the type of employees they hire and train. Alternatively, if the leadership assumes that people are fixed, it might attempt to modify the organization.

Representative of studies that examine the construct of fit between an individual and an institution or organization is the work of Matteson and Ivancevich (1982). These researchers studied the fit, or lack thereof, between type A or type B behavior patterns in employees and type A or type B patterns in the organizations in which these employees worked. Dependent measures consisted of various health indices. As predicted, type B employees in type B organizations reported the fewest negative health symptoms, whereas type A employees in type A organizations reported the most negative health symptoms. Type B employees in type A organizations and type A employees in type B organizations reported an intermediate level of symptoms, as hypothesized, thus supporting the "fit" model.

Stages of Organizational Growth and Decline

Just as an organism develops and declines, so do organizations. Six stages of organizational growth and decline are described here: new venture, expansion, professionalization, consolidation, early bureaucratization, and late bureaucratization. These stages are adapted from Sperry (1990) and are based on the work of Greiner (1972), Adizes (1988), and Miller (1989).

Stage I: New Venture

Stage I of an organization involves the conception of a new venture. The critical tasks at this stage include defining a target group (e.g., hospital patients, high school seniors, middle managers) and developing a service that targets such a group. Accomplishing these tasks requires the ability to extend or create a market need; the willingness to make a risky investment of time, energy, and money to create an organization that satisfies the unmet need; and the ability to create an embryonic organizational structure that can provide that service to the target group. These abilities are characteristic of the entrepreneurial leader, and the entrepreneurial leadership style is most compatible with this stage.

Adizes (1988) notes three distinct leadership roles and patterns: entrepreneur, performance, and administration. Gerber (1986) similarly refers to these roles as entrepreneur, technician, and manager. The *entrepreneur* is the visionary and risk taker who is creative and innovative. The entrepreneur craves change and control over people and events and can easily transform an idea into reality and single-handedly give birth to an organization. The *performer* is the doer or task-focused leader who is diligent, dedicated, and loyal to the assigned task and focuses exclusively on what needs to be done. The *administrator* focuses on how things should be done. He or she craves order and the status quo and manages operating systems better than either the entrepreneur or the performer and is comfortable with bureaucratic matters. The more the leader is able to adapt his or her leadership style to the needs of the organization, the more valuable and effective the leader is.

Stage I primarily involves developing a basic system for day-to-day operations and finding individuals to staff the organization. At first the organization is likely to be quite small in terms of members and clientele, and thus its structure can be flexible and informal. Often there is little role differentiation among leaders and followers. Also the planning and development functions do not need to be formalized at first, and on-the-job training is prevalent.

Entrepreneurial leadership, especially when combined with performance-style leadership, is particularly effective in keeping the vision and embryonic organizational structure viable. The entrepreneurial leadership pattern lends itself to the autocratic or benevolent organizational style. Because of their visionary and risk-taking stance and their hard-won success, entrepreneur-performer leaders easily become the object of admiration. They tend to attract members who are in awe of the founder's success (Sperry, 1990). These members readily accept a dependent stance and easily acquiesce to the demands of the entrepreneur-performer leader.

Stage II: Expansion

Stage II is the stage of rapid growth. It either commences very quickly or after the organization has been in Stage I for a number of years. The major problems that occur in Stage II involve growth, rather than survival: Organizational resources are stretched to their limits as a new wave of members join the organization, demands for services increase, and the organization's rather primitive day-to-day operating system becomes overwhelmed. Organizational "growing pains" are disturbingly present. Growing pains signal that changes are needed and cannot be ignored; they imply that the organization has not been fully successful in developing the internal system it needs at a given stage of growth.

If the founder of the organization is unable to cope with the management problems that arise in Stage II, the organization is likely to flounder and even fail. Not surprisingly, the critical task at this stage is to develop an infrastructure of operating systems that results in efficiency and effectiveness. As this more complex operating system develops, the organizational structure becomes more differentiated. Basic human resources and management training become a necessity at this stage. Whereas little formal management structure beyond "doing what the owner said" was needed in Stage I, more managerial structure is needed in Stage II, particularly with delegation of authority.

Entrepreneurs tend to be less interested in the nonglamorous challenge provided by Stage II, as compared with Stage I. Thus, there is a need at Stage II for the administration dimensions of leadership to blend with the entrepreneurial. The entrepreneur-administrator style and the turmoil wrought by growing pains at this stage almost guarantee that members will begin to become disenchanted with leadership and dissatisfied with the organization itself. Member turnover and rebelliousness are manifestations of counter-dependency, particularly when leaders are slow to decentralize and share power or when they vacillate by proposing and then rejecting initiatives to delegate and decentralize the process (Sperry, 1990).

Stage III: Professionalization

Stages I and II represent the entrepreneurial organization. Even though they may have lacked well-defined goals, policies, plans, or controls, organizations in these stages have prospered. But once a critical size has been achieved, the structure and operating system must be further formalized. Another wave of new members requires more formal planning, defined roles and responsibilities, performance standards, and control systems. Developing a strategic planning and management system then becomes the critical task at Stage III. This, in turn, requires some sort of organizational development effort that provides the concurrent level of skill training needed to implement this management system.

Those in leadership must change and increase their skills and capabilities. The *integrative* leadership pattern is characterized by sensitivity and an orientation to people. Optimal leadership at Stage III involves a mixture of the administrative and the integrative styles.

Not surprisingly, an organizational climate that encourages consultative and participative management matches well to those who are able to function relatively interdependently.

Stage IV: Consolidation

After transitioning to a professionally managed system, the organization can focus its efforts on consolidation. Consolidation means maintaining a reasonable increase in growth while developing organizational culture. In Stage I, the organization's culture was transmitted by contact between the founder(s) and the members. In Stages II and III, the first wave of members transmitted the culture to the next wave or generation. But this informal mode of socialization becomes much less effective and less adequate with the subsequent waves of members. Culture becomes a critical concern in Stage IV.

Thus, in Stage IV, a more conscious and formal method of transmission is needed. Otherwise members may no longer share a vision of what the organization is or where it is going. As a result, members can begin interpreting culture in ways that meet their own needs but not those of the organization. So, first the organization's culture must be assessed, and the underlying beliefs and norms of the particular organization must be elicited. Examples of unhealthy beliefs and norms include: "Avoid conflict," "Set unrealistic performance expectations," "Avoid accountability," or "Poor performance is tolerated." Next, the organization must decide on a more appropriate and healthy cultural form; for example, "Two-way communication and conflict-reclamation are high priorities," "Set realistic performance expectations," "Quality is a concern," "Innovation is encouraged," or "Poor performance is not tolerated."

The organizational structure of Stage IV is a further enhancement and articulation of the organizational structure of Stage III. Knowledge of and commitment to the organization's mission statement and implementation strategies must be widespread throughout the organization. The mission statement must be reflected in both the orientation for new members and newsletters to existing members. Members are respected and prized, and, thus, human resources development and employee assistance programs (EAPs) will become integrated parts of the organization. Also members' horizons, knowledge base, and skills are regularly upgraded.

Leadership that combines entrepreneurship and integration is most compatible with Stage IV functioning. Note that while administrative leadership had professionalized the organization in Stage III, entrepreneurial leadership is needed to rekindle and augment the original dream and to motivate and challenge the organization, especially the fourth wave of new members. At Stage IV, individual members who are able to function interdependently with superiors, coworkers, and subordinates are most compatible with the organization's collaborative or participative styles.

The challenge of effective leadership is to assist the organization to arrive at this stage and to remain, and it requires considerable effort to grow and adapt to the constantly changing external environment—the suprasystem—in which the organization finds itself. As a result, self-renewal becomes the organization's basic strategy. Failure to strategically plan and manage the corporation can result in the organization's downward trend and decline. Stages V and VI describe this downward trend, which can result in the eventual death of the organization.

Stage V: Early Bureaucratization

As the organization makes the transition to Stage V, there is a subtle but clear shift from substance to form. Status seeking, "business as usual," and appearances characterize the behavior of members. The organization is usually well endowed at this stage and may be cash rich for the first time in its history.

Later in Stage V, the focus shifts to internal turf wars. Backbiting, coalition building, and paranoia are common. Growing pains are particularly intense as members' dissatisfaction mounts. In some organizations, negativity threatens to poison the organization's climate. Leadership, which at first was content to rest on the organization's laurels, must now shift to a self-protective mode. Cliques become the usual mode of communication. The best and brightest start leaving the organization. The emphasis has clearly shifted from growth and maintenance to decline. The structures and the planning and development functions are much less responsive than in previous stages. Leadership is marked by administration and, in the later part of this stage, by inefficient administration. Decentralization and delegation become increasingly threatening to leadership, and efforts to recentralize power are expected behaviors. Counter-dependency behavior, including passive-aggressivity, becomes commonplace, reflecting demoralization among workers as well as among managers.

Stage VI: Late Bureaucratization

Many of the subunits and subsystems of the organization become clearly dysfunctional during Stage VI. Miscommunication is commonplace, and two-way communication is limited or nonexistent. Coordination and follow-through are the exception rather than the rule: "My right hand is seldom aware that a left hand exists, much less knowing what it is doing." New members are no longer informed of the mission statement and strategy, and, for all members, the organizational culture reflects a sense of helplessness and a lack of common direction. "Come late, leave early," "Do as little as you have to," "Don't try to change anything," "Protect job security at all costs" are attitudes reflecting the organizational culture in Stage VI.

The critical function at this stage is to forestall and avoid extinction, as the organization is figuratively in intensive care and is being maintained by external life-support systems. The corporate subsystems are conflictual and nonresponsive to the needs of both members and clientele. Little if any training and development occur. Administrators struggle to buy time and prolong the organization's life, but inefficiency and ineffectiveness are to be expected. Clients find little access to responsive subsystems.

Not surprisingly, the reemergence of dependency among members complements the autocratic leadership style. The eventual demise of the organization seems inevitable, and consultants report that the prognosis for organizations in Stage VI is poor, even with heroic interventions (Adizes, 1988). As noted earlier, however, organizational decline and poor person–organization fit are not inevitable. A strategically managed corporation is able to adapt to changing times and circumstances and is able to renew itself and achieve a new level of homeostasis.

Adaptation-Strategic Planning Process

Adaptation is the organizational system's capacity for change and development. It is brought about by positive feedback, which leads to a better adjustment or "fit" to the environment and accounts for the ability to meet developmental crises and create new forms. *Strategic planning* is a process and a form of organizational adaptation. Strategic planning is defined as "the process by which the guiding members of an organization envision its future and develop the necessary procedures and operations to achieve that future" (Pfeiffer et al., 1989, p. 12).

There are various models of strategic planning (Birnbaum, 1990; Pfeiffer et al., 1989; Steiner, 1979). A process involving seven steps of strategic planning is described here (Figure 3.2).

Step 1: Decision to Plan and Allocate Resources

The decision to plan and allocate resources is the first step in strategic planning. Assuming that corporate leaders recognize the

FIGURE 3.2

Steps in the Strategic Planning Process

Decision to plan

Situational analysis

Mission statement

Goal setting

Strategy development

Strategy implementation

Evaluation

value and need for strategic planning and can dedicate the resources of people, place, time, and money, the process can begin in earnest.

Step 2: Situational Analysis

The second step is situational analysis. This is also called an environmental scan and internal review by some (Birnbaum, 1990). The basic question to be considered at this second step is, Where are we today? By reviewing the threats and opportunities from the suprasystem or environment and the strengths and weaknesses of the subsystems, this question can be answered.

Step 3: Mission Statement

The third step is the specification of the vision, or mission statement. A *mission statement* is a brief, clear statement of the objectives of an organization. This statement crystallizes the organization's vision and serves as a guidepost for present and future decisions about structure, power, and resources. A truly effective mission statement succinctly specifies, in 20 words or less, what functions the organization will perform for whom. The questions to be answered are, "What should our business be?" and "Who are our customers?" Establishing an effective mission statement is probably the most important task of an organization and, initially, is one of its most difficult. Accomplishing this task requires that leaders relinquish any fuzzy or grandiose thinking about organizational goals as well as personal agendas that could undermine the organization and its vision (Sperry, 1991a).

A critical key to an organization's effectiveness is clarity of its vision and articulation of its mission. Members of an organization need to know and understand what their organization is about and how its values drive the organization. Without such knowledge and understanding, members cannot develop commitment and loyalty to the organization or toward its success. The consequences of having no vision or a blurred one, no mission statement or a poorly articulated one, can be quite serious (Pfeiffer et al., 1989). Decreased outcomes, productivity, and morale as well as loss of the most able, committed, and psychologically healthy members are some of the most obvious consequences of this blindness. When an organization's mission is not clearly stated, there can be no way to determine when and if the mission will be accomplished.

An effective mission statement provides a template for the behavior of the entire organization. Each member should know what is expected of him or her; therefore, the overall organizational mission statement needs to be tailored to the particular responsibilities of the different units or segments of the organization. Furthermore, accountability is easier to articulate when the mission statement is reflected in organizational job descriptions and performance standards.

An effective mission statement also sounds a rallying cry that directly involves and energizes organization members—both leaders and followers—to accomplish their mission (Sperry, 1991a). Rallying cries reinforce commitment to the vision. And when this envisioning process is coupled with strong leadership that articulates the vision in word and deed, the organization's commitment translates into the accomplishment of its mission.

So what is an example of a mission statement? Page and Selden (1987) provide the following one for People Express Airlines: "Our mission is to market lower airfare in densely populated regions. Our niche will be people who seldom fly and frequent fliers in search of bargains" (p. 56). This statement clearly answered the business and customer questions for People Express. Unfortunately, this airline seemed to have forgotten its mission, when in 1985, it acquired ailing Frontier Airlines. Frontier had built its reputation on providing upscale services. The acquisition of Frontier was clearly not in accord with the People Express mission statement. Not surprisingly, this acquisition eventually led to the demise of People Express.

Step 4: Goal Setting

This step addresses the question of goals, which can be stated as, Where do we wish to arrive, and when? Donald Burr, the founding president of People Express, chose the company name to underscore the firm's commitment to a people-oriented management philosophy. Corporate slogans and ads such as, "Teamwork takes on a new meaning at People Express" and "People Express is growing fast because we put people first" became goals. Burr established an adaptive network rather than a hierarchical organizational structure to "create an environment which would enable and empower employees to release their creative energies." Another stated goal was that employees would participate directly in decision making (Levering, 1988, p. 164). These goal statements appear to reflect a bottom line for both profit and employees, and, as a result, employees placed their trust in People Express. Most organizations specify only business goals, indicating that there is little, if any, priority in translating slogans into meaningful changes in the organization's subsystems.

Step 5: Developing Strategy

Step 5 involves the question, "How do we get from here to there?" This is the basis for developing the corporate strategy. When People Express began, its strategy was to develop a market for discount flying by finding every conceivable way to reduce costs and to offer dramatically lower fares than anyone else (Page & Selden, 1987).

Step 6: Implementing Strategy

Step 6 involves implementing the strategic plan. This step involves revising other subsystems, particularly structure, to maximize the probability that the strategy can be achieved. It also involves developing an operational plan and tactics. The *operational plan* is the game plan for implementing the strategy. The tactics of the operational plan are the action steps: the how-to-do-it, the who-does-it-and-when, and the what-are-the-resources-required steps. The operational plan is developed by those closest to the "action." Whereas strategic plans may have a 3- to 5-year time span, an operational plan has a time span of I year or less (Birnbaum, 1990).

Step 7: Evaluation

Step 7 involves assessing and monitoring the effectiveness of implementing the strategy. Both short-term and long-term feedback loops, as noted in Figure 3.2, are important (Birnbaum, 1990). Comparing strategy implementation with the mission statement is crucial. Had Donald Burr compared the mission of People Express with that of Frontier and noted the obvious incompatibility, the story might have had a different ending.

The example of People Express permits some speculation about linking a business plan—mission, goals, and strategy—with a people plan. The early years were an exciting time for the employees of People Express. They could not have been more committed to the corporate vision and mission. Yet the astonishing rate of growth, prompted by Burr's obsession to expand, meant that employees worked longer, uncompensated hours because the airline was consistently understaffed. The stressors were immense, precipitating among employees, numerous divorces, health problems, and demoralization. Why did these problems occur? One explanation is that there was no grievance system. Initially, Burr and his top executives had an open-door policy, but as the airline expanded exponentially, there was no visible mechanism for employee complaints or concerns. In short, members and leaders of the structure subsystem did not configure with the strategic subsystem. The fit was poor. Ultimately, trust was betrayed. One commentator noted that there was a "clear conflict between Burr's 'winning-is-everything' attitude and his espousal of humane leadership" (Levering, 1988, p. 168).

Organizational Health and Dysfunction

Work organizations can be thought of as being situated on a continuum from health to dysfunction. Organizations can become dysfunctional and self-destructive in a relatively short period. Or organizations can develop into profitable and efficient operations and appear to be healthy for years and then become dysfunctional almost overnight. Still other organizations begin as healthy enterprises and are able to maintain their health, remaining in the consolidation stage. The demise of People Express, however, probably occurred in the expansion stage, primarily due to problems in strategy implementation.

In Search of Excellence, the 1982 runaway best-seller by Peters and

Waterman, describes 43 "excellent" corporations that had at least 20 years of demonstrated superiority over competitors, as measured by six financial yardsticks. But by 1987, two thirds of these same corporations had slipped, and only 14 were rated as excellent (Pascale, 1990). In *The 100 Best Companies to Work for in America* (1985), by Levering and colleagues, the rating system used includes financial markers and several psychosocial markers. In *A Great Place to Work* (1988), Levering reports on a follow-up study of the top 20 of the original 100 corporations reported in the 1985 book. Based on this more in-depth evaluation, he recites three characteristics from an employee's perspective that made these corporations great places to work: (1) you can trust the people you work for, (2) you have pride in what you do, and (3) you enjoy the people you work for.

In addition, Levering (1988) notes several categories on a "checklist for a great place to work." In the category of *basic terms of employment*, fair pay and benefits, commitment to job security, and commitment to a safe and attractive working environment are listed. The *job* category includes maximized individual responsibility for how the job is done; flexible work hours; and opportunities for growth, such as promotion from within and recognition that mistakes are part of learning. The category *workplace rules* includes reduced social and economic distinction between management and other employees; the right to due process, information, and free speech; the right to confront those in authority; and the right not to be part of the family/team. In the category *stakes in success*, shares rewards from productivity improvement, shares profits, shares ownership, and shares recognition are listed.

Furthermore, Levering indicates that all 20 of these corporations were financially profitable in addition to having formally integrated a "people plan" with their business plan. Even though not all corporations shared all the previously mentioned categories, three patterns were noted: employees trusted those they worked for, they took pride in the work they did, and they enjoyed their relationship with other employees and managers.

Levering also lists four patterns characteristic of *bad* workplaces: (1) exploitative (arbitrary rules, abusive supervisors, and disregard for employee well-being), (2) mechanical and depersonalizing, (3) entrepreneurial, and (4) paternalistic. Jaques and Clement's (1991) description of a healthy, or "requisite," organization is surprisingly similar to that of Levering. According to Jaques and Clement, the healthy organization embraces a number of core values that are fundamental to developing effective working relationships, including (1) mutual trust, confidence, and reliability; (2) fairness and justice, whereby recognition is related to personal effectiveness; (3) dignity and respect for employees; (4) openness, with freedom from fear and from central decree; and (5) the expectation of the following from employees: integrity, commitment, reliability, initiative, and cooperativeness.

Are there other characterizations and explanations for health and pathology in organizations? Kets de Vries and Miller (1984, 1987) describe different types of dysfunctional organizations, which they call "neurotic organizations." Their observation is that organizational pathology is a primary function of the neurotic personality of the top leader. The Appendix to Chapter 4 describes five "problematic corporate cultures" based on their research.

In Miller's unique research project, published as *The Icarus Paradox: How Exceptional Companies Bring About Their Own Downfall* (1990), the basic thesis is that successful corporations, like Icarus of Greek mythology, are highly prone to failure. Their victories and strengths can seduce them into excesses that cause their downfall. Miller identifies four variations on this theme—"trajectories" or types that he labels *focusing, venturing, inventing,* and *decoupling.* What is particularly useful about these trajectories is that each constitutes a specific configuration or consistent pattern within the organization's subsystems. Miller details the leadership, cultural, structural, and strategic subsystems for each of these organizational types and how these four subsystems appreciably change and reconfigure into rigid and self-defeating patterns during the process of decline.

Microview: Worker, Job, Organization, and Family

So far we have been describing the macroview: the subsystems and stages of a work organization. A shortcoming of this perspective is that it tends to minimize the individual worker. Thus, the purpose of this section is to describe the microview, that is, the relationship of the individual worker to job, coworkers, and family, as well as to the rest of the organization. Let's view this relationship with a specific example.

In 1936, Charlie Chaplin's award-winning film *Modern Times* premiered. In it Chaplin portrays a hapless worker who tightens bolts on products whizzing by him on an assembly line that is arbitrarily speeded up by a "big brother" company president who monitors his employees from his office while he amuses himself assembling kid's puzzles. Chaplin's work team consists of contentious and unsupportive assembly workers supervised by a demanding and critical line foreman. One day a device that automatically pushed and poured food into the worker so that his hands would be free to continue working is field-tested during the lunch break. The president "volunteers" Chaplin for the demonstration. In slapstick fashion the device malfunctions and literally assaults Chaplin who later that day becomes so traumatized that "men in white coats" are called to carry him off to an insane asylum.

In many respects this film reflects a contemporary view of the impact of organizational change on worker health and well-being: that stress engendered by organizational changes—such as a merger or downsizing—can combine with already stressful job demands and low supervisory and peer support to result in impaired physical and psychological health.

This section next describes the interaction of four variables: job, organizational change, worker, and family. This interaction is illustrated in Figure 3.3.

Job

Chaplin's job was inherently stressful and impairing, given its unrealistically high demands for production with very little control or decision-making input over it. Recall that the company president controlled the speed of the assembly line. Job demand and control decisions are two factors in the job strain model developed by

FIGURE 3.3

**The Interaction of Job, Worker, Family/Coworker Support System
and Organizational Dynamics**

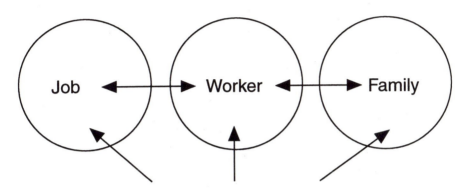

Organizational Dynamics

researchers Karasek and Theorell (1990). Job strain is defined as the short-term physiological, psychological, and behavioral manifestations of stress resulting from a job where psychological demands are high, and control over the job is low. All job classifications can be thought of in terms of the degree of demand and control. Essentially, the demand/control model articulates a 2 × 2 contingency table of high and low demand on the horizontal axis and high and low control on the vertical axis.

Thus job classifications like telephone lineman and machinist, which have low demand and high control, are considered low-strain jobs, while assembly worker and telephone operator are considered high demand, low control jobs. However, even though job demands are high, the extent to which workers can make decisions about how to plan and execute their jobs attenuates the extent of stress and impairment they experience. For example, a study of over five thousand Swedish and American men found that the lower tenth of workers, measured by their inability to control their own jobs, were five times more likely to develop heart disease than the top tenth of the workplace hierarchy, who had the greatest control over their job (Karasek & Theorell, 1990). Other job factors that have been related to health problems are occupational and safety hazards and shift work. Shift work, particularly rotating shift work, can significantly impact physical as well as psychological well-being. Workers who choose fixed shift work experience better health than those on rotating shifts where choice is limited and social and physiological adjustments are difficult (Jamal & Jamal, 1982).

Organization and Organizational Change

Chaplin's company epitomized Taylor's (1911/1967) "scientific management" approach wherein workers were trained to be efficient and productive "cogs in the corporate machine" while managers assumed all planning and decisional responsibilities. Subsequently, when organizational change is considered, management has total responsibility for its implementation. Chaplin was literally the victim of the president's decision to implement the automatic "feeding machine."

The most prevalent forms of organizational change today are mergers, downsizing, and layoffs. To the extent that workers are not active participants in the change process, they experience varying degrees of victimization ranging from stress symptoms, such as insomnia, irritability, and anxiety, to Anxiety Disorders including posttraumatic stress syndrome. Marks and Mirvis (1986) describe the "merger syndrome," which consists of anxiety, dysphoria, stress reactions, worry and preoccupation, constricted communications, "we-theyism," crisis management, and culture clash.

They suggest three strategies to reduce merger syndrome. First, during the initial deliberations for corporate mergers, top management must carefully consider the human implications along with the financial and business aspects. A transition team with members focusing on the people side of the merger is then formed. Second, emotional preparation of workers is accomplished through a pre-merger workshop. Third, counseling is made available for workers at all levels who have experienced difficulty coping with the syndrome. McCann and Gilkey (1988) found that establishing effective two-way communications—upward and downward—is of paramount importance in short-circuiting the merger syndrome.

Worker

Chaplin's character showed a marked degree of vulnerability, and thus, his "nervous breakdown" was not unexpected. There are several descriptors or markers to describe individual vulnerability. Two of the most widely studied markers are hardiness and optimism. Hardiness is a marker of personality reflecting how individuals view themselves and the world. Stress-hardy individuals show high levels of control, commitment, and challenge. Those who are high in control have a strong belief they can exert influence on their surroundings. Those high in commitment tend to fully engage themselves in what they are doing, while those high in challenge see change as a natural part of life that affords opportunities for growth.

Maddi and Kobasa (1984) found that high levels of hardiness are more important than a strong body constitution in buffering stress and impairment. In a prospective study, 259 workers were rated on their level of hardiness and studied for five years. Under equal amounts of stress, those with hardy personalities experienced half the illness episodes of those with little hardiness (Maddi & Kobasa, 1984). Additional data reported by these same researchers shows that hardiness could be bolstered by exercise, diet, and a nurturing support system.

Optimism is related to hardiness in that while optimists tend to attribute or explain bad events as externally caused, time limited, and having minimal impact on their lives, pessimists tend to explain the same event as internally caused (they blame themselves), stable, and global in its impact. The pessimistic explanation can result in helplessness, depression, and physical illness. Seligman's (1989) research shows that workers with a pessimistic style have compromised immune function and subsequently suffer more illness than those with an optimistic style. Similarly, those with a pessimistic style develop chronic degenerative illness, such as hypertension and heart disease, earlier in life and die at a younger age than those with an optimistic style (Seligman, 1989). Like hardiness, a more optimistic style can be learned.

Family

In addition to having little peer support on the job, the Chaplin character had no family support. Research shows a link between the presence of social support and health maintenance, particularly among married men (Bjorksten & Steward, 1985). McCubbin and Thompson's (1989) extensive study of stockbrokers and their families shows that workers' health and well-being could be maintained under great duress when the worker experienced the job supervisor's support as well as nurturing, supportive communication from his spouse and high levels of family hardiness and optimism. On the other hand, the worker's health deteriorated when there was little or no job supervisor support, an incendiary, harsh, critical, "blaming-spousal" communication pattern, and low levels of family hardiness.

Gottman (1991) reports that another type of spousal communication pattern can greatly impact health. He describes something akin to the "pursuer-distancer" interaction pattern (Guerin, Fay, Burden, & Kautto, 1987) wherein physiological arousal predicated marital dissatisfaction, separation, and divorce. To the extent that the pursuing spouse "attacked" the distancing spouse who experienced high physiological reactivity and engaged in "stonewalling"– avoiding eye contact, limiting vocalization, and refraining from other indications of response–the researchers were able to predict not only separation or divorce within a four year period, but also deterioration of the distancer's physical health (Gottman & Levinson, 1988).

In closing, research data now supports the clinical observation that corporate change can greatly impact worker health and well-being, and that job factors, workers' characteristics and family factors can either exacerbate or buffer the extent of distress and impairment experienced by the worker. It is fascinating that a movie produced 66 years ago so clearly captured a truth which the behavioral science literature is now documenting.

MODELS FOR UNDERSTANDING ORGANIZATIONAL DYNAMICS

The study of organizations and organizational behavior has a fascinating history traceable back to the ancient civilizations of the Egyptians, Babylonians, Greeks, Chinese, and Romans (Van Fleet, 1988). However, the scope of this book permits only a brief, thematic overview of how behavior in organizations has been understood in the 20th century, during which leaders of organizations have faced the challenge of reconciling organizational needs with human needs, particularly productivity with job satisfaction. Three models are notable in the quest to meet this challenge: the rational, the nonrational, and the integrative.

The Rational Model

One way of reconciling organizational and human needs is to subordinate workers' needs to the organization's goal of optimal productivity and to accomplish this with a logical and scientific method. This is the basic theme of rational approaches to the management of organizational behavior. At the turn of the 20th century, the scientific management perspective prevailed. In this perspective, workers were perceived as cogs in the organization's machine. Taylor (1911/1967) assumed that workers would become more productive if they became technically competent and used proper tools in a prescribed standard manner. Thus, time-and-motion studies were done to establish the prescribed standard for each job classification. Taylor believed his approach took the human elements of error, laziness, and inefficiency out of the work process. However, while productivity was clearly increased by this approach, both quality and job satisfaction were not.

A second version of the scientific management perspective viewed the well-oiled bureaucratic organizational machine as the key to productivity. According to Max Weber (1947), hierarchical authority with a well-defined chain of command, specific rules and procedures, and a division of labor based on specialized work functions were the basic strategies for ensuring productivity and efficiency. The factory assembly line reflected these two views of scientific management well.

A third version of the rational perspective is the introduction of management by objectives (MBO), developed by Peter Drucker (1954). In MBO, worker behavior is conformed to organizational needs by written goals or standards of performance for a job. More humane than scientific management, the MBO system is based on mutual agreement between superior and subordinate on the goals in individual goal-setting meetings and periodic reviews to evaluate achievement of the objectives. MBO and Drucker are well known both inside and outside the business world. The performance appraisal or merit rating system is a variant of MBO.

Less well known are two other rational approaches: operations research (OR) and management information systems (MIS). In addition, the "rational manager" (Kepner & Tregoe, 1954) further reflects the rational model wherein the leader bases decision making on complete and accurate information and workers have specified job objectives and standards, rules, and procedures to guide their activity. Basic to this model is the belief that the manager knows best and must ultimately control the worker and that nonrational elements must be delimited as much as possible.

A consultant operating from the rational model would "fit" best in rational corporations, which expect "expert" consultation. At the turn of the 20th century, expert consultants performed time and motion studies, whereas today they implement and/or evaluate MBO, MIS, OR, or strategic planning and management systems.

The Nonrational Model

Elton Mayo became famous for his research at the Hawthorne plant of Western Electric that enunciated the Hawthorne Effect, which indicates that nonrational factors such as prestige, social contact, and recognition influence productivity more than so-called rational factors. In fact, Mayo (1933) assumes that workers are not very rational and that "the administrators of the future" would apply methods of behavioral science to guide and direct these workers. As a result of the studies at the Hawthorne plant, management largely shifted to view organizational success as a function of individual motivation and interpersonal relationships. Thus began the focus on the nonrational aspects of leadership.

McGregor (1960) continues the nonrational tradition by contrasting Theory X—the rational, machine view of the worker as a passive, outer-directed cog—with Theory Y—a nonrational, more humanistic view of the worker as a potentially active, inner-directed, trustworthy, and growth-oriented individual. McGregor's Theory Y was based, in part, on Maslow's (1954) hierarchy of needs. Theory Y leadership assumes that overcontrol of the worker is not needed when the worker's lower-level needs, like safety and wages, are met and the workplace provides sufficient challenge, so workers can satisfy their higher needs for affiliation, self-esteem, and self-actualization.

Tannenbaum and Schmidt's (1958) participative style and Blake and Mouton's (1964) managerial grid were described earlier in the chapter. Both of these approaches, as well as T-group or sensitivity training, Herzberg's "satisfies/dissatisfies," and organizational development (OD) are manifestations of humanistic psychology, which emphasizes the nonrational. Other nonrational approaches include the various psychoanalytic approaches propounded by Levinson (1981), Hirschhorn (1988), and Kets de Vries (1989; Kets de Vries & Miller, 1984, 1987), as well as the Gestalt approach (Merry & Brown, 1987) and the Adlerian view (Cox, 1974, 1990).

Probably the most well known contemporary adherent of the nonrational model is Tom Peters, coauthor of *In Search of Excellence* (Peters & Waterman, 1982) and *A Passion for Excellence* (Peters & Austin, 1985). Peters believes that excellence occurs when managers exercise the "technology of enthusiasm" and use motivational techniques like inspiration, passion, and enthusiasm to overcome conflict between management and worker: The excellent manager "manages by wandering around" (MBWA) and "pushing authority far down the line." Essentially, Peters believes that the interests of workers and management are basically the same and that motivation is basically about finding the right irrational "buttons to push."

The consultant, operating from a nonrational approach like OD, would likely assess worker and leadership perceptions of work conditions, communication patterns, conflicts, and leadership process through surveys and interviews with individuals or focus groups. Utilizing the method of process consultation—defined as the set of activities utilized by a consultant to aid a client to perceive, understand, and act on the process events that occur in the client's environment (Schein, 1987)—the consultant might suggest ways to improve the communication, leadership, and decision-making processes in the organization.

The Integrative Model

Adopting either a rational model or a nonrational model seems cavalier amid the complexity of today's corporate world. Unquestionably, both views—especially the most recent approaches in each model—offer important knowledge and techniques, but both are insufficient and somewhat simplistic. Thus, the integrative model has emerged. It consists of approaches that combine and synthesize elements of both the rational and the nonrational models, as well as other input. Currently, there are four contemporary approaches that are integrative, in varying degrees: systems theory, contingency theory, Theory Z, and the Deming method.

Systems theory is based on the premise that a system has four elements: inputs, a transformation process, outputs, and feedback from the environment. As noted earlier in this chapter, the concepts of the organization interacting with its environment, the interdependence of subsystems, and synergy are critical to understanding organizations.

Contingency theory is an eclectic view of management premised on the beliefs that there is no best way to lead, nor is each organization unique. It argues that the most appropriate leadership actions in groups of situations depend on, or are contingent on, the elements of each of the particular situational groups (Van Fleet, 1988).

Theory Z suggests that a flexible managerial approach with elements of both structured (type A, for American) and relaxed (type J, for Japanese) organizations leads to success (Ouchi, 1981). McGregor, Bennis, and McGregor (1967) also describe a Theory Z to reconcile the Theory X and Y opposites (Pascale, 1990). However, Ouchi's view includes such elements as group consensual decision making and achievement, lifetime employment, and quality circles. All three of these elements have their roots in Japanese culture and custom. Various efforts have been made for transporting Theory J to America. This transported synthesis is called *Theory Z* (Ouchi, 1981) or *quality circles*. Quality circles refer to small groups of employees who engage in quality improvement activities (Pascale, 1990).

Finally, the *Deming method* embodies the notions of statistical quality of control and quality circles. Deming articulated 14 points on the "multitudes for management of productivity and quality" (Deming, 1982), which emphasize both quality assurance and worker well-being.

In short, the integrative approaches attempt to combine rational and nonrational elements, and particularly Ouchi's Theory Z and the Deming method, to emphasize the elements of trust, pride, and worker satisfaction and enjoyment that seem to be essential to healthy workplaces (Levering, 1988).

To enlarge the perspective further, it might be useful to briefly contrast the American view of leadership and organization with other views. Essentially, the American view is largely centered on the leadership style and on the leader's action orientation. This orientation is quite rational, individualistic, and behavorial, focusing largely on benefits and bottom lines. Nonrational elements of leaders and organizations are seldom recognized.

On the other hand, the Japanese view is more oriented toward feelings and focused on the achievement of the work team or group rather than on the individual. As noted earlier, this view reflects basic Japanese culture and values of achievement through group and company loyalty, which contrasts with the rugged individualism of many Western countries.

Contrasted with both the American and Japanese views is the European or Continental view, articulated by Jaques and Clement (1991). Rather than being centered on action or feeling, this approach is based on thinking, particularly on the individual's cognitive complexity. *Cognitive complexity* is the capacity to abstract and envision the task in terms of the present and the future. Needless to say, a truly integrative and mature theory of organizational behavior will likely incorporate features of all three of these widely different viewpoints.

CONCLUDING NOTE

Although the preceding section on models for understanding organizations and organizational behavior is necessarily brief, it does provide an overview and perspective on organizations and organizational behavior that can be elaborated by additional reading. Chapter 4 continues the discussion of organizations and organizational dynamics by focusing on the assessment of organizational behavior also called organizational diagnosis.

4

Organizational Diagnosis

Among the most important consultation skills is organizational diagnosis or assessment. Methods of organizational diagnosis have been described by Levinson (1972), Harrison (1987, 1994), and Manzini (1988), but some of these approaches will seem foreign to the new clinician-consultant. The exception is Levinson's *Organizational Diagnosis* (1972), since it is primarily written from the clinician-consultant perspective. There are, however, a number of parallels between organizational diagnosis and the individual diagnostic evaluation routinely performed by clinicians.

This chapter points out these parallels and suggests a concise interview format for performing a basic organizational diagnosis. Whether the nature of the consultation request is for team building, corporate strategic planning, individual consultation or coaching, or even full scale organizational development, this interview format can serve as the basis for an organizational diagnosis, which can be tailored and/or supplemented with questionnaires and standard inventories measuring leadership style, organization climate, conflict resolution patterns, or the like. Before describing the interview format, individual diagnosis will be compared to organizational diagnosis and a model for organizational diagnosis will be discussed.

PARALLELS BETWEEN INDIVIDUAL AND ORGANIZATIONAL DIAGNOSIS

Although the content differs, there are close parallels between elements of an individual diagnostic evaluation and an organizational diagnostic evaluation. The elements of the individual diagnostic evaluation include identification of the patient and chief complaint; history of present illness; past history, including past psychiatric history and developmental history; family and social history; mental status exam; and diagnostic impression (Andreasen & Black, 1991). I conceive of organizational diagnosis in terms of five elements: situation and stressors; subsystems and suprasystem; stages; synchronism; and organizational-diagnostic impression.

The organizational situation and stressors refer to specific concerns or crises, such as decreased productivity, loss of market share, low morale, merger, downsizing, and impaired functioning of a particular work team or individual. This dimension is parallel to identification of the patient, chief complaint of symptoms, and history of the present illness in the individual diagnostic evaluation. Stages refer to the stages of organizational growth and decline that currently characterize the organization. Organizational stage parallels the history of past psychiatric illness and developmental history in the individual diagnostic evaluation.

Subsystems and suprasystem refer to the six interrelated components of the organizational system that reflect the organization's unique identity and mode of operation. Subsystems in the organizational diagnostic evaluation roughly parallel the family and social history of the patient in the individual diagnostic evaluation. Synchronism refers to the degree of "fit" among the various subsystems and stages of the organizations, with regard to its present situation and stressors, and parallels the mental status exam in the individual diagnostic evaluation. Table 4.1 summarizes these parallels between the individual and organizational diagnosis.

Finally, the organizational diagnostic impression is the consultant's view of the extent of the organization's symptoms and pain and level of functioning with regard to its developmental history. It is equivalent to the diagnostic impression—usually a five axis diagnosis in DSM-IV terms—that the clinician uses to summarize the clinical data. Since there is currently no organizational equivalent to DSM-IV, organizational diagnostic impression is usually a brief summary of the organization's pain, situated in terms of the lack of synchronism among stage, subsystem, and stressors.

TABLE 4.1

Parallels Between the Elements of Individual and Organizational Diagnosis

Individual Diagnosis	*Organizational Diagnosis*
1. Identification of patient and chief complaint; history of present illness	1. Situation and stressor(s)
2. Past history: History of psychiatric illness and developmental history	2. Stage of organization
3. Family and social history	3. Subsystems
4. Mental status exam	4. Synchronism/Fit
5. Diagnostic impression	5. Organizational diagnostic impression

THE FOUR-S METHOD OF ORGANIZATIONAL DIAGNOSIS

As noted in the previous section, a basic organizational diagnosis involves four "s's": situation and stressors; sub-system; stages; and synchronism, summarized by an organizational diagnostic impression. The interview format that follows permits the consultant to assess the first three s's, while synchronism is derived from a consideration of the "fit" among the various subsystem components. Finally, the diagnostic impression is a brief statement that summarizes the organization's symptoms and problems in terms of the four s's. A number of queries are provided to aid the clinician-consultant's assessment of fit.

Since fit or synchronism is central to this method of organizational diagnosis, a brief discussion of fit is in order. As stated earlier, organizational subsystems are interrelated and influence one another. For instance, while environment shapes strategy, organizations are also shaped by their environment. The organization's structure and culture affect members' behavior, i.e., productivity, satisfaction, and health, but their behavior also impacts structure and culture. Similarly, there should be a reasonable degree of fit between the stage of an organization's development and the subsystems. An obvious example is fit between an entrepreneurial leadership style and an organization in the Birth and Expansion Stage. On the other hand, a poor fit would be an entrepreneurial leadership style in the Consolidation Stage. Thus, consultants need to carefully assess the relationship and degree of fit between and among these subsystems and stages.

With such a perspective the consultant should be able to anticipate the impact of a change of one or more subsystems on the organization at different stages of development and decline. For example, management's plan to acquire a new information system to enhance accountability could be perceived as a threat to job security and part of labor–management relations in an organization in the Early Bureaucratization Stage but be applauded as consistent with the organization's strategy for facilitating communications in an organization moving into the Professionalization Stage.

A corporation's success and viability depends largely on its ability to adapt to its internal and external environment at a particular stage. Fit refers to the compatibility of requirements of subsystem components and stage. The better the fit, the higher productivity, job satisfaction, and overall health, while decreased productivity, satisfaction, and health induces higher job stress associated with poor fit (Beer, 1980; Muchinsky, 1993).

ORGANIZATIONAL DIAGNOSIS INTERVIEW FORMAT

The following interview guide is designed to be used to develop an initial diagnostic impression of an organization. Included are a list of open-ended questions for each of the six organizational subsystems. Depending on the degree of elaboration, the interview could last from 30 to 120 minutes, and interviews with only one or several members may be planned. Typically, though, the first interview is with the client who makes the consultation request. The format of questions is designed to be used as a general guide rather than as a rigid script. As noted earlier, this basic interview format may be supplemented with additional lines of inquiry—such as financial factors—and with other data sources: direct observation, questionnaires, and standard inventories.

Strategy

- What would you say is the overall mission or purpose of this organization?
- Who is responsible for developing it?
- Who is responsible for articulating it and gaining member support for it?
- What percentage of members know it and follow it?
- Does each group or unit of the organization have its own mission and strategy derived from the overall organizational mission?
- Do group members know it and utilize it as a basis for work task decisions and actions?

Structure

- How is the work in your part of the organization (work team, unit, department, division) organized and structured, and how does it fit into the whole organization? *(Elicit the formal organizational structure, including leaders and reporting relationships. If appropriate, ask the interviewee to draw an organizational chart for the organization. Organizations have an informal as well as a formal structure.)*
- What is the informal structure here? *(Look for cliques, links between and within departments, social networks based on ethnic background, sports interest, and the like.)*
- What task does your group (team, department, division) perform?
- What are the main methods and means used?
- How does your job fit into the work done here?
- With whom do you work to accomplish it?
- How do you communicate with them?
- Do you feel your group is operating effectively?
- What do you mean by effective?
- What kind of problems do you face here?
- How do you handle them?

- Are there barriers to getting tasks accomplished or doing them the way you would like to?

Culture

- What aspects of work are most emphasized in this organization—i.e., speed, quantity, quality, customer satisfaction, innovation, worker safety, and so on?
- If you were telling a friend what it is really like to work here, how would you describe the atmosphere in your group? In the whole organization? *(Look for norms, assumptions, rituals, beliefs about the nature of work and how it should be done, along with what member's involvement should be, and rewards and sanctions.)*
- Does it pay to take risks around here, like making suggestions or giving feedback? *(Probe for support for initiative, creativity and risk taking, as well as organizational attitudes toward criticism and feedback.)*

Leadership

- Who is your superior?
- How closely do you work with him/her?
- What is it like to work with him/her?
- In general, how much say do you have in the decisions your superior makes? *(Probe for leadership style in terms of both the leader-centered [autocratic] versus the member-centered [participative] continuum, as well as on the people versus task continuum.)*
- How does his/her style compare with other bosses here? *(Look for overall pattern of leadership style favored by the organization.)*
- What kind of things does your superior do to help you in your job? *(Probe for functions such as coach, mentor, or career developer versus disciplinarian, know-it-all, or self-promoter.)*

Member

- In general, how do employees feel about working here? *(Probe for job satisfaction and worker-management communications and relations.)*
- What are workers' main concerns here? *(Listen for worries and fears such as job loss, downsizing, rapid turnover of employees, wage and benefits, potential for violence, and management's response to these concerns.)*
- How long have you been in your work group (team, division, department)? What is it like to work with other people in your work group? *(Look for nature and quality of interpersonal relations: trust level, helpfulness, etc.)*

Environment

- What is the competition for your product (or service)?
- What is the community's view of and attitude toward this organization?
- What are some of the potential threats to the organization's well-being now and in the future? *(Probe for factors like government regulations, changes in industry procedures, changes in market share, or stakeholder demands and/or dissatisfaction.)*
- What are the growth opportunities?
- What do you imagine this organization will be like in five years?

Strategy–Structure Fit

This represents the degree to which the organization's strategy and objectives are supported and facilitated by the organization's structure.

- Are procedures for coordinating work and communication/information flow appropriate to the tasks and technology?

- Are members who must work together closely grouped in teams, units, or otherwise linked structurally?
- Are there tasks and functions that no one is doing adequately and others in which members or units unnecessarily overlap?
- Do members have sufficient decisional control and resources to accomplish their tasks adequately?

Strategy–Culture Fit

This represents the degree to which shared norms, beliefs, values, symbols, and rituals positively support and reflect the organization's vision, mission, and strategy.

- Do members regard official rules, policies, and procedures as sensible and fair?
- Are sanctions and rewards applied consistently, and do they encourage behavior and group norms compatible with the organization's goals and purposes?
- Is the "psychological contract"—which prescribes appropriate behaviors between members and organization as well as expectations about job advancement and security—upheld or arbitrarily changed by management?

Strategy–Leadership Fit

This represents the degree to which management behaviors responsibly support and facilitate the accomplishment of the organization's strategy.

- To what extent does leadership articulate the organization's mission and goals and the expectation that the organization's primary purpose is to accomplish the mission?
- Does leadership act in ways that galvanize a sense of mission and identity among members? Do members perceive

leadership as facilitators or stumbling blocks to accomplishing the mission and strategy?

Strategy–Member Fit

This represents the degree to which members are aware of, committed to, and actually achieve the organization's mission and strategy.

- Do members' skills and training fit their job requirement?
- Are the best people attracted and retained?
- Do members have sufficient job challenge and decisional latitude to increase job satisfaction and decrease job strain and boredom?
- Are members' work behaviors and decisions blocked by needless conflicts or power struggles? Does inappropriate competition between teams or units of members exist?

Strategy–Environment Fit

This represents the degree to which the organization interfaces with its internal and external environment in accomplishing its strategy objectives.

- Do the organization's strategy objectives and tactics help it gain and maintain a favorable position in its external environment?
- Is the organization's internal physical and emotional environment sufficiently safe to support members' work efforts?

DIAGNOSIS OF ORGANIZATIONAL STAGE OF DEVELOPMENT

The clinician-consultant should think developmentally when making an organizational diagnosis and planning organizational interventions. Flambolz (1990) provides a developmental perspective in which specific problems can be viewed in terms of the organization's overall development. This perspective is a lens through which an organization can provide a common framework for understanding developmental issues. Flambolz suggests that many organizational problems are the result of the organization not having made the transition effectively from one stage of growth to the next. These developmental programs may be likened to conflicts in the various stages of human development that must be resolved to achieve individual growth (Erikson, 1980).

Flambolz (1990) describes six key tasks/sequential steps that must be performed in an integrated fashion in order for an organization to develop properly and function successfully. All six are essential to the functioning of the firm at any given time, but each develops to a different degree at different stages in an organization's growth process. The six tasks are: identifying and defining a market niche; developing products and services; acquiring resources; developing operational systems; developing management systems; and developing a corporate culture.

These six tasks can be correlated with the stages of an organization's development described in Chapter 3. At Stage I, New Venture, the critical task is markets and products. At Stage II, Expansion, the critical task is the development of resources and operational systems. At Stage III, Professionalization, the key task is the development of management systems. At Stage IV, Consolidation, the critical task involves management of the organization's culture. Finally at Stages V and VI, Early Bureaucratization and Late Bureaucratization, the critical task involves organizational revitalization. If consultants understand the framework, they will be able to orient their organizational development efforts to the appropriate focus. Table 4.2 illustrates the specific tasks for each developmental stage.

Most organizations face some degree of difficulty in managing the transitions required between stages of growth. When the transition between stages has not been made successfully, the organization experiences what Flambolz (1990) calls a "developmental gap." This developmental gap, in turn, produces what he has termed "organiza-

TABLE 4.2

Developmental Stages and Tasks of an Organization

Stage	Task
I. New Venture	Product development and market
II. Expansion	Operational systems
III. Professionalization	Management system
IV. Consolidation	Culture system
V. Early Bureaucratization	Strategic review and modification of stages I–IV (organizational transformation)
VI. Late Bureaucratization	Forestall demise and attempt stage V

tional transition pains." The transition pains may be viewed as symptoms that an organization experiences because of a failure to develop an infrastructure appropriate to its stage of growth. In this context, organizational infrastructure can be operationally defined as resources, operational systems, management systems, and corporate culture.

There are two different types of transition pains that can occur because of a discrepancy between an organization's infraructure and its stage of growth. Type I, which Flambolz calls "organizational growing pains," emerges during Stages I to IV because the infrastructure has not been sufficiently developed. Type II, which he labels "organizational aging pains," emerges during Stages V and VI when the organization is in decline.

In addition, Flambolz has developed a 10-item instrument, called the "Organizational Growing Pains Questionnaire," to measure growing pains. These growing pains are not merely problems in themselves but symptoms of a deeper systemic problem. The basic underlying problem is that the organization has outgrown its infrastructure, which produces a "developmental gap" that results in growing pains. Similarly, Flambolz has identified 10 symptoms of organizational aging pains. Like growing pains, aging pains are not simply problems in themselves but symptoms of an underlying systemic problem, namely, that the organization's infrastructure has become bureaucratic and is causing the company to choke on its own systems.

Finally, clinician-consultants must appreciate what will happen when an organization has failed to match its infrastructure to its developmental stage. To summarize, the result will be a predictable set of growing pains and/or aging pains that must be understood not only as problems per se but as symptoms of underlying systemic issues involving the overall development of an organization.

FIVE TARGETS FOR ORGANIZATIONAL DIAGNOSIS AND INTERVENTION

The problem areas that form the basis for organizational diagnosis and intervention reflect five domains of organizational functioning. The first involves the exercise of power/authority, while the second relates to morale/cohesion. The third is centered on problems arising from norms/standards of conduct, and the fourth comprises any issue involving goals/objectives of the organization. Blake and Mouton (1976, 1983) contend that all organizational problems can be subsumed into one of these four domains. Goodstein (1978) disagrees and contends that a fifth domain—roles/communication—is an additional necessary and distinct domain of organizational functioning. I have found that these five domains, described below, can be viewed as focal targets that are quite useful in formulating a diagnosis and intervention strategy.

1. **Power/Authority.** Power refers to the capability of having an effect, and authority refers to the right to exercise power. Power/authority issues revolve around whether power and authority are used effectively in both formal and informal matters within an organization. Power/authority issues can arise over the ways power and authority are in fact used or over the ways their use is perceived by those who are not in positions of power within an organization. *Power/authority* issues are the most common focal targets, outnum-

bering others by a frequency of about three to one (Blake & Mouton, 1983).

2. **Morale/Cohesion.** Morale is a state of high, positive mental energy among members of an organization. Cohesion refers to the degree to which members of a group experience a positive sense of togetherness and unity. *Morale/cohesion issues* concern how members perceive the organization and its direction as well as the degree to which members see themselves as part of a "team."

3. **Norms/Standards.** Norms are the "rules" that govern appropriate behavior by members of all, or some, part of the organization. Standards are the criteria organizations use for measuring quality. *Norms/standards issues* are frequently raised when an organization is forced to cope with internal and/or external changes, and both are usually difficult to change.

4. **Goals/Objectives.** Goals are the aims and purposes of an organization, and objectives are those things that are accomplished when goals are met. Goals/objectives issues are frequently related to norms and standards issues and typically arise when goals and objectives are either poorly defined or have not been achieved. *Goals/objectives issues* frequently surface during investigation of norms/standards issues.

5. **Roles/Communication.** Roles are expected behavior patterns attributed to a particular position in an organization. The structure of an organization specifies the reporting relationship of all roles within a given organization. Roles, along with the policies and procedures for communication, are essential in achieving the organization's tasks and goals. Communication is the transmission of information and understanding among individuals in various roles in the organization. *Roles/communication issues* arise as roles become less clear and boundaries blur, particularly with the roles of manager and subordinate.

Power/authority, morale/cohesion, norms/standards, goals/objectives, and roles/communication are actually interdependent phenomena. This means that initiating a change in one domain will subsequently result in changes in the other domains as well. For instance, a reduction of a manager's unilateral use of power/authority may increase morale/cohesion among staff members.

The focal target is the domain of the organization causing or exacerbating a particular problem or concern. Though these five domains are interdependent, it is important that the clinician-consultant identifies the underlying problem and domain so that interventions can be effectively focused. It is equally important for the consultant not to confuse surface problems with underlying problems.

When compared with power/authority, other focal targets might seem less important, but such a conclusion would be unwarranted. Expecting that all organizational problems can be solved by imposing an intervention targeted at the power/authority domain is a mistake that novice consultants often make. When an underlying problem is mistakenly identified, the intervention that is implemented will often backfire. For example, a clinician-consultant may diagnose a clinic group's practice style as disorganized and unpredictable and then mistakenly plan an intervention to impose order via the power/authority domain instead of addressing the real underlying problem—the norms/standards domain. But in due time, the group's response to this intervention may engender an additional set of problems, this time clearly reflective of power/authority issues. Had the clinician-consultant accurately diagnosed the underlying problem as one of norms/standards and provided the clinic staff with a structured format for discussing the situation so that constructive norms/standards would emerge, a quicker and more effective solution could have been reached.

Blake and Mouton (1983) report an actual consultation with a grocery chain that further illustrates the failure to identify the underlying target problem and the subsequent failure of the intervention. They describe how the consultants assisted the organization to change its structure so that the corporate office could provide its outlet chains with a fuller range of marketing and distribution services. This change involved the norms/standards for operating the organization's structure. In hindsight, however, the consultants were stunned by their failure to recognize power/authority as the underlying problem. Because power/authority was not the focus of the intervention strategy, the intervention did not produce the expected outcomes. Yet, had the intervention been initially directed at the power/authority focus, the consultants might then have shifted to a focus on norms/standards as a second phase of the consultation. Skill in identifying the basic focal target(s) is, thus, one of the important competencies of the effective clinician-consultant.

A DIAGNOSTIC CLASSIFICATION SYSTEM

As more clinician-consultants interface with organizational and workplace concerns, the necessity and value of a diagnostic classification system for workplace behavior and functioning becomes more evident. There have been a few previous efforts to specify such a classification system. Cowan (1993) describes what he calls an "organizational problem map" of 11 interrelated problem categories noted in a survey of corporate executives. These include problems with communication, strategy, marketing, management information systems (MIS), operations, accounting, production, management, environment, customers, and personnel. As noted in the previous section, Blake and Mouton (1983) indicate that all issues involving organizational behavior and functioning can be subsumed under four categories or domains: power/authority, morale/cohesion, norms/standards, or goals/objectives. Lowman (1993) describes, in some detail, two classes of work dysfunctions: disturbance in the capacity to work and dysfunctional working conditions.

While each of these efforts is noteworthy, none of these schemas is sufficiently comprehensive and inclusive to be useful for those involved in clinical consultation. This section describes a more inclusive, comprehensive classification system.

The proposed classification system is based on several premises. The first premise is that psychopathology and medical problems are both brought to and result from the work setting. The second is that any organizational component or process, such as structure, culture, or leader–worker interaction, can trigger or "cause" physical and psychological distress or symptoms. This distress can be manifested as somatic, psychological, or psychosomatic symptoms. A third premise is that these symptoms vary in severity from situational stress to work-related anxiety, depression, or somatization to full-blown DSM-IV Axis I, II, and III disorders that often present to medical and psychiatric consultants for disability evaluation and management. One final premise is that workplace problems or dysfunction span a continuum from "technical" to "personal-behavioral," wherein "technical" or structural problems are typically less complex and require less effort and time to ameliorate than "personal-behavioral" dysfunctions, which are much more complex and require significant effort and time to modify.

Table 4.3 on pp. 86–87 in the Chapter Appendix, presents the "Taxonomy of Organizational and Work Dysfunction." Two main categories are delineated: "Dysfunctional Organizational Work Context" and "Dysfunctional Work Capacity." Nine categories articulate dysfunctional organizational work contexts—the first four categories are primarily "technical" issues, while categories 5–9 are both "technical" and "personal-behavioral." Four categories articulate "Dysfunctional Work Capacity." All four are primarily "personal-behavioral."

Typically, management consultants focus on what have been designated as "technical" problems, while the majority of organizational psychologists and organizational development consultants usually focus on "personal-behavioral" problems or issues. Actually, since technical problems and dysfunctions (i.e., merger and downsizing) nearly always create a variety of psychological and somatic symptoms or disorders, clinician-consultants could be involved with all the technical categories. Their involvement might be as a member of the consultation team, if not as the main consultant, as they would be for all the personal-behavioral categories.

Appendix to Chapter 4

Taxonomy of Organizational and Work Dysfunction

The appendix to this chapter describes each of the thirteen categories and subcategories of the Taxonomy of Organizational and Work Dysfunction in some detail. These descriptions are not intended to be formal case definitions but rather clinical descriptions of these phenomena. Table 4.3 and this appendix are offered as a taxonomy or "diagnostic system-in-process," based on over 20 years of clinical and consultation experience, rather than as a definitive classification derived from an extensive data-based investigation and theory. The field desperately needs a data-based theory of organizational and work dysfunction. In the interim, theories and models, such as the one presented in this chapter, will serve a practical as well as heuristic purpose.

I. DYSFUNCTIONAL ORGANIZATIONAL WORK CONTEXT

1. Strategy/Structure Mismatch

Strategy involves the organization's long-term goals and objectives, while structure is the way the organization is put together to administer the strategy. Chandler (1962) was one of the first to insist that structure must follow strategy. By this he meant that an organization must establish its strategic plan prior to forming its organizational

TABLE 4.3

Taxonomy of Organizational and Work Dysfunction

I. DYSFUNCTIONAL ORGANIZATIONAL WORK CONTEXT

1. Strategy/Structure Mismatch
  A. Incompatible Organizational Design

2. Structural Problems
  A. Operational and/or Management System Incompatibility
  B. Role Conflict/Role Ambiguity/Reporting Relationship
  Problems

3. Environmental Problems
  A. Internal
    1. Toxic Exposure or Occupational Hazards
    2. Extreme Physical Conditions
    3. Organizational or Workplace Crises
  B. External
    1. Increased Competition/Decreased Market Value

4. Job Design Problems
  A. High Job Strain
  B. Role Overload
  C. Ergonomic Incompatibility
  D. Worker–Job or Worker–Organizational Mismatch
  E. Schedule/Shift Problems

5. Restructuring Problems
  A. Merger Syndrome
  B. Downsizing Syndrome

6. Problematic Corporate Cultures
  A. Confident Culture
  B. Survivor Culture
  C. Conscientious Culture
  D. Sedentary Culture
  E. Solitary Culture

7. Dysfunctional Interpersonal and Team Relations
  A. Interpersonal Conflict
  B. Team Conflict
  C. Intergroup Conflict

8. Defective Supervision
  A. Unqualified for position
  B. Improper/Inadequate training

9. Authority Problems and Issues
A. Leadership–Followership Style Conflicts
B. Unresolved Family-of-Origin Conflict
C. Personality Disorders or Characterological Problems

II. DYSFUNCTIONAL WORK CAPACITY

10. Undercommitment and Overcommitment Patterns
A. Undercommitment Patterns
  1. Underachievement Patterns
  2. Temporary Production Impediments
  3. Procrastination
  4. Fear of Success
  5. Fear of Failure
B. Overcommitment Patterns
  1. Work Addiction
  2. Type A Behavior Pattern
  3. Burnout

11. Problematic Work-Personality Styles
A. Sensitive Style
B. Adventurous Style
C. Mercurial Style
D. Devoted Style
E. Dramatic Style
F. Self-Confident Style
G. Conscientious Style
H. Vigilant Style
I. Leisurely Style
J. Solitary Style
K. Idiosyncratic Style

12. Life-Role Conflicts
A. Career Decision and Development Problems
B. Work–Family Conflicts and Issues
  1. Inflexible Scheduling and Leave Policies
  2. Career Dysynchrony Between Married Spouses
  3. Child or Elder Care Issues
  4. Chronic or Terminal Illness of a Family Member

13. Other Work Difficulties/Disorders
A. Perceptual Inaccuracies
B. Performance Anxiety
C. DSM-IV Psychiatric Disorder

structures and that whenever corporate strategy changes, structural changes must also take place. The assumption is that a good match between strategy and structure will result in increased organizational performance and decreased problems, while a mismatch will result in more problems and less productivity. Such a mismatch is called an **incompatible organizational design**. Certain strategies lend themselves to certain structural designs. For example, a high-tech manufacturing corporation in a fast-changing market would fare better with a more flexible, organic structural design than with a hierarchial, bureaucratic structural design.

2. Structural Problems

Organizational structures include operational systems and management systems. Operational systems include accounting, billing, personnel, training, production, sales, and related systems, while management systems include planning, organizing, control, and management development. Operational and management systems must match organizational strategy as well as facilitate each other's functioning. Structural problems arise when there is an incompatibility, such as when the corporation's new strategy is impeded by an outmoded management information system (MIS), or when a compatible MIS system is being improperly utilized because workers have not been adequately trained in its use. This is referred to as **operational** or **management system incompatibility**.

Organizational structures also specify the way the organization achieves its intended goals and tasks. Work tasks are divided into jobs or roles, which are grouped as teams, departments, or divisions. Structures specify the reporting relationship of these various roles, their span or control and authority, and their hierarchial location in the organizational chart. Structures further specify the expectation of each role, as well as policies and procedures for communicating with others in the performance of the task. **Role conflict** occurs when two or more expectations occur simultaneously so that complying with one makes accomplishing the other more difficult.

Role ambiguity refers to the differences between what management expects workers to do and what workers feel they should do.

Reporting relationship problems refer to communication difficulties between worker and superior, either because of person or structural issues. Structurally, workers who have a reporting relationship to two or more superiors can experience problems. For example, in a health care setting, a nurse would report both to a nursing department supervisor and a treatment team leader, who might be a physician. Role conflict, role ambiguity, and reporting relations problems can greatly impact job performance, job satisfaction, and worker health and well-being.

3. Environmental Problems

Environmental problems can be either internal or external. **Internal environmental problems** include various physical stressors in the workplace, such as exposure to toxic substances or fumes; extreme physical conditions, such as noise, heat, cold; or multiple stressors, such as combined heat and noise. They can also include various workplace crises, such as a union strike, death of a beloved senior executive or foreman, or violent episodes like a holdup, shooting, or hostage taking. **External environmental problems** result from outside economic, legal, or sociocultural factors. They include forced product recalls because of product tampering or safety concerns, a hostile takeover, or the unexpected loss of a major contract. Furthermore, increased competition, changes in market share, and the like can significantly impact corporations and the people working for them.

4. Job Design Problems

Job design refers to the process by which management specifies the contents, methods, and relationships of jobs to satisfy both organizational and individual requirements. In short, it is the process of arranging the components of the job/task in the most efficient manner. Common job design problems are high job strain, role overload, ergonomic incompatibility, worker–job or worker–organizational mismatch, and schedule/shift problems.

Job strain refers to the physiological, psychological, and behavioral manifestations of stress arising from an imbalance between the demands and control or decision latitude with a given job. **High job strain** results from jobs with high demands and low control, such as those of telephone operators, machine-paced assemblers, and video display terminal operators. The less control or decision latitude associated with a job, the higher the probability of psychological symptoms such as depression and anxiety, as well as stroke, heart disease, and hypertension (Karasek & Theorell, 1990).

Role overload refers to excessive expectations and demands associated with an individual's job. As corporations have downsized, more workers are now not only expected to increase their job productivity but also to assume additional role functions and tasks that were previously part of other job descriptions. For example, many managers and other professionals now have the added responsibility of doing filing and word processing previously done by clerical staff.

Ergonomics, or human factors engineering, is the adaptation of work conditions to the physical and psychological requirements and well-being of the worker. When the design of a job poorly matches an individual worker, it is called **ergonomic incompatibility**.

Worker–job or worker–organizational mismatch. The concept of "fit" or match between worker and job or organization is a useful framework for thinking about human behavior in organizations (Muchinsky, 1993). Generally speaking, the better the match between worker aptitudes, values, and attitudes and the job's requirements and the organization's culture, the more likely the worker will be productive and satisfied (Lowman, 1993).

Work schedules can impact job productivity, commitment, and job satisfaction as well as worker health. For some workers, flexible work hours offer an alternative to the traditional fixed working schedule and provide workers some choice in arrival and departure times. For other workers, work schedules include second shift, night shift, or rotating shift work. Research indicates that many shift workers experience problems with health and social adjustment. Because of an interruption in circadian rhythm, shift workers often complain of lack of sleep, fatigue, appetite loss, and constipation. They also experience family and marital difficulties (Muchinsky, 1993). In short, **schedule/shift problems** affect worker productivity, health, and interpersonal relationships.

5. Restructuring Problems

As corporations attempt to become more strategically focused and globally competitive, they tend to engage in restructuring activities. Currently, planned changed efforts such as "reengineering," "downsizing," "mergers," and "organizational transformation" are popular. The sequelae of these planned changed efforts are broad and pervasive and can significantly affect the health and well-being of involved workers. **Merger syndrome** is the result of either an unexpected hostile takeover or a merger and acquisition that was inadequately planned. The symptoms experienced by a majority of workers involve anxiety, dysphoria, insomnia, and various somatic concerns. These have been likened to posttraumatic syndrome. Because they have not adequately been psychologically prepared, workers experience fear of the unknown, grief at the anticipated change, loss of "psychological contract" with their employer, and the like (Mirvis, 1991).

Downsizing syndrome involves similar symptoms plus guilt feelings, specifically the guilt associated with being a survivor. It has also been called "layoff survivor sickness" (Noer, 1993). When a corporation downsizes, certain workers are laid off, usually permanently, while other workers retain their jobs, at least for a while. Those that are laid off or fired experience the sequelae of the job loss syndrome (Kates, Greiff, & Hagen, 1990) and may be aided by outplacement counseling. Those that survive the layoff can experience downsizing survivor syndrome.

6. Problematic Corporate Cultures

Kets de Vries and Miller (1984, 1987) describe five corporate cultures that engender difficulty for corporate members and stakeholders. The following problematic cultures are based on their research.

The confident culture. This organization, also called the **dramatic organization**, is often headed by ambitious leaders and tends to be hyperactive, impulsive, dramatically venturesome, and dangerously uninhibited. Audacity, risk taking, and diversification are corporate themes, and power tends to be centralized with the top decision makers. The merger mania of the 1980s, often financed by leveraged buyouts, epitomized the dramatic organization, in which a few ambitious executives and financiers were able to control unheard of sums of capital. Often in this culture, sensible expansion gives way to uncontrolled greed.

The survivor culture. This organization, also called the **paranoid organization**, emphasizes organizational intelligence and control. Sophisticated and elaborate information systems reflect the organization's desire for perpetual vigilance and preparedness for emergencies. In this type of organization, key executives model and reinforce an "institutionalization of suspicion." The merger and takeover boom of the 1980s endangered paranoid organizations: These corporations spent inordinate time tracking and fighting their enemies to such an extent that they ultimately neglected the needs and wants of their customers. Advisedly, a climate of suspicion is not unusual within many firms that are candidates for takeover. However, within survivor culture organizations, suspiciousness takes hold, and eventually fight and flight considerations supersede manufacturing or service and marketing strategies as fears became institutionalized.

The conscientious culture. Like the survivor culture organization, the conscientious culture organization, or the **compulsive organization**, also emphasizes formal controls and information systems but for different reasons. In the compulsive organization, controls are designed to monitor internal operations, productivity, costs, and scheduling of projects, rather than external conditions, as in the paranoid corporation. Thoroughness, completeness, and conformity to established procedures characterize the compulsive firm. Its organizational structure is strictly hierarchical, reflecting top leadership's concern with control. Not surprisingly, corporations that value precision, such as engineering and valuation companies, tend to be compulsive organizations. They epitomize the quest for being "rational managers" and thus allocate considerable time and effort to strategic planning and management.

The sedentary culture. This organization, also called the

depressive organization, tends to be a well-established firm serving a mature market. It is characterized by inactivity, lack of confidence, and extreme insularity and passivity. Pessimism and helplessness prevail. This sense of defeatism is usually caused and contributed to by a stagnating business environment. Corporations like General Motors and Ford Motor Company in the 1980s acted as moribund bureaucracies in which complacent and conservative chief executive officers (CEOs) let manufacturing and design capacities stagnate as overseas competition overwhelmed them.

The solitary culture. The solitary culture organization, or the **schizoid organization,** is like the sedentary organization in that it suffers from a leadership vacuum. Because of past disappointments, the CEO in this organization withdraws from contact with others, believing that most contacts will end painfully and is inclined instead toward daydreaming and reverie. Second-level executives tend to fill the leadership void and "carry" the CEO. Unfortunately, this often leads to political infighting as this second tier of leaders vies to win favor from an unresponsive CEO. Consequently, strategy making vacillates between the proposals of one favored subordinate and those of another. The corporation thus drifts or bounces along, depending on the energy of one group, and then reverses itself when a new group of executives wins favor. Not surprisingly, effective coordination and communication are impossible. And because the corporation's focus has become so internally focused, the solitary organization tends to lose sight of valuable external information. Accordingly, its business suffers.

7. Dysfunctional Interpersonal and Team Relations

Working relations among organizational members assume a certain degree of conflict, given the complexity of role and task demands, and some conflict is necessary and useful. For example, in the formation of a work group or team, various stages can be observed: forming, storming, norming, and performing. The last stage, performing, indicates the group is moving to a point of full productivity and collaboration without need for struggles and adaptation.

Interpersonal conflict can result between two coworkers or a worker and a superior. This conflict can arise from differences of opinion, style, values, or mannerisms. It can also arise because of role conflict, role ambiguity, or role overload. Verbal, physical, or sexual harassment can be a factor, and sometimes personality factors are involved. Ordinarily, personality factors are considered secondary to role factors, when analyzing conflict in an organizational setting.

Team conflict. Approximately 60 percent of the length of any team project, from start to finish, is taken up with the forming and storming group stages. In the storming stage, conflict among team members is a "necessary" period of stressful negotiation of the terms under which the team will work together (Robbins & Finley, 1995). In other instances, team conflict may arise from inadequate or inconsistent leadership; misalignment of team goals and objectives with corporate goals and objectives; or scapegoating, stereotyping, or other communication problems. Inadequate resources or skill deficit among one or more teams members can be another cause.

Intergroup conflict refers to conflict between two or more work teams or corporate units/divisions. It can be constructive, such as in the healthy competition to meet production quotas, or unhealthy, as when one group sabotages the efforts of another. Feldman (1985) describes several types of such conflict and a taxonomy of conflict resolution strategies.

8. Defective Supervision

A worker's immediate superior or supervisor can either enhance or detract from the worker's job productivity, organizational commitment, and sense of job satisfaction and well-being. Ineffectual or troublesome supervisors can either be **unqualified for their position** or have received **improper/inadequate training**. Personality factors, including personality-disordered behaviors, may also be involved.

9. Authority Problems and Issues

Authority problems in a work context appear to stem from the same dynamics as authority problems in other contexts, such as marital and family relations. Two contributing factors to evaluate in authority problems are the role of the work situation itself and the role of predispositional factors (Lowman, 1993).

Leadership–followership style conflicts. Jobs vary in the degree of supervision required, the manner in which supervision is implemented, and in the match between leadership and followership styles. The greater the "fit" or match in leader–follower relations, the less conflict is to be expected; while the poorer the match, the more conflict is to be expected. Some supervisors are better at exercising authority than others, possibly because their influence and control are more implicit than explicit.

Leader–follower relationships have the potential for reenacting family-of-origin dynamics. Individuals with **unresolved family-of-origin conflicts** are likely to experience problems with authority or may create such a problem, if it does not already exist. What the worker brings to the work organization in terms of prior authority problems—particularly unresolved conflicts with parental figures—will influence the likelihood and types of conflicts.

Similarly, authority problems may reflect longstanding **personality disorders** or **characterological problems** of workers or supervisors. The evaluation of authority conflicts should begin with the realities of the complaint. If multiple complaints of abuse of authority originate from a particular organizational unit of a certain supervisor, the issue is less likely to be the worker's personality and more likely the supervisor's characteristics.

II. DYSFUNCTIONAL WORK CAPACITY

10. Undercommitment and Overcommitment

Patterns of undercommitment reflect a tendency to be underinvolved in work in a way that makes the worker less effective than his or her abilities or career profile suggest. It implies that the pattern has become sufficiently dysfunctional to interfere with the worker's day-to-day job tasks. The basic issue in patterns of undercommitment is a failure to commit to requirements of the work role such that potential is not reached, or there is a significant discrepancy between required job duties and acceptable levels of job performance. Under-commitment patterns can be cyclical, occurring at sporadic intervals, or they can be persistent and typically characteristic of the individual's job performance. Both the worker and the organization suffer in not obtaining the best the worker is capable of on the job (Lowman, 1993).

In **underachievement patterns,** there is a chronic discrepancy between the worker's ability to do the job and how he or she actually performs the job. Underachievement can be caused by a variety of issues, including passive-aggressive behavior.

Temporary production impediments refers to a temporary or cyclically periodic inhibition in performing a work role in a worker who formerly performed at a higher level. Common examples are writer's or painter's blocks.

Procrastination refers to a persistent and/or cyclical pattern in which a worker, who is otherwise capable of doing a job, repetitively avoids timely initiation and/or completion of work assignments or activities that must be initiated or completed by a particular deadline, real or perceived.

Fear of success is noted when a worker underachieves because of consciously or unconsciously perceived negative consequences associated with being "successful," including the perception that significant others may be dissatisfied or unhappy with the achievements.

Fear of failure refers to the belief that one will not be able to reach a desired or previously set goal or success and, as a result, will be a failure, especially in the eyes of others.

Patterns of overcommitment refer to an intense identification with and involvement in the work role such that a worker's psychological (and sometimes physical) health is potentially impaired. Overcommitment becomes a work dysfunction when it is perceived by the employee as a problem or when the health consequences of the overcommitment become problematic.

Work addiction, or workaholism, is a preoccupation with work tasks characterized by overwork, obsessiveness, inability to relax, denial, difficulty with intimacy, mental preoccupation with the future, perfectionism, self-esteem problems, and a narrow range of outside interests. Work productivity of these individuals is often less than that of nondriven workers.

The **type A behavior pattern** describes the individual who is aggressive, driven, ambitious, competitive, task oriented, and constantly on the move. This individual chronically struggles to complete as many tasks as possible in the shortest period of time.

Burnout is a debilitating psychological condition caused by unmanaged work stress resulting in depleted energy levels, decreased immunocompetence, increased dissatisfaction, pessimism and absenteeism, as well as inefficiency at work. Burnout is more commonly noted among those working in the helping professions and in the service sector (Lowman, 1993).

11. Problematic Work-Personality Styles

Personality-related problems create some of the most emotionally volatile and difficult to manage workplace concerns. They often affect not only one worker but others in the work team or organizational unit as well. Usually these difficulties are blown out of proportion into the precipitating conflict as individuals get locked into dysfunctional interactions and as the conflict becomes publicly manifest (Lowman, 1993).

It would be simple and convenient to assume that the designation "Personality Disorders" in DSM-IV is directly applicable in the workplace. By definition DSM-IV requires that a Personality Disorder be an enduring pattern that deviates from cultural expectations and is inflexible and pervasive. Pervasive means the pattern is operative in the family, in social settings, and *on the job*.

Fortunately, not all individuals who meet criteria for a DSM-IV Personality Disorder experience difficulty on the job or in a specific work role. For example, a hardworking, dedicated accountant, who seems to meet the criteria for an Obsessive-Compulsive Personality Disorder, may find that the culture of his accounting department rewards him for his accuracy and perseverance, whereas his wife and family find his orderliness, perfectionism, and feeling avoidance extremely disturbing.

To be considered a problematic work-personality style, the problematic behavior should be persistent across a variety of workplace situations, appreciably interfere with the implementation of the work role, and be relatively unresponsive to change efforts, such as coaching and performance contracting (Lowman, 1993). The following 11 work-personality styles are described in detail in Chapter 7, including their corresponding DSM-IV designation. They are the **Sensitive Style; Adventurous Style; Mercurial Style; Devoted Style; Dramatic Style; Self-Confident Style; Conscientious Style; Vigilant Style; Leisurely Style; Solitary Style; and Idiosyncratic Style.**

12. Life-Role Conflicts

Difficulties in the work role may lead to stress in one's nonwork life, just as nonwork life stress can cause or exacerbate job stress. The interaction between job, career, and personal life is decidedly complex. Yet, these three intersecting factors must be considered when evaluating a worker or planning an intervention. Greenhaus (1987) and Arthur, Hall, and Lawrence (1989) adequately address job career and personal/family issues, particularly **career decision** and **development problems.** Certain individuals are chronically dissatisfied with their career status because of failure to take realistic risks or failure to implement and follow through with career training and decisions.

Work–Family conflicts and issues span the continuum from work scheduling to elder care issues. Zedeck (1992) provides a comprehensive treatment of job and personal–family conflicts. **Inflexible scheduling and leave policies** may be stressors for some workers, particularly women who have child rearing responsibilities. Flextime scheduling, a shortened work week, or a shared job may be a reasonable option in such cases. Nevertheless, because of fear of job loss or being branded as someone demanding special privileges, some workers will be reluctant to make such requests.

Career "dysynchrony" between married spouses is an increasingly common cause of concern and conflict among dual career couples. Dysynchrony occurs when the worker's or the couple's experience is "off schedule" in relation to some sort of "timetable" of career, family, or individual development. Thus, individuals who marry late and have children late experience considerably more stress when living through other out-of-sync decisions, such as a career change, than those who are "on schedule" (Sekaran & Hall, 1989). There appears to be more social support for workers who are on schedule or in sync, and such support reduces stress.

Child or elder care issues can also be stressors. Finding adequate and affordable care for the children and aging parents of workers is not only an individual worker's concern but an increasing concern for corporations. **Chronic or terminal illness of a family member** can be a considerable stressor affecting not only a specific worker but others on the work team or organizational unit as well. Since the worker with a sick family member may be absent often—using all or many sick days to care for their relative—productivity and team morale may suffer. Creative solutions for this and other work–family conflicts are needed.

13. Other Work Difficulties/Disorders

Perceptual inaccuracies occur in work situations in which there is a considerable discrepancy between consensually validated views of the situation and the worker's perception. They are neither psychotic nor as pervasive as the perceptual distortions of the Paranoid Personality-Disordered worker. An example is the manager who continually thinks that her superior is angrily opposed to her ideas, when in fact it is the manager who is angry (Lowman, 1993).

Performance anxiety is an anxious reaction that is situation specific and usually directly relevant to job performance. It can affect a variety of performance areas or be limited to certain aspects of work (Lowman, 1993). Unlike DSM-IV social phobias, performance anxiety does not lead to significant impairment in functioning or in marked distress. For example, a design engineer who is otherwise well suited to design engineering and well regarded for his technical competence may experience stage fright when making a formal presentation to his peers at a scientific meeting.

While this taxonomy has been developed to assess and evaluate the normative range of organizational behavior and functioning, it is conceivable that a worker could be diagnosed with a concurrent **DSM-IV Psychiatric Disorder** that may or may not affect job performance. Furthermore, what first appears as a work dysfunction or disorder might be a subclinical manifestation as a DSM-IV Axis I or II disorder that later manifests as a full-blown clinical disorder.

5

Organizational Interventions

Traditionally, organizational interventions have been assumed to be only the domain of internal and external organizational consultants, or other specialists with specific training and experience in organizational dynamics and organizational diagnosis, and not that of clinicians, who would have had no formal training in these interventions and little or no experience with them. As noted in Chapter 1, however, this assumption is no longer tenable. Today, clinician-consultants may routinely administer some or all of these interventions.

Organizational interventions refer to the structured activities in which consultants and clients participate during the course of an organizational consultation. These activities are designed to improve the organization's functioning, and in some instances, individual functioning as well. More specifically, organizational interventions are a set of structured activities that are focused at selected organizational units: individual, team, or the entire organization. Table 5.1 lists ten common organizational interventions utilized in individual, team, or organization-wide contexts.

These ten interventions are discussed in subsequent sections of this chapter. Each intervention is described from the consultant's perspective: his/her role, goal, and task. It is hoped that this overview will provide the reader with an appreciation of the potential tools that are available to corporate change agents. Key resource materials are referenced for each intervention in the Recommended Reading list at the end of each section. Some of these intervention strategies are also illustrated in case examples in Chapters 8 and 9.

TABLE 5.1

Organizational Interventions

Individually Focused Interventions

1. Executive Assessment Consultation
2. Executive Coaching and Consultation
3. Career Development Counseling and Consultation
4. Retirement Counseling and Consultation

Team-Focused Intervention

5. Team Development Consultation

Organization-Focused Interventions

6. Management and Leadership Development Consultation
7. Strategic Planning Consultation
8. Organizational Restructuring and Transformation Consultation
9. Stress Management Consultation
10. Performance Appraisal System Consultation

INDIVIDUALLY FOCUSED INTERVENTIONS

Executive Assessment Consultation

The executive assessment is to a normal population what the clinical assessment is to an abnormal population. The executive asssessment emphasizes health rather than pathology, and it has dramatically more wide-ranging potential. It is an in-depth, comprehensive assessment of a person's overall functioning, assessing the person's capacities, styles, level of emotional maturity, and the degree to which he or she capitalizes on basic potentials. It is the consultant's way of gathering a maximum of data, usefully integrating that data, and predicting future functioning.

The executive assessment serves many purposes: as a descriptor and predictor of performance, as a developmental manual for the individual's supervisor, as an inventory of organizational talent, and as the beginning of a trusting relationship with the consultant.

Tobias (1990) provides a descriptive and useful outline for organizing the report of the executive assessment in terms of six characteristics:

1. *Intellectual Characteristics:* indicating the degree and kinds of intelligence, cognitive styles, and the extent to which the individual works up to capacity
2. *Emotional Characteristics:* indicating emotional stability, maturity, modes of adjustment, ego strength, core values, degree of integration, stamina, and so forth
3. *Motivational Characteristics:* indicating level of drive and psychological needs
4. *Insights into Self and Others:* indicating extent of flexibility, objectivity, self-scrutiny, defensiveness, receptivity, sensitivity, perceptiveness, psychological-mindedness, and empathy
5. *Interpersonal Characteristics:* indicating adaptability, dominance, friendliness, cooperativeness, tact, and poise
6. *Vocational Characteristics:* indicating technical skills; leadership skills; ability to organize, coordinate, direct, plan, and take charge; managerial style; and organizational strengths and shortcomings. In addition, this part of the report highlights the implications the foregoing material has for on-the-job performance, person–job fit, and ways of shaping context and environment to best suit the individual.

This outline has the advantage of starting with deeper personality characteristics, moving through the bridge of insight, and ending with the social and occupational manifestations of personality in behavior.

Executive assessment reports of prospective workers usually include a recommendation section, which reflects the consultant's judgment of the psychological fit between the applicant and the job in question. In reaching this judgment, the consultant needs to consider the promotability of the candidate; the nature of the organizational culture; the characteristics of the applicant's prospective manager, coworkers, and subordinates; and barriers or special circumstances that could affect the applicant's performance, as well as the nature of the job itself. In addition, the consultant should take into account the inevitability of change and adversity in all of these areas, as well as in the applicant's personal life and the corporation's future. Finally, a prediction of how the individual will likely respond under conditions of crisis, stress, temptation, pressure, uncertainty, disappointment, rejection, loss, failure, or lack of control are critical considerations.

Executive assessments are typically reported in both oral and written form. The oral presentation has the virtue of immediacy, informality, give-and-take between psychologist and evaluee, and the ease of shifting focus from broad to narrow, from abstract to concrete, and from the descriptive to the experiential. The written report allows for comprehensiveness, subtle differentiation, and a consistent message and tone for anyone who reads it. An oral report without a written one is apt to lack comprehensiveness and to be imprecise. However, a written report without oral feedback does not have the advantage of further clarification and reader input, and it tends to be felt as impersonal.

Recommended Readings

Special Issue: Issues in the assessment of managerial and executive leadership. (1994). *Consulting Psychology Journal, 46* (1).

Tobias, Lester. (1990). *Psychological Consulting to Management: A Clinician's Perspective.* New York: Brunner/Mazel.

Executive Coaching and Consultation

As an organizational intervention, coaching involves the consultant working with executives to help them lead and relate more effectively to others and learn or modify specific skills, such as assertive communication, active listening, negotiation, or handling difficult employees. In the process, they are helped to see themselves as others see them, and they are encouraged to explore new ways of behaving. Throughout, the emphasis is upon giving nonevaluative feedback to the individual.

A second important feature of this intervention is the joint exploration of alternative behaviors. The consultant responds to the executive's questions, such as "What do you think I should do to improve my performance?" by suggesting alternatives raised by the executive himself or herself and then assisting the executive to evaluate the costs and benefits of the various alternatives. The consultant stresses that implementation of any behavioral change is the executive's responsibility and that the consultant's role is to provide accurate feedback by asking questions and increasing the executive's choices.

Executive consultation is less concerned with the executive's leadership and relational skills and more with the executive's own concerns. The consultant's role here is rather one of listener, confidant, and personal adviser. Essentially, the consultant serves as a sounding board and as an objective and trustworthy source of feedback. Such consultation sessions consist of directed discussions initiated by the executive who sets the agenda. Discussion might focus on a staff conflict, morale in a division, a merger, office relocation, or a personal concern. The session might last 20 minutes or six hours. Although sessions usually take place in the executive's office, they might also take place on the phone or at the executive's club.

Recommended Readings

Durcan, Jim, & Oates, David. (1994). *The Manager as Coach.* London: Pittman.
Singer, E. J. (1979). *Effective Management Coaching.* London: Institute.
Special Issue: Consulting to senior management. (1991). *Consulting Psychology Bulletin, 43* (1).

Career Development Counseling and Consultation

Career development counseling and consultation is a generic term referring to an array of intervention strategies that have an individual focus. Career development is the process by which a corporation promotes its workers' growth inside the organization. This might involve career counseling or career planning. The purpose of these activities is to help individuals focus on their life and career objectives and assist them to better control their career and future. Issues dealt with in career development include an evaluation of one's career history, a formulation of clear personal goals for the future in terms of desired lifestyle and career path, and a plan of action aimed at achieving the specified goals.

Career counseling interventions focus on separate functions

including career planning, career decision making, career adjustment, and career effectiveness. These interventions may be delivered
individually, in groups, programmatically, or in various combinations of the three, and they draw heavily upon techniques of vocational assessment, occupational information, labor market trends,
and information about personal attributes as they relate to work.

Individual approaches to career counseling and career development
have been characterized by a series of interactions with workers that
usually range from two to five interviews. These interviews are typically phased as follows:

1. An intake interview in which the career counselor or consul-
    tant and worker establish a working relationship such that
    some working hypotheses about the worker's needs and
    well-being can be formulated.
2. A phase involving what might be called "problem defini-
    tion" in which the worker's major concerns are made more
    explicit than in the initial interview, and a priority order
    of these concerns is established.
3. An assessment phase that involves some more or less sys-
    tematic appraisal of the worker's attributes that seem to be
    most closely related to the defined problem or problems.
    This assessment can be done using interview methods or
    might involve a rather extensive variety of psychological
    tests and inventories (Lowman, 1991). Furthermore, the
    assessment phase can include work simulation or job sample
    tasks and techniques.
4. A feedback phase in which the consultant reports back to
    the worker the results and the potential meaning of the
    previous phases, particularly the assessment phase.
5. Finally, an implementation phase in which the worker's
    main responsibility is to make decisions pertinent to putting
    into action, in appropriate ways, some of the major informa-
    tion and attitudes gleaned from the previous four phases.

In a comparison of individual, group, and programmatic approaches
in career development, one finds that programmatic approaches are

used when anticipating normal career growth and development, without the presence of a problem; individual approaches are typically used with individuals who need extra help in dealing with normal career decision problems; and group approaches include both a high proportion of individuals with normally developing careers and individuals with career problems.

Recommended Readings

Greenhaus, Jeffrey. (1987). *Career Management.* Chicago: Dryden Press.
Lowman, Rodney. (1991). *The Clinical Practice of Career Assessment.* Washington, DC: American Psychological Association.
Schein, Edgar. (1978). *Career Dynamics: Matching Individual and Organizational Needs.* Reading, MA: Addison-Wesley.

Retirement Counseling and Consultation

Usually retirement is thought of as having four facets: scheduled retirement, planned early retirement, forced retirement, or semi-retirement. With 28 extra years added to life expectancy during the past century, the average American now has a choice of growing old or using these extra years to plan different scenarios. Until now, it was assumed that an individual would follow the "linear life plan," in which childhood and adolescence are a time of education and job preparation, followed by a career and family life, and then death. Longer life expectancy allows more flexible life and career planning, which is aptly referred to as the "cyclic life plan."

Individuals will now have the option of having several different careers and jobs in their lifetime interspersed with periodic time off for further education or retraining, as well as planned sabbaticals and leaves of absence for extended leisure activities. A Rand Corporation study predicted that by the year 2020, the average worker will need to be retrained up to 13 times in his or her lifetime (Dychtwald & Flower, 1990). Also, because of downsizing, many workers in their 50s are taking early retirement, along with those in their 60s and 70s.

Many corporations have preretirement planning programs, which are primarily developed for the older retiree. The majority of these programs emphasize information on pensions, health insurance, medicare, and retirement timing options (Morrow, 1985). These services often include a group format in which retirees-to-be meet with program personnel and "successful" retirees to discuss how to maintain and enhance identity, self-esteem, intimate and social relations, and other retirement issues (Greenhaus, 1987; Lewis & Lewis, 1986; Morrow, 1985). What is currently needed, however, is retirement counseling and consultation that is more comprehensive and that includes the unique developmental issues of this stage of life as well (Bronte, 1993).

Recommended Readings

Bronte, Lydia. (1993). *The Longevity Factor.* New York: HarperCollins.
Fyock, Catherine, & Dorton, Anne. (1994). *Unretirement.* New York: AMACOM Books.

TEAM-FOCUSED INTERVENTION

Team Development Consultation

Team development is a general category of organizational interventions intended to enhance the effective operation of organizational subgroups or teams (Dyer, 1977). These interventions aim to improve the ways in which individuals work together as a cohesive team. The activities involved may relate to task issues, that is, to the way things are done and the skills needed to accomplish the tasks, or they may relate to the nature and quality of the relationships between the team members or between the members and the team leader.

There are different types of interventions for different types of teams. For *new teams* the manager and the new team members develop a common framework and common goals toward which they can work. The strengthening of *existing teams* is accomplished by the team evaluating its recent past to identify strengths and problems in the way it conducts business and then developing action plans to solve the problems and to capitalize upon team strengths.

Finally, another type of intervention is used for *reforming teams*. The approach is similar to that used in strengthening teams, except that the members may have worked with each other previously. The groups themselves may be formal work teams, such as managers heading different committees, temporary task forces, or social groups. A wide variety of different activities are used in this intervention. Some focus upon problem diagnosis of group work, task accomplishment, team relationships, and team and organizational processes.

Team development activities usually include problem diagnosis and problem-solving sessions. A facilitator is utilized when appropriate. Data are gathered about the relevant problems and the issues to be addressed. The sessions themselves include feedback from the data, problem prioritization, problem diagnosis, and planning (Reddy, 1994). Although team development approaches differ, they all have common characteristics and similar stages. They frequently begin by gaining top management's commitment to the project and then that of the supervisor. The goal here is to improve communication, reduce conflict, and improve productivity. The next step is to hold workshops for teams throughout the organization in order to improve teamwork and the understanding of each other's problems. Finally, follow-up meetings are scheduled to help keep the momentum of change going.

Recommended Readings

Dyer, W. G. (1977). *Team Building.* Reading, MA: Addison-Wesley.
Katzenbach, Jon, & Smith, Douglas. (1993). *The Wisdom of Teams: Creating the High Performance Organization.* Boston: Harvard Business School Press.
Reddy, W. Brendan. (1994). *Intervention Skills: Process Consultation for Small Groups and Teams.* San Diego: Pfeiffer.

ORGANIZATION-FOCUSED INTERVENTIONS

Management and Leadership Development Consultation

U.S. corporations spend approximately 1 percent of their total revenues for the training and development of their managers, amounting to about $40 billion annually (McCall, Lombardo, & Morrison, 1988). Traditionally, these management development programs have concentrated on building and upgrading a set of generic management competencies, such as interpersonal skills and financial analysis, in a course or seminar format. The underlying assumption is that course work fosters executive performance because it facilitates the manager's ability to gain technical knowledge, understand management models and theories, solve and frame problems, and develop self-confidence and judgment skills. But the assumption that this form of learning significantly impacts executive functioning and is cost-justified is questionable. Others argue that the most effective and useful way to learn about management is on the job rather than in the classroom. However, there was no definitive research to address this concern until McCall, Lombardo, and Morrison published *The Lessons of Experience-How Successful Executives Develop on the Job* in 1988.

Data for this research was generated from four separate studies, encompassing 191 successful executives from six major corporations. It concluded that the process of executive development occurs during the course of 10 or 20 years of progressive job experience. The report also noted that not all work experiences are the same. Some experiences engender more developmental impact than others. Further, the lessons taught are not random, and certain things are far more likely to be learned from one kind of experience than another. The research describes in addition five sets of lessons successful executives had learned on the job and five developmental events that spawned these lessons. The five lessons are: setting and implementing agendas; handling relationships; basic values; executive temperament; and personal insight.

Besides the context for executive training and development, contemporary management and executive development programs are also reflecting other changes in philosophy and design. For instance, training is become less trainer directed and more self-directed; less theory based and more strategically based; less activity focused and more outcome or results focused. Furthermore, management development training is increasingly being referred to as a "management development system" (Potts & Sykes, 1993). Based on extensive research, Stumpf and Mullen (1992) describe six strategic management skills. These skills involve the manager's ability to: (1) know the business and markets; (2) manage subunit rivalry; (3) find and overcome threats; (4) stay on strategy; (5) be an entrepreneurial force; and (6) accommodate adversity.

Executive development programs are being designed to help managers develop a capacity to manage strategically. Because traditional educational methods have been inadequate in teaching strategic leadership, other approaches—such as coaching, mentoring, and simulation—have become commonplace. The consultant's use of coaching and mentoring are described earlier in this chapter.

Organizational simulations, including computer simulations and simulated company work experiences, have been found to be extremely effective learning experiences (Stumpf & Mullen, 1992). Each manager's experience in a simulated organizational environment is real for him or her, since it provides an opportunity to exercise skills in pursuit of a wide range of goals through different strategies. Each manager determines the mission, vision, and objectives of the firm, which can include expansion or contraction of specific parts of the business, diversification into other lines of business, an increase in customer service, and/or the development of the firm's human resources or community relations. As a result of the simulation experience, the manager is able to develop strategies for attaining each of these objectives.

The power of organizational simulations is that they are comprised of a representative work environment and management issues, just as flight simulators are comprised of a representative airplane environment and flying issues. They are realistic contexts in which managers think, act, and interact in much the same way as they do on their real jobs. In contrast to their real jobs, however, they receive quick and rich feedback from self-assessment, peer assessments, and instructors' evaluations on their strategic leadership abilities.

In short, whereas before the consultant's role in management and executive development had been to teach or facilitate management seminars, now the consultant's role is more likely to involve designing learning experiences that are strategically focused or utilizing coaching or simulation activities.

Recommended Readings

Hague, Hawdon. (1974). *Executive Self-Development: Real Learning in Real Situations.* New York: Wiley.

McCall, Morgan, Lombardo, Michael, & Morrison, Ann. (1988). *The Lessons of Experience: How Successful Executives Develop on the Job.* Lexington, MA: Lexington Books.

Potts, Tom, & Sykes, Arnold. (1993). *Executive Talent: How to Identify and Develop the Best.* Homewood, IL: Business One Irwin.

Strategic Planning Consultation

The successful performance of strategic planning consultation is the acid test for any organizational consultant (Greiner & Metzger, 1983). In strategic planning, the consultant must be able to analyze facets of a client's business from not only an organizational perspective but also from the perspective of the corporation's product, market, and competition. In short, strategic planning consultation requires broad business knowledge and analytical skills. The effective consultant must also have the ability to work on a peer basis with senior executives and be able to confront them with hard facts and bad news while also leading them to new insights. Finally, the consultant must be able to translate intellectual understanding into concrete recommendations that still retain the emotional commitment of senior management.

Since strategic planning usually occurs in a group context, the consultant will function best in the role of facilitator. In this role, the consultant develops the agenda and subject matter to be covered and ensures that discussion moves creatively toward the objectives. The challenge is to steer discussion away from destructive company political issues and fights, while still encouraging open debate and, at the same time, facilitating the less vocal to share their ideas.

If the participants are well prepared, knowledgeable, and can work together constructively, the consultant's role can be unobtrusive and minimally participative. Often, however, long silences and irrelevant or paternalistic monologues occur. Senior managers who are unsure of the role they should play or who are insecure when facing new and threatening issues will tend to look to the CEO to lead every discussion and resolve every issue. In such instances, it is the role of the consultant to open up the discussion by arguing for the sake of argument and/or asking others for their opinions.

It is very difficult for one consultant to manage strategic planning sessions alone. The value of having more than one consultant present at these sessions is, that as one takes notes and monitors the agenda or discussion outline, the other is guiding the actual discussion, participating in the arguments, and watching the interactions between the participants. Also as one consultant facilitates the discussion, the other can write down thoughts and ideas expressed on "flip chart" pages, which are then torn off and taped to the walls of the conference room. Following the sessions, the consultant should transcribe the notes into a memorandum to all participants that can be used later as an implementation guide and monitoring device to assure follow-up.

Once the goals and objectives of the corporation have been developed, the consultant can be of further assistance in assuring that the written and verbal conclusions from the session are, in fact, implemented. It begins with a top management meeting after the session to develop action assignments with agreed upon responsibilities for each member set within realistic time frames. Then, the consultant should work with each senior manager and his or her respective subordinates to "infuse" goals and objectives downward and to return upward with a list of support and resource needs required to carry out these goals. This downward, upward, downward movement of ideas, plans, and needs provides a positive, dynamic set of interactions, which in turn gives a sense of purpose and direction to the corporation.

A consultant who is able to orchestrate these complex communications effectively has done a successful job. He or she has revitalized and helped to create a supportive climate for everyone involved and has assisted the corporation to refocus its energy (Pfeiffer, et al., 1989).

Recommended Readings

Greiner, Larry, & Metzger, Robert. (1983). *Consulting to Management.* Englewood Cliffs, NJ: Prentice-Hall. (Chapter 6)
Pfeiffer, J. William, Goodstein, Leonard, & Nolan, Timothy. (1989). *Shaping Strategic Planning.* Glenview, IL: Scott, Foresman.

Organizational Restructuring and Transformation Consultation

There is considerable interest among corporate leaders about organizational restructuring and transformation. Two common forms of restructuring are total quality management and reengineering.

Total Quality Management (TQM)

Also referred to as continuous quality improvement, total quality management is an organization-wide approach to change that combines a number of organizational interventions, including the use of quality circles, statistical quality control, self-managed teams and task forces, and employee participation. TQM's goal is to transform the organization. Interest in TQM stems largely from the critical need for American corporations to compete on a global scale, particularly with the Japanese who have had great success in managing quality.

The following seven features characterize TQM. First, *a primary emphasis on customers:* This calls for development of an organizational culture in which employees at all levels, including the CEO, give paramount treatment to customer needs and expectations. Second, *the daily operational use of the concept of internal customers:* Emphasis is placed on the concept that work flow and internal interdependencies require that organizational members treat each other as valued customers across functional lines as well as within units. Third, *an emphasis on measurement using both statistical quality control and statistical process control techniques:* Statistical quality control is a method of measuring and analyzing deviations in manufactured products; statistical process control is a method of analyzing deviations in manufacturing processes. Fourth, *a shift toward participative management:* This includes extensive delegation and involvement and a coaching, supportive leadership style. Fifth, *an emphasis on teams and teamwork:* Typically this includes self-managed teams. Cross-functional and multilevel task forces are also used extensively. Sixth, *a major emphasis on continuous training:* This means learning new and better ways of doing things and adding new skills. In many organizations it is reinforced by changes in the reward system, for example, the introduction of skill-based or knowledge-based pay. And finally, *top-management support on an ongoing basis:* This requires a long-term perspective and a long-term commitment on the part of top management.

Some version of total quality management is being used in virtually all types of organizations today. Organizations as diverse as health care organizations and the U.S. Navy have become involved. A U.S. General Accounting Office (GAO) study found that total quality management is useful for both large and small organizations. The GAO reported that sufficient time needs to be allowed for gains to appear—on the average, companies required two and a half years to improve their performance. Thus, TQM requires a long-term perspective, as it is a long-term, continuous process.

Reengineering

Recently, considerable interest has been generated in reengineering, which Hammer and Champy (1993) define as the fundamental rethinking and radical redesign of business processes to achieve dramatic improvements in critical, contemporary measures of performance, such as cost, quality, service, and speed. Reengineering is not appropriate for making incremental improvements but rather for large-scale, divisional, or organization-wide changes.

Reengineering seeks to streamline an organization to be more efficient by combining, eliminating, or restructuring activities without regard to present hierarchical or control procedures. Downsizing, or selective permanent layoffs, is a basic strategy for accomplishing the goal of reengineering. For workers, reengineering is commonly synonymous with job loss. Thus, it should not be surprising that workers have strong feelings and convictions against reengineering. Accordingly, they may consciously or unconsciouly undermine reengineering efforts.

Reengineering, as it is presently conceptualized, pays little attention to the social system of organizations relative to change processes and the redesign of work. In contrast, organizational development interventions, such as social–technical systems, emerged out of the realization that the interdependence and "fit" of the technical and social systems of organizations were extremely important. As such, reengineering is distinctly different from the organizational development activities of many psychologically trained consultants.

Reengineering is essentially a top-down intervention that assumes that neither an upward flow of involvement nor consensus decision making will work to accomplish dramatic changes. Proponents of reengineering contend that people lower down in the organization do not have sufficient perspective to visualize the changes that are needed. However, they do point out that it is important to pay attention to the corporation's human resource and organizational infrastructures. Finally, they see the role of the manager changing from being that of a superior that of a coach, which is consistent with the experience of organizations that move toward self-managed teams.

Needless to say, both reengineering and TQM require considerable consultant skill. Furthermore, organizational restructuring efforts usually involve a team of organizational consultants and other expert consultants.

Recommended Readings

Hammer, Michael, & Champy, James. (1993). *Reengineering the Corporation: A Manifesto for Business Revolution.* New York: HarperCollins.
Lawler, Edward, Mohrman, Susan, & Ledford, Gerald. (1992). *Employee Involvement: Total Quality Management.* San Francisco: Jossey-Bass.
Wall, Bob, Solum, Robert, & Sobel, Mark. (1992). *The Visionary Leader.* Rocklin, CA: Prima.

Stress Management Consultation

There are two rather different approaches to stress management consultation. The first approach assumes that "context" and "stressors" are givens and that stress reactions in the workplace are primarily a function of limited coping ability and heightened "vulnerability" in the individual. In this view, the individual has defective or inadequate coping skills that stress-management programs should remediate (Roskies, 1987). Most books and prepackaged stress management programs are based on this set of assumptions. The second approach, however, assumes that organizational structures, such as job design and policies, are the primary cause of workplace stress. Stress management consultation should thus be focused on the "reconstruction of work life." (Karasek & Theorell, 1990).

Individual stress-management interventions include training in such knowledge and skill areas as diet, exercise, time management, assertiveness, support groups, relaxation/meditation, biofeedback, autogenic training, and cognitive restructuring. Of these interventions, exercise, relaxation, biofeedback, time management, and cognitive restructuring have been found to have positive stress reduction effects (Matteson & Ivancevich, 1987). However, in terms of long-range results, relaxation was found to result in lower absenteeism in workers for the first year only (Murphy & Sorenson, 1988), and only those who were trained one-on-one spent increased time in managing stress after training (Jenkins & Calhoun, 1991). In a review of the outcome data from 19 work-site stress programs, of which 80 percent used relaxation/meditation, the most common finding was that subjective feelings of anxiety were reduced, while physiological measures did not show continued benefits (Pelletier & Lutz, 1991).

Organizational interventions address stressors by using management action to reduce the harmful effects of stress. Primarily preventive in nature, such interventions center on eliminating or reducing stressors before they can function as sources of stress. Organizational interventions include such programs as corporate restructuring/job redesign/job enrichment; compensation/reward systems; participative decision making; team building/outdoor leadership courses/executive retreats; management and supervisory training; recruitment/orientation and organizational socialization; career development; change of workloads and deadlines; change in work schedules/flex-time/summer hours/sabbaticals; casual-dress days; and wellness programs/fitness centers.

From this variety of organizational interventions, goal setting, participative decision making, job enrichment, change in work schedule, and survey feedback systems have some scientific proof of effectiveness (Matteson & Ivancevich, 1987). Qualitative positive results have been found for sabbaticals, flexible work schedules, summer hours, casual-dress days, executive retreats, outdoor leadership courses, fitness centers, and community involvement in the companies that used these methods of reducing organizational stress (Landon, 1990).

Finally, outcome research shows that commonly used prepackaged stress management programs do not appear to be either health or cost effective. According to Pelletier and Lutz (1991, p. 202), the "best health and cost efficacy data indicate that stress management is most effective with an identified high risk or symptomatic employee population utilizing traditional, problem focused, brief psychotherapy with an emphasis upon developing stress management skills." These researchers also noted that "whether group or individual approaches are employed, it is also essential to modify hazardous working conditions" (p. 202).

Recommended Readings

Karasek, R. A., & Theorell, T. (1990). *Healthy Work: Stress, Productivity, and the Reconstruction of Working Life.* New York: Basic Books.
Moss, Len. (1981). *Management Stress.* Reading, MA: Addison-Wesley.
Pelletier, Kenneth, & Lutz, Robert. (1991). Healthy people–Healthy business: A critical review of stress management programs in the workplace. In Steven Weiss, J. Fielding, & A. Baum (Eds.), *Health at Work* (pp 189–204). Hillsdale, NJ: Erlbaum.
Quick, James, Nelson, Debra, & Quick, Jonathan. (1990). *Stress and Challenge at the Top: The Paradox of the Successful Executive.* New York: Wiley.

Performance Appraisal System Consultation

Performance and productivity, along with accountability, are core values in this era of organizational restructuring and transformation. Two systems of accountability are the performance appraisal and the performance management system. The traditional mode of performance appraisal is the one that occurs between a worker and the immediate superior. Essentially, all performance appraisal approaches contain a number of key rating scales, checklists, rankings, or essay appraisals as the basis for the assessment. After its completion, the appraisal is checked for accuracy and for its recommendations by a third party, who is usually the assessor's superior. The final stage is the feedback interview or discussion with the worker. The purpose of this session is to provide feedback to workers on their performance for a given time period, motivate them to do a better job by clarifying expectations, coach them on needed improvements, strengthen the senior–subordinate relationship, and facilitate their comments about their work and their performance.

A more contemporary view of performance accountability conceptualizes it as a management system. Performance management is a managerial and supervisory system that involves continually assisting those supervised to improve their personal performance as well as the corporation's overall operation. It involves planning, collaborative objective setting, delegation, work program development, work facilitation, two-way feedback between manager and worker, monitoring of key performance outcomes, training and development, appraisal, and recognition and reward (Egan, 1993).

An effective performance management system is much more than an appraisal system. Appraisal is retrospective, as it occurs after the fact. Performance management is prospective, and its purpose is not to appraise but rather to facilitate and improve performance. Moreover, a performance management system is a system for developing people, rather than a system for controlling people. Performance management is the responsibility of every manager. If the performance management system would be administered by a human resources department it would revert to being exclusively an appraisal system. At its best an effective performance management system is a collaborative process to improve the business.

Recommended Readings

Egan, Gerald. (1993). *Adding Value: A Systematic Guide to Business-Driven Management and Leadership.* San Francisco: Jossey-Bass.

Henderson, Robert. (1984). *Practical Guide to Performance Appraisal.* Englewood Cliffs, NJ: Prentice-Hall.

Latham, Gerald, & Wexley, Kay. (1981). *Increasing Productivity Through Performance Appraisal.* Reading, MA: Addison-Wesley.

6

Clinical-Organizational Interventions

Clinical-organizational interventions refer to the structured activities in which clinician-consultants and clients participate during the course of a clinical-consultation. These activities are designed to improve the organization's functioning, and in some instances, individual functioning as well. Unlike traditional organizational interventions that were presumed to be the domain of specially trained organizational consultants, clinical-organizational interventions are much closer to the clinician's formal training and clinical experience. In fact, because of the clinical expertise required to utilize these intervention strategies, most traditionally trained organizational consultants would not be able to competently provide these services. Consequently, it should be relatively easy for clinician-consultants to extend their previous knowledge and skill base and become proficient in these interventions. Futhermore, unlike most traditional organizational interventions, clinical-organizational interventions can be utilized in either a clinical or organizational setting.

More specifically, clinical-organizational interventions are a set of structured activities that are focused at selected targets: individual, team, or the entire organization. Table 6.1 lists 14 clinical-organizational interventions utilized in individual, team, or organization-wide contexts.

These 14 interventions are discussed in subsequent sections of this chapter. Each intervention is described from the clinician-consultant's perspective: his/her role, goal, and task. It is hoped that this

TABLE 6.1

Clinical-Organizational Interventions

Individually Focused Interventions

1. Hiring, Discipline, and Termination Consultation
2. Work-Focused Psychotherapy
3. Outplacement Counseling and Consultation
4. Stress-Disability and Fitness-for-Duty Evaluation and Consultation

Team-Focused Interventions

5. Dual-Career Couples Counseling and Consultation
6. Conflict-Resolution Consultation with Work Teams
7. Conflict-Resolution Consultation in a Family Business

Organization-Focused Interventions

8. Crisis Intervention Consultation or Critical Incident Stress Debriefing (CISD)
9. Consulting on Resistance to Planned Change Efforts
10. Merger Syndrome Consultation
11. Downsizing Syndrome Consultation
12. Treatment Outcomes Consultation
13. Mental Health Policy Consultation
14. Violence Prevention Consultation

overview will provide the reader with an appreciation of the potency of these intervention strategies and their utility in a variety of clinical and organizational contexts. Key resource materials are referenced for each intervention in the Recommended Reading list at the end of each section. Some of these intervention strategies are illustrated in case examples in Chapters 8 and 9.

INDIVIDUALLY FOCUSED INTERVENTIONS

Hiring, Discipline, and Termination Consultation

Corporations will benefit from establishing an ongoing relationship with a clinician-consultant who has some experience with troubled and disgruntled workers as well as violence in the workplace. He or she could be an internal or external consultant who has some experience in the field, on-the-job training, and real, practical experience with actual incidents. Ideally, the clinician-consultant who does the preemployment screening and helps with the hiring practices for the corporporation would be the same professional who establishes an ongoing relationship with the people working there. He or she should also be involved in the training and development of the corporation's managers. And ultimately, this person would also be involved with any workplace violence or other crises.

In summary, the clinician-consultant helps to hire workers; offers training to deal with personnel, supervisory, and human resource issues; and provides individual or group therapy or coaching at all levels of the organization. This bond with the corporation makes it easier for the clinician-consultant to intervene before, during, or after potential workplace violence episodes. This section emphasizes the clinician-consultant's role with regard to the hiring, disciplining, and terminating of difficult workers.

Consulting on Hiring Issues

The clinician-consultant's role in the process of screening job applicants is expanding at a time when state and federal statutes—particularly the Americans with Disabilities Act (ADA)—are radically altering previous hiring practices. Until recently, many corporations utilized pen-and-paper psychological tests for all applicants for specific positions. For instance, in some organizations, jobs involving security clearances or major financial transactions required these kinds of tests. But the use of written psychological screening tests is not without its perils. Recent court rulings have banned the use of some standard instruments, such as the Minnesota Multiphasic Personality Inventory (MMPI) because of the invasiveness of certain questions on matters of sexuality, religion, bodily functions, and the like.

Since corporations may no longer be able to rely on psychological screening inventories as they have in the past, it means that the job interview will become even more important in hiring decisions. And because of their expertise in diagnostic interviewing, clinician-consultants can play a crucial role in screening job applicants. This includes both establishing interview guidelines and protocols for personnel specialists to screen for severe Personality Disorders and other Paranoid and Delusional Disorders and for conducting follow-up interviews on questionable job applicants. Mantell (1994) provides specific interview guidelines and questions useful in screening for Antisocial, Paranoid, and Borderline Personality Disorders, as well as for Paranoid Schizophrenia and Delusional Disorders.

Consulting on Disciplinary Matters

The consultant's role in a potentially difficult discipline meeting cannot be underestimated. As an expert in distressed human behavior, the consultant can intervene to reduce or contain the worker's threats, aggressive behavior, rage, or paranoia. The discipline meeting may require the presence of two or more supervisors in the room with the worker and a security guard posted near the door.

Disturbed or disgruntled employees are not usually passive. Their words and their actions telegraph their potential for acting out. When the consultant helps management to establish a force-presence, it communicates to the disturbed worker, in clear terms, that the purpose of the meeting is to talk about his or her behavior and how it will need to change if he or she wishes to remain employed at the firm.

Disturbed Employee Terminations

When a seriously disturbed worker will not accept a discipline order, management can legitimately ask the worker to accept a mandatory referral to a clinician-consultant for an evaluation. In these highly charged events, management needs to determine whether the worker is dangerous to himself/herself or others or if he or she can successfully return to work. Using the clinician-consultant as a buffer between the supervisor and the disturbed employee enables management to identify the root of the worker's problems.

In instances when the worker is uncooperative, and termination appears to be the only alternative, the consultant can assist management by explaining the risk of termination to the worker as well as the choices open to him/her. For instance, the worker can submit to drug testing, accept a short- or long-term suspension, make significant behavioral changes, or be fired. Meetings between the worker and the clinician-consultant can take place on corporate premises or at an office away from the company. By foreshadowing the possibility of termination at these meetings, the consultant can lessen the impact, prepare the employee for what is to come, and deal with the worker's feelings of rage or anger at the immediate moment.

In a worst-case scenario, the highly disturbed worker will refuse to cooperate with any suggestions. When termination appears to be the only option, corporate security guards—or if danger seems imminent, the local police—will escort the worker off the premises permanently.

Recommended Readings

Mantell, Michael. (1994). *Ticking Bombs: Defusing Violence in the Workplace.* Burr Ridge, IL: Irwin.

Work-Focused Psychotherapy

Psychotherapy can be directed toward general treatment goals or more focused goals. Lowman (1993) made the case for focal psychotherapy addressing work and work dysfunction. He defines work dysfunction as any persistent difficulty or failure in the work site associated with psychological characteristics of the individual. These dysfunctions can be independent of or interactive with the nature of the worker's job or the organizational context in which the work takes place. Lowman proposes a classification of work dysfunction and differentiates psychopathology and work dysfunctions with the understanding that the two types of problems can coexist. The clinician-consultant's first task is to assess the presence of psychopathology and its relation, if any, to work functioning, while also assessing the presence of work dysfunction and its impact on psychopathology.

The classification or taxonomy of work-related dysfunctions (see also Chapter 4) includes patterns of undercommitment (i.e., underachievement, procrastination, organizational and/or occupational misfit, fear of success, and fear of failure); patterns of overcommitment (i.e., workaholism, type A behavior pattern, and job and occupational burnout); work-related anxiety and depression (i.e., performance anxiety, generalized anxiety, and work-related depression); personality dysfunctional patterns (i.e., problems with authority and personality disordered work behavior); life-role conflicts (including work–family conflicts); transient situational stress; and perceptual inaccuracies. A final category of the taxonomy is dysfunctional working conditions (i.e., defective job design, defective supervision, and dysfunctional interpersonal relationships).

For most individuals, issues involving work and the workplace are resolved in a relatively nonconflictual manner. Individuals typically find a career or job that is, to some degree, satisfying and fulfilling, and they are able to function reasonably well in a work setting. It is the failure to find, implement, or sustain a satisfactory work role or a change in the person or the work situation that creates psychological difficulties known as work dysfunctions. Clinicians are consulted by management for those individuals who experience work dysfunctions or by the dysfunctional workers themselves. The clinician-consultant's goal is then to assist such individuals in understanding and changing what is dysfunctional about their personality, work, or work environment.

Short-term, behaviorally focused interventions seem to be particularly effective in treating many work dysfunctions, provided that more complicated psychopathology or severe Personality Disorders are not present or, at the least, that the broader, contextual issues are kept in mind (Sperry, 1995a). Lowman (1993) believes that metaphorical approaches that encapsulate a central dynamic of the person through the presenting work concerns are also effective. The clinician-consultant may need to work around lifelong characterological issues when working with individuals experiencing both Personality Disorders and work dysfunctions.

Finally, practical career counseling and career management can be quite beneficial to certain individuals, including those with relatively pervasive Personality Disorders. For instance, specific directives and warnings about the real-life work consequences of continued aberrant work behavior may be as instructive and influential in working with certain Personality Disorders as long-term psychotherapy. Such workers may be strongly motivated to comply with such directives when a prospective job loss or restriction looms before them.

Recommended Readings

Lowman, Rodney. (1993). *Counseling and Psychotherapy of Work Dysfunctions.* Washington, DC: American Psychological Association.

Outplacement Counseling and Consultation

Outplacement counseling is a process of helping workers whose jobs have ended to face the crisis of job loss with renewed self-esteem. The aim is to enable such individuals to conduct their own job search or retraining plans to lead to new jobs. Outplacement counseling is essentially a human resources intervention; it represents a point at which the interests of the worker and the company converge. The need to remove a person from his or her job, apart from economic reasons, represents an individual's or a company's failure. Brammer and Humberger (1984) estimate that half the reasons for the dismissal of workers are their failure to produce, to get along with others, or to develop in their job. Other dismissals, according to Brammer and Humberger, represent an organization's failure to select, train, counsel, or evaluate the employee successfully. The remaining reasons for employee dismissal rest with economic rather than individual or organizational factors. Today, for example, corporate downsizing accounts for a significant number of permanent layoffs.

The goal of outplacement counseling is reemployment. It focuses on rebuilding the individual's self-esteem, giving new meaning to the worker's life, and helping to establish balance between work and family life. Outplacement counselors and consultants are retained by corporations to provide brief counseling, with job relocation and to job retraining. Such organizations will also use outplacement as part of a general strategy to increase productivity, deal with problem employees, or reduce staff. Outplacement counseling then benefits not only the terminated worker, but also the organization. While the clinician-consultant might actually engage in the practice of outplacement counseling, consultation to employees or outplacement counseling firms is also possible. Rudisill, Painter, and Pollock (1992) indicate four consultation interventions clinician-consultants can provide to employers and outplacement firms: (1) firing prevention, (2) exit interviewing, (3) outplacement evaluation, and (4) consultation for outplacement staff. They believe that consultation provided to the staff of outplacement firms can improve outplacement programs and provide accessible resources for these programs.

Recommended Readings

Brammer, L. M., & Humberger, F. H. (1984). *Outplacement and Inplacement.* Englewood Cliffs, NJ: Prentice-Hall.
Morin, W., & Yorks, L. (1982). *Outplacement Techniques.* New York: AMACOM Books.
Rudisill, John, Painter, Albert, & Pollock, Susan. (1992). Psychological consultation to outplacement firms. *Innovations in Clinical Practice, 11,* 425–430.

Stress-Disability and Fitness-for-Duty Evaluation and Consultation

A case can be made for the position that stress-disability evaluations are essentially a clinical intervention rather than a clinical-organizational intervention since there are some clinicians with little knowledge or experience of organizational dynamics whose entire practice involves disability evaluations. Nevertheless, if the disability claimant contends that the alleged disability was caused or triggered by workplace factors or organizational dynamics, it would seem that an adequate disability/fitness-for-duty evaluation would involve at least a minimal assessment of workplace and organizational factors. Such an assessment means that the evaluation would thus be a clinical-organizational intervention.

Psychiatric Disability Evaluation

The profile of typical stress disability claimants includes female employees, white-collar workers, and people over age 30. Job pressures are cited as the main reason for 70 percent of the claims, with harassment accounting for the other 30 percent (Boustedt, 1990). Furthermore, these individuals tend to hold jobs that are psychologically demanding but over which they exercise little or no control, and consequently, they feel powerless (Karasek & Theorell, 1990).

There are several issues pertinent to performing a psychiatric evaluation of a claimant for disability compensation. As background, the evaluator will need to become familiar with the appropriate standards of workers' compensation law in the state or jurisdiction in which he or she practices. Furthermore, the evaluator must become conversant with disability concepts such as work functions, residual function capacity, levels of impairment, and work factors (Enelow, 1991; London, Monana, & Loeb, 1988). Finally, the evaluator must consider the unique ethical, legal, and malpractice issues associated with this type of evaluation, not the least of which is confidentiality.

There are several excellent sources that describe the psychiatric disability examination process and report (Grant & Robbins, 1993; Larsen & Felton, 1988; and Meyerson & Fine, 1987). A useful report will include:

- A brief summary of the legal situation and the context for the evaluation.
- A detailed history of the alleged work-related injury, including symptoms, associated features, and events, in a clear, outlined, and numerically sequenced format.
- A review of records, including summary facts from various sources and comments on discrepancies between sources.
- A summary of the issues discussed in the clinical evaluation interview(s).
- The results of the mental status examination.
- A review of psychological, neurological, and workplace testing.
- A diagnosis, including a full five-axis DSM-IV diagnosis, briefly explaining how the diagnostic criteria were fulfilled.
- A statement of disability, including the degree, extent, and duration of the impairment. The prognosis and type of treatments recommended must be specified. Furthermore, the cause of the current mental disorder and whether it

arises "out of" or "in the course of" employment should be noted.

- Responses to other specific questions asked by the referral source.
- A concluding statement in which all pertinent material about diagnosis, prognosis, treatment recommendations, and the evaluation of impairment and disability is noted. This statement should briefly summarize the clinical reasoning the evaluator utilized in coming to his or her clinical opinion (London et al., 1988).

Such an evaluation and report may take 4-6 hours, which includes the actual evaluation and time to review case records, test reports, and the like and to formulate and dictate the report (Whyman & Underwood, 1991).

Fitness for Duty Evaluations

Fitness to work, or "fitness for duty," refers to the employee's capability of performing an assigned job within the required standards of attendance, quality, efficiency, safety, and conduct. Because fitness for work is in part related to an individual's global level of functioning, Axis V of DSM-IV, as delineated specifically by Gordon and Gordon (1991), can be useful. The severity of impairment and its impact on the social and occupational functioning of the worker-patient should be estimated. Often, the determination of fitness will be linked to certain contingencies, such as an alternative work placement or the specification of restrictions on the worker's previous job.

Establishing work prognosis should be done separately from illness prognosis. Usually, the clinician-consultant is requested to provide both short-term and long-term prognoses. A short-term work prognosis is an estimate of the span of time before the employee-patient is fit to return to work. Specific target dates are preferable to "unspecified" or "indefinite." Long-term work prognosis refers to how well the employee-patient will adjust after the initial return to the workplace. This is usually assessed based on information about past work adjustment and behavior, particularly regarding job history, attendance, and previous disability (Rigaud, 1989). The report of such an evaluation is a confidential document that should be well structured, include relevant data and observations, and be couched in language that medical and other health care providers can understand.

Rigaud (1989) offers a useful outline protocol for structuring the evaluation interview and the work prognosis report. Six elements are suggested:

1. The reasons and questions that initiated the referral are specified, along with a summary of the conclusion that the clinician-consultant has drawn from a review of the employee-patient's records.
2. The employee-patient's presenting problems and concerns are noted, along with a description of the individual's lifestyle and any current treatment in which he or she is involved.
3. Significant data regarding the individual's prior occupational; medical, surgical, and psychiatric; and developmental, familial, and socioeconomic histories are summarized.
4. Pertinent findings from the clinical evaluation and mental status examination are described.
5. The evaluating clinician-consultant's case formulation, which should include diagnosis and prognosis and therapeutic and occupational recommendations, is stated. Ideally, this would be an integrative biopsychosocial formulation (Sperry et al., 1992).
6. Specific suggestions for placement and, if necessary, for additional investigations or measures are noted.

Recommended Readings

Grant, Brian, & Robbins, David. (1993). Disability, workers' compensation and fitness for duty. In J. Kahn (Ed.), *Mental Health in the Workplace* (pp. 83–105). New York: Van Nostrand Reinhold.

Larsen, Robert, & Felton, James. (Eds.). (1988). Psychiatric injury in the workplace (special issue). *Occupational Medicine: State of the Art Reviews, 3* (4).

Meyerson, Arthur, & Fine, Theodora. (Eds.). (1987). *Psychiatric Disability: Clinical, Legal and Administrative Dimensions.* Washington, DC: American Psychiatric Press.

TEAM-FOCUSED INTERVENTIONS

Dual-Career Couples Counseling and Consultation

The number of dual-career couples is increasing dramatically. When both spouses hold jobs outside the home, the marital relationship is called "dual earner." But, when both spouses hold professional or executive-level positions, their relationship is referred to as "dual career." The workplace implications of conflict among dual-career couples are profound, and clinician-consultants who can effectively engage these couples therapeutically can greatly impact their lives. This intervention is different enough from individual psychotherapy and traditional marital therapy to be considered an area of subspecialization.

Stoltz-Loike (1992) notes six underlying themes related to effective dual-career couple functioning. The first theme is that couples must establish boundaries between themselves and others. Second, spouses must be able to express supportiveness—both emotional and physical—to each other. Third and fourth, effective couple relations depend on mastering and using both basic communication skills and conflict-resolution skills. Fifth, dysfunctional couple patterns can be framed as problems in need of solutions. And sixth, effective couple relations involve the process of change, which couples tend to fear and resist.

Depending on the level and severity of conflict, treatment can range from simply psychoeducational interventions, to focused systemic interventions, or to more in-depth psychodynamic interventions. While psychoeducational and systemic strategies aim to teach relational and coping skills or how to achieve adaptive solutions, these approaches tend to be of limited use in helping dual-career couples work through resistance to change or the developmental blocks which lead to relational and therapeutic impasses. Therapeuti-

cally confronting these resistances and impasses may require exploring issues from early childhood in each spouse's development.

Confronting and resolving unfinished development in one or both
spouses is often part of the process of becoming a mature, dual-career
couple. Developmental issues underlie the six common conflict areas
for dual-career couples (Glickhauf-Hughes, Hughes, & Wells, 1986).
Three of these: power conflicts, competition, and commitment, will
be briefly described.

Power conflicts often reflect each spouse's childhood experience
that others cannot be counted on to meet their needs; as adults they
are likely to develop a look-out-for-number-one attitude. In addition,
when parents are insensitive to their children's needs and frustration
level, these children will likely become adults who have difficulty
tolerating the frustration of unmet needs. Thus, compromise with a
spouse may be both difficult and painful, since it is associated with
loss rather than mutual gain.

Equity is often proposed as the corrective solution for resolving
power conflicts or struggles. But this solution requires several provisions: the spouse should (1) keep the other's needs in mind, (2) be
able to tolerate the frustration of not getting one's own needs met
immediately, and (3) be able to view a spouse's requests as legitimate
and not as attempts at control or domination. In terms of Erikson's
stages of psychosocial development, the resolution of power conflicts
by equity is difficult if either or both spouses have insufficiently
mastered the developmental tasks of trust and autonomy.

Another common conflict of dual-career couples is competition.
The opposite of competition is cooperation or collaboration. Collaboration requires the capacity to separate one's own feelings from one's
spouse's feelings and behavior, the ability to sustain and augment
self-esteem via encouragement, and an acceptance of competitive
feelings, both within oneself and in one's spouse. The developmental
obstacle that can impede a couple's resolving conflicts about competition results from insufficient mastery of the tasks of autonomy and
initiative by one or both spouses.

A third common conflict involves commitment. Since many dual-
career spouses value success, achievement, and independence and
respond more to external rather than internal validation, these indi-

viduals find it easy to "hedge their bets" about relationships and thus place a higher priority on personal attainment and satisfaction. To commit oneself to another requires the ability to be intimate, to develop an internal reward system, and to make the spousal relationship a priority. The developmental tasks that must be mastered in this conflict involve industry and intimacy.

Essentially, psychodynamic intervention strategies are necessary when problem solving and communication training are not working or are only partially effective because of resistances and impasses secondary to more basic developmental issues (Rice, 1979).

Recommended Readings

Rice, David. (1979). *Dual-Career Marriage: Conflict and Treatment.* New York: Free Press.
Stoltz-Loike, Marion. (1992). *Dual-Career Couples: New Perspectives in Counseling.* Alexandria, VA: American Counseling Association.

Conflict-Resolution Consultation with Work Teams

Conflict is commonplace in the corporate world, and it can be either constructive or destructive to the functioning of a work team. When it is too high or too low, it hinders performance. An optimal level is one in which there is enough conflict to prevent stagnation, stimulate creativity, allow tensions to be released, and initiate the seeds for change, yet not so much as to be disruptive. Clinician-consultants are consulted regularly by managers faced with excessive team conflict. Unfortunately, there is no single formula to resolve destructive conflicts. Rather, the consultant should select the conflict-resolution techniques appropriate for a given situation. Feldman (1985) has developed a taxonomy of conflict-resolution strategies that frequently are used in organizations and discusses the circumstances in which each strategy is most effective. He describes four classes of strategies: conflict-avoidance, conflict-defusion, conflict-containment, and conflict-confrontation.

The primary dimension in which intergroup conflict-resolution strategies vary is how openly they address the conflict. The chief characteristic of conflict-avoidance strategies is that they attempt to keep the conflict from coming into the open. The goal of conflict-defusion strategies is to keep the conflict in abeyance and to "cool" the emotions of the parties involved. Conflict-containment strategies allow some conflict to surface but tightly control which issues are discussed and the manner in which they are discussed. Conflict-confrontation strategies are designed to uncover all the issues of the conflict and to try to find a mutually satisfactory solution. Which strategy is most effective depends on how critical the conflict is to task accomplishment and how quickly the conflict must be resolved. If the conflict arises from a trivial issue and/or must be resolved quickly, a conflict-avoidance or conflict-defusion strategy is likely to be effective. But if the conflict centers around an important work issue and does not need to be solved in a short period of time, conflict-containment or conflict-confrontation strategies will most likely be effective.

Two very commonly utilized conflict interventions are third-party peacemaking and the no-lose method. The purpose of *third-party peacemaking interventions* is either to control a conflict or else to resolve it. It utilizes a third party—such as a consultant—to help in the diagnosis and resolution of difficult human problems within or between two work teams. The third-party approach allows those in conflict to gain an outside perspective on their problem and to use the third party as a trusted agent to begin rebuilding the relationship between them. A key feature of this approach is confrontation, that is, the parties involved must be prepared to recognize that conflict exists between them as well as the consequences of the conflict. The clinician-consultant uses confrontation tactics to make the conflict visible and susceptible to examination and diagnoses the conflict by means of a schema that considers conflict issues, the precipitating circumstances, the conflict-relevant acts, and the conflict's consequences. In intervening, the clinician-consultant's role is to structure confrontation and communication between the antagonists.

According to Walton (1969), productive confrontation requires both parties to be equally ready to confront and suggest initiatives and to have adequate time available to work through their antagonisms.

The clinician-consultant faciliates the process of developing norms of openness and reassurance between the parties. Each party should understand the other, and each should experience moderate stress. First they should clarify the differences that divide them, and then they should process their negative feelings about each other. Finally, they should identify what they have in common, as well as their positive feelings toward each other. Throughout this process, the clinician-consultant's role is to assist the parties, either directly or indirectly. Direct intervention may require that the consultant set an agenda. Indirect intervention may entail scheduling a meeting on neutral ground and setting time or topic boundaries.

No-lose conflict resolution is another well-known approach to negotiation and conflict reduction. Although there are a number of versions, only the one developed by Gordon (1977) will be described here. Acknowledging the negative consequences that arise from a win–lose resolution approach, this technique aims to bring mutual satisfaction to both the parties. Gordon argues that one of its benefits is the generation of increased commitment among the parties to carry out the decision. Additional benefits include higher quality and quicker decisions, closer relationships between the parties, and no need to "sell" any benefits to the other side. The steps in the process, as outlined by Gordon, include identifying and defining the problem; generating alternative solutions; evaluating the alternative solutions; seeking, by both parties, a commitment to one solution; implementing the solution (deciding who does what by when); and, finally, the follow-up and evaluation of the agreed-upon solution.

Recommended Readings

Feldman, Daniel. (1985). A taxonomy of intergroup conflict resolution stategies. In L. Goodstein & J. Pfeiffer (Eds.), *The 1985 Annual: Developing Human Resources* (pp. 169–175). San Diego: University Associates.

Gordon, Thomas. (1977). *L.E.T.: Leader Effectiveness Training.* New York: Putman.

Walton, Richard. (1969). *Interpersonal Peacemaking: Confrontation and Third-Party Consultation.* Reading, MA: Addison-Wesley.

Conflict-Resolution Consultation in a Family Business

Most people associate "family business" with "mom-and-pop" operations, such as small independent grocery stores or hardware stores. Although many family businesses are small, a large number are major corporations, including 175 of the Fortune 500 companies. In fact, 95 percent of all businesses in the United States are family owned—over 10 million in fact—and they generate about 50 percent of the total wages paid in this country (Ward, 1987). Unlike other corporations, family business issues involve two sets of roles and dynamics: organizational roles and dynamics and family roles and dynamics. Not surprisingly, the complexities of family and corporate role demands and intertwining dynamics result in considerable conflict between and among family members.

Fortunately, there are various conflict-resolution intervention options for family businesses. Traditional marital or family therapy can offer insights into the nature of family dynamics and can provide needed skills for resolving interpersonal conflicts. A management consultant might advise bringing in another partner, providing a separate salary to both spouses, or restructuring the business to decrease conflict and tension. Also a family's accountant or attorney might make recommendations to the CEO or to the board of directors to rearrange the management team. Or a clinician-consultant, knowledgeable in family business, could be consulted. Clinician-consultants who are knowledgeable about individual and family dynamics, have done some marital and family therapy, and have some experience with team or organizational dynamics are uniquely qualified to consult on family business matters, particularly conflict resolution.

Kaye (1991) describes a model of conflict resolution particularly valuable in family business consultation. The model makes three assumptions: (1) conflicts within family businesses are essentially different from conflicts between nonfamily or "separate parties," who will have no ongoing personal relationships after the dispute is settled; (2) conflicts within families follow a dynamic pattern that is circular rather than linear and the repetitive sequences created by the family members sustain the conflict over time; and (3) an analysis of the family's typical pattern is an essential element in resolving conflict and improving communication and interactions.

According to Ward (1987) there are four common sources of conflict in family businesses: (1) succession, that is, who will next take charge of the firm, when will it occur, and how will it occur; (2) participation, that is, who can and cannot join the business, what preparation is required to join, and, what to do if the newly joined party doesn't work out; (3) compensation, that is, who can own stock and how are family members evaluated and paid; and (4) responsibility, that is, what happens if there is a divorce, what responsiblity is there to the community, what responsibility is there to long-term employees, and what responsibility is there to other family members.

Such conflicts not only represent the defensive reactions of one individual to others, but also are collusive-mechanisms to protect the family system from something they fear—a fear more threatening to the family system than the ongoing disputes. The hostile behavior may be unconsciously motivated, just as the underlying dread may be in the realm of the unspeakable. Unlocking the "real fears" among those in the family system holds the key to working through the conflicts that have been utilized to camouflage their core concerns.

Recommended Readings

Rosenblatt, P. C., de Mik, L., Anderson, R. M., et al. (1985). *The Family in Business: Understanding and Dealing with the Challenges Entrepreneurial Families Face.* San Francisco: Jossey-Bass.
Ward, J. L. (1987). *Keeping the Family Business Healthy: How to Plan for Continuing Growth, Profitability and Family Leadership.* San Francisco: Jossey-Bass.

ORGANIZATION-FOCUSED INTERVENTIONS

Crisis Intervention Consultation

Crisis intervention consultation or Critical Incident Stress Debriefing (CISD) is an effective method of providing early intervention for employees who have experienced a workplace trauma. Popularized by Jeffrey Mitchell, Ph.D., CISD is a group format that facilitates the ventilation of emotions and other reactions to a critical incident and includes an educational component to assist those affected to deal with their responses. CISD is not group therapy. Instead, it is a focused group process designed to put the crisis in perspective. The two major goals of debriefing are to reduce the impact of a critical event and to accelerate the recovery of these people who are suffering through normal but painful reactions to abnormal events.

CISD's main value is its proactive approach to coping with stressful events that could have long-term sequelae. Essentially, it helps prevent and reduce the psychological effects of traumatic events, while also providing an early opportunity to identify those at high risk for severe impairment along with potential candidates for Posttraumatic Stress Disorder (PTSD).

Mitchell and Bray (1990) divide CISD into several phases, including the cognitive, emotional, and educational phases. The *cognitive phase* begins with the least threatening element of the crisis, as the group members respond to two factual questions: "What was your job at the time of the event?" and "What did you see?" These questions facilitate some initial ventilation and identification and help ease the group members into further processing the critical event. The next question, "What was the first thought that you had during the event?" assists the participants in facing and articulating the more distressing aspects of the trauma.

The *emotional phase* involves gently challenging participants to acknowledge and express their emotional responses to the critical incident. The question posed is, "What was the worst thing about the event for you?" Next the group members are asked to identify the symptoms and responses they experienced as a result of the trauma. They are asked, "What did you experience in the first 24 hours after the event?," "What did you experience in the next day or so?," and "What symptoms do you have now?" In addressing these questions, the participants come to recognize that they are not alone, unique, or flawed.

In the *education phase* there is a normalizing of the variety of reactions reported by group members. These reactions include sleep problems, irritability, concentration problems, survivor guilt, startle reactions, preoccupation with the incident, and intrusive memories. The facilitator then educates the group about stress reduction methods and self-care guidelines. The self-care guidelines include information about exercise, alcohol, and drugs; talking; and spending time with other group members. Group members who exercise regularly are advised to stick to their normal routines, while those who seldom exercise are encouraged to establish a sensible exercise regimen.

The facilitator also educates the group about the numbing effects of alcohol and drugs and explains how they actually retard the body's ability to recover from stress. Nonchemical alternatives for stress reduction are then recommended and explained. Group participants are next advised to talk about their feelings and reactions to the critical incident, particularly with coworkers, supervisors, and family members. Finally, group members are informed that, while it is normal to withdraw and isolate oneself following exposure to a traumatic event, isolation is counterproductive. Workers are advised to spend time with whomever they feel the most safe and comfortable.

In the wrap-up phase, the clinician-consultant summarizes the reactions expressed by group members and also verbalizes and normalizes the feelings that the participants have likely held back. Positive coping skills are emphasized and group members are told that it will take some time before they can expect to feel "normal" again. The consultant may distribute handouts with self-care guidelines, lists of expected symptoms and reactions, and telephone numbers for further assistance.

Prior to the CISD debriefing session, the clinician-consultants would conduct an assessment, usually by the end of the first day of the incident, or the next morning at the latest. He or she obtains a thorough description of the event from the managers-in-charge and key employee witnesses. The clinician-consultant then establishes rapport with the work-group leaders, explains the role he/she will take, sketches out a suggested plan for further action, and enlists the support of key managers in initiating the plan. He or she reassures management that resuming normal operations is not only good for the corporation but also therapeutic for the workers. The clinician-consultant also helps restore the flow of work by making special services available to victims at their work site.

The clinical-consultant, in addition, should pay special attention to high-risk workers following a traumatic event. These include workers who are experiencing intense survivor guilt, were unable to help others in danger, had close relationships with any deceased or seriously injured coworkers, the direct supervisors of affected workers—who may themselves be traumatized—and workers who are absent the day or days following the incident.

The clinician-consultant will need to meet individually with a limited number of workers to assist them with their more painful reactions and to assess the quality of their personal support system, augmenting it where necessary. Anger at the corporation, whether reasonable or irrational, is also best handled in this format. Personal histories of prior trauma or tragedy should also be assessed, weighing their potential contribution to reactions to the current incident.

Finally, individuals who will require ongoing psychotherapy beyond the internal trauma-response program should be identified. These workers will require therapy of varying length, often determined by their prior history or personality structure. Clinician-consultants can serve an organization very effectively by administering this referral process.

Recommended Readings

Mitchell, Jeffrey, & Bray, Grady. (1990). *Emergency Services Stress.* Englewood Cliffs, NJ: Prentice-Hall.
Psychological Consequences of Disasters: Prevention and Management. (1992). Albany, NY: World Health Organization.

Consulting on Resistance to Planned Change Efforts

Achieving large-scale planned change in an organization is a time-intensive process that may take 2–5 years. And not all organizations that begin the process complete it. In fact, the majority abandon the effort—in part or entirely—at about 18 months into the planned change process (Wall, Solum, & Sobol, 1992). There are a number of reasons for this failure to achieve planned change. Argyris (1985) contends that *resistance* is a major factor in these failures and goes on to describe "defensive routines" as a common form of resistance to change. Argyris defines defensive routines as "thoughts and actions used to protect individuals', groups', and organizations' usual way of dealing with reality" (p. 5).

Defensive routines are common in organizations and include passive resistance to authority, mixed messages, and rationalizations. Argyris believes these defensive routines are automatic reponses that are learned early in life and function as threat reducers and face savers. Such defenses are dangerous to the long-term health and well-being of an organization because they distort the truth in the name of helping others. Argyris also believes these defensive routines may or may not be responses to pathological or unjust actions. They are taken for granted in organizations because they are as inevitable as power, scarce resources, coalitions, and other features of everyday life in organizations. Essentially, their purpose is to protect self and others. Unfortunately, these behaviors inhibit learning, are difficult to change, and become self-reinforcing.

Argyris analyzes the way in which defensive routines undermine the strategic planning and strategic implementation process in organizations and offers consultants 11 strategies for diagnosing and modifying the defensive routines commonly associated with organizational change. Specific tactics for reducing and preventing defensive routines with individuals and work teams are also described. Argyris illustrates this clinical-organizational intervention with numerous case examples, including transcriptions of specific consultation sessions.

Connor (1993) deftly distinguishes negative and positive resistance to change. He describes negative resistance to change in terms of five phases similar to Kubler-Ross's five stages of death and dying. He then identifies five phases of positive resistance to change: uninformed optimism, informed pessimism, hopeful realism, informed optimism, and completion. Then he offers a strategy for reducing negative resistance and facilitating the process of positive resistance, which he contends is essential to managing the change process.

Another way of conceptualizing resistance to planned change is in terms of personality style and disorders. Sperry (1990, 1993) describes predictable ways in which different personality styles and disorders obstruct or hinder the process of planned change, specifically, the strategic-planning process. Individuals with paranoid, narcissistic, obsessive-compulsive, and passive-aggressive styles commonly resist and undermine planned organizational change efforts for reasons that are predictable based on their specific personality dynamics.

Clinician-consultants can be of enormous assistance to organizations experiencing resistance to planned change because of their ability to recognize defensive routines, personality dynamics, and other causes of resistance and can intervene accordingly. Other types of organizational consultants tend to be confused and ineffectual with the phenomenon of resistance. Unlike nonpsychologically trained consultants who function from a rational model of organizational behavior, clinician-consultants more readily understand and appreciate unconscious and nonrational determinants of behavior, such as resistance.

Recommended Readings

Argyris, Chris. (1985). *Strategy, Change and Defensive Routines.* Boston: Pitman.
Connor, Daryl. (1993). Resistance to Change. In *Managing at the Speed of Change.* New York: Villard Books.

Merger Syndrome Consultation

Recently, "mergers and acquisitions" and "hostile takeover" have become household terms. Large as well as small corporations attempt to use mergers or acquisitions to increase their competitiveness and profitability in a swiftly changing world economy. The combining of two corporations, however, almost guarantees a "reduction in work force" or "downsizing" because fewer employees and managers are needed. Also corporations have high hopes for the outcomes of mergers and acquisitions, which seldom are met. For individual executives and employees, mergers and acquisitions can be extreme stressors, whether their jobs are eliminated or retained.

The mere rumor that a merger is under consideration can send shock waves throughout both organizations involved. However, the aftermath of the actual sale and the process of combining people from different corporations often result in a protracted turmoil called the "merger syndrome" (Marks & Mirvis, 1986). This syndrome is characterized by distractibility; preoccupation; constricted upward and downward communication in the organization; stress reactions including anxiety, depression, somatic complaints, and withdrawal; and crisis management.

While much has been written about the human and cultural symptoms of mergers, there is little documentation regarding interventions to minimize merger stress or culture clash as companies combine. Largely, this is because management is usually more focused on the financial and structural components of the merger, rather than on the human component.

Early interventions should focus on employees' immediate feelings and concerns about what *the merger* will mean for them and the organization. These interventions are most useful soon after an intended merger is announced. During this period, management usually knows little about when the merger will actually happen and which primary postmerger interventions can have the most positive impact on the integration process, since the focus at this point is usually on the exchange of valid information between merging partners. Primary postmerger interventions should take place then during the transition period that occurs immediately before and just after the merger receives legal approval. Postmerger interventions should next focus on assessing and correcting maladaptive behaviors in the merger parties. These interventions usually are confrontational and should occur anywhere from six months to a year and a half after the merger.

Corporations often use internal organizational development staff augmented by external consultants for merger work, so clinician-consultants need legitimacy and a clearly demonstrated capacity to undertake the important and sensitive tasks involved with mergers and acquisitions. Usually the tasks require the clinician-consultant to function in the roles of adviser, observer, and process facilitator. McCann and Gilkey (1988) note that the process facilitator's client is usually the transition team itself—that is, the merger specialists, lawyers, bankers, CEOs, and even middle-level managers. In the pressure-cooker atmosphere of a merger or acquisition, transition teams often get caught up in counterproductive dynamics. Therefore the role of the process facilitator is crucial before, during, and after the merger acquisition process to minimize these effects (Schein, 1987).

Premerger workshops can be held for all employees, in which company philosophy, goals, changes in compensation and work scheduling, and training and development plans are discussed. In addition, stress management training, in the form of voluntarily attended workshops or one-on-one sessions, should be offered along with individual counseling for personal adjustment or career issues related to the merger. Finally, outplacement services may be offered to executives (Matteson & Ivancevich, 1990). McCann and Gilkey (1988) add that establishing effective two-way communication—upward and downward—is of paramount importance in short-circuiting the merger syndrome.

Sometime after the merger is finalized, a "postmerger syndrome" may emerge. This is recognized by lowered productivity and morale problems (McCann and Gilkey, 1988). During this time, EAPs and corporate mental health services report sizable increases in referral utilization rates. It is important that clinician-consultants reinforce the notion that cost cutting and underbudgeting for mental health services is a temptation that must be avoided.

Recommended Readings

Mirvis, Philip H. (1991). *Managing the Merger: Making It Work.* Englewood Cliffs, NJ: Prentice-Hall.
McCann, Joseph, & Gilkey, Roderick. (1988). *Joining Forces: Creating and Managing Successful Mergers and Acquisitions.* Englewood Cliffs, NJ: Prentice-Hall.

Downsizing Syndrome Consultation

In the process of corporate downsizing, inevitably some workers are permanently laid off—while others survive the layoff. Those who survive are prone to what is called "layoff survivor sickness" (Noer, 1993). Layoff survivor sickness is a generic term that describes a set of attitudes, feelings, and perceptions that occur in employees who remain in organizational systems following involuntary employee reductions. The symptoms of layoff survivor sickness are anger, depression, fear, distrust, and particularly guilt—guilt that some workers retained their jobs while their friends or coworkers did not. Those with survivor sickness are often described as having a reduced desire to take risks, a lowered commitment to the job, and a lack of spontaneity. Besides workers, managers may also experience this syndrome. This is particularly evident among caring and concerned managers who are forced to make workforce reduction decisions without any guidance, training, or support.

As a result of downsizing, open hostility among workers is becoming more commonplace. Not suprisingly, it is directed toward the corporation rather than toward the competition or the marketplace where such energies can be more productively channeled. The amount of suppressed, covert hostility lurking just below the surface in many surviving workers is also common. Unfortunately, much of the frustration, anger, and depression is taking its toll on the nonwork lives of these surviving workers. Frequently, its manifestations are deteriorating physical and psychological health. The impact of downsizing on managers' health cannot be ignored and may be approaching crisis proportions. This is particularly important in that symptoms of depression among managers are very common.

Nevertheless, intensive, focused interventions have been demonstrated to be effective in resolving layoff survivor sickness or downsizing syndrome. Noer (1993) describes four levels of intervention needed for dealing with this syndrome. Level 1 interventions deal with the process—the way layoffs take place from the survivors' perspective. These interventions do not provide a cure for survivor sickness but keep survivors from sinking further into survivor symptoms. Level 2 interventions help survivors to grieve. These interventions deal with repressed feelings and emotions and provide the opportunity for a catharsis that releases the energy that has been invested in emotional repression. Level 3 interventions help survivors recapture their sense of control and self-esteem from the organization.

Finally, Level 4 interventions create the structural systems and processes that immunize people against survivor sickness.

Although this four-level "pyramid" is a stage model—Level 1 interventions proceed to Level 2, and so on—utilized to convey the increasing depth and breadth of each successive intervention, clearly the
real world is much more dynamic than any model. For example,
Level 1 process interventions sometimes lead directly to Level 4
system changes without going through Levels 2 or 3. Reducing overdependency on the organization—Level 3—often stimulates Level 2
grieving and vice versa. Noer's (1993) four-level model postulates
that process interventions are less complex and deep than those that
facilitate grieving; interventions that reduce organizational dependency are yet deeper and broader than the first two; while interventions that change organizational systems from those that reinforce
the old paradigm to those that encourage the new are the most
difficult of all.

Because of their training and experience in therapeutically dealing
with loss and grieving, clinician-consultants are in a unique position to
positively impact the health and well-being of workers in corporations
that have downsized or will downsize their workforce. Currently, treatment of downsizing syndrome, or layoff survivor sickness, is largely accomplished in group settings (Noer, 1993), and most of the treatment is
now done after layoffs have been announced. It seems likely, though, that
preventive measures could be extremely effective. These might include
coaching managers responsible for notifying workers that they will be
laid off as well as preparation sessions for workers slated for layoff.

Ultimately, layoff survivor sickness is a complex phenomenon that
does not lend itself to a simple solution. It contains conflicts of values
centered on overdependency on the organization as well as self-empow-
erment. Developing organizational systems that will prevent the reoc-
currence of this sickness ought to be one of the most fundamental
priorities of organizational leaders.

Recommended Readings

Noer, David. (1993). *Healing the Wounds: Overcoming the Trauma of
    Layoffs and Revitalizing Downsized Organizations.* San Francisco:
    Jossey-Bass.

Treatment Outcomes Consultation

History will likely show that the 1990s were the most challenging of times for clinicians. They currently face unprecedented pressure from many quarters, including managed care organizations, to provide results-oriented treatment that is effective, affordable, and long lasting. Also a paradigm shift is now occurring in the way behavioral health services are being conceptualized, delivered, and remunerated. Even though some clinicians have vowed to fight this paradigm shift, in time, this "protest stage" will give way to new ways of training and practice for clinicians or, the likely preferred designation, "behavioral health providers."

Since combined treatment has been shown to be both cost-effective and treatment efficacious, combining two or more treatment modalities, such as individual therapy and medication or group or family therapy, will become more common. Clinicians will need to become competent with specific strategies for tailoring and combining treatment. They will also be expected to measure, monitor, and manage the outcomes of such treatment, along with the illness; the therapeutic setting; treatment modalities; and the patient's readiness and expectation for treatment. Finally, because clinician practice styles and clinic patterns will have significantly changed, many clinicians and clinic groups will need both expert and process organizational consultation to accommodate and adjust to these changes. In short, it appears that at least three types of consultation are needed: instructional, clinical research, and organizational.

Regarding instructional consultation, enterprising clinician-consultants will need to establish training programs and seminars for practicing clinicians on a wide variety of topics. This training, or more accurately "retraining," will range from current topics, such as time-limited therapy, solution-focused treatments, cognitive-behavioral therapy strategies, and the like to strategies for tailoring and combining various treatment modalities. Training in the use of computer-assisted assessment and diagnosis, interactive video treatment methods, as well as in the effective utilization of time-limited couple and group treatments, will be additional topics that clinicians, clinics, and other health care organizations will perceive as necessary competencies. While some entrepeneurs will develop individual study materials or large workshops, which may or may not involve continuing education credits, clinician-consultants will establish contractual relations with health care systems to evaluate their training needs and tailor various educational programs and experiences to meet those needs. Of course, an understanding of organizational behavior and dynamics will be invaluable in this process.

With regard to the clinical research dimension of treatment outcomes, some clinician-consultants will be able to establish a reputation for expertise in this particular niche. To many clinicians and managed care organizations, measures of treatment outcomes have progressed no further than patient satisfaction surveys. Because of response bias and questionable relationship to other outcome measures, patient satisfaction surveys appear to have limited utility and value. Of more value and utility are measures of treatment effectiveness that involve ratings of client-patient symptom severity, global functioning, and the like. Some managed care organizations have begun monitoring outcomes before, during, and after the course of treatment to predict patterns involving relapse and recurrence. A few managed care organizations are attempting to manage outcomes. That is, they are profiling client-patient presentations and comparing the efficacy and efficiency of specific treatment protocols and then profiling providers to predict the best match among client-patient, provider, and treatment protocol (Sperry, Brill, Howard, & Grissom, 1996).

While both of these instructional and clinical research efforts largely involve expert consultation, clinician-consultants can provide more process-oriented consultation in assisting clinicians and provider organizations to change their professional practice styles and patterns. Because of the extensiveness of such changes, many clinicians will need to grieve the loss of the way they practiced and functioned previously. Furthermore, the organizational culture and dynamics of clinics, practice groups, and provider organizations will also be changing. And, like other organization-wide planned change efforts, organizational restructuring and transformation usually requires the assistance of consultants. In short, clinician-consultants can positively impact the changes occurring in their own profession.

Recommended Readings

Sederer, L., & Dickey, B. (Eds.). (1996). *Outcomes Assessment in Clinical Practice.* Baltimore: Williams & Wilkins.

Sperry, Len. (1995). *Psychopharmacology and Psychotherapy: Strategies for Maximizing Treatment Outcomes.* New York: Brunner/Mazel.

Sperry, Len, Brill, Peter L., Howard, Kenneth, & Grissom, Grant R. (1996). *Treatment Outcomes in Psychotherapy and Psychiatric Interventions.* New York: Brunner/Mazel.

Mental Health Policy Consultation

Although most corporations have elaborate policies for the recognition and treatment of the mental health concerns of workers, most have no consistent policy for executives. Because of this, some clinician-consultants have established a reputation for mental health policy consultation (Speller, 1989). To be effective and useful, a corporate policy for the detection and management of relational, substance use, and psychiatric problems in distressed and impaired executives must specify a number of contingencies, articulate the overall mission and justification, and clearly delineate the roles and responsibilities of key parties.

Such a policy must reflect at least four beliefs. The first is that the performance of senior executives is critical to the corporation's long-term well-being. Experienced, productive, and loyal executives are the corporation's most basic strategic asset. The second belief is that relational, substance use, and psychiatric disorders are not willful forms of conduct and do not reflect moral weakness. The third belief is that any delay in taking appropriate action relative to these disorders is counterproductive and inappropriate. And, fourth, in order to avoid or reduce long-term disability and eventual separation from the corporation, all executives must make it their responsibility to promptly take action so that distressed and impaired executives get treated, recover, and return to work in a timely manner.

The policy should specify which level or levels of management are covered by this policy. Because middle-level and senior executives tend to avoid using EAP services, a separate and distinct policy and set of procedures are warranted. Some firms specify that the executive policy is only for vice presidents and higher executives or for the top management of major divisions or subsidiaries, with all other managers covered by the EAP policy. The policy statement should also operationally define "executive impairment," and this definition should include reference to DSM-IV Axes I and II as well as useful descriptions, like the policy of the National Council on Alcoholism, wherein the alcoholic is described as "an individual whose drinking interferes in a continuing and growing way with the components of the individual's lifestyle, family, friends, and work, usually in that order."

Furthermore, the policy must specify where the program is to be located in the corporate structure. Usually it is located in the senior personnel executive's office, even if the corporation has several subsidiaries and is geographically diverse. The clinician-consultant should work with and directly report to this senior executive, to ensure that recommendations are given support from the highest levels of the organization.

The policy should also include the commitment of senior management to the policy, especially regarding the matters of early detection, documentation, and reporting of impaired behavior to the senior personnel officer; review of the data in conjunction with the clinician-consultant; confrontation of the impaired executive; referral and treatment follow-up; and reintegration of the treated and recovering executive into the corporation.

The roles of the key players should be specified in the policy. It must be understood that all executives are expected to monitor their own performance and voluntarily seek help from the supervising executive or senior personnel officer. Likewise, the supervising executive is expected to monitor, evaluate, and document job performance of workers they supervise and to report signs of distress and impairment to the senior personnel officer. The senior personnel officer is expected to advocate the use of the program by all covered executives and to oversee the implementation of the policy—which usually specifies orientation sessions.

Regarding distress issues, this implementation means reviewing issues of executive–job "fit" with the clinician-consultant and offering appropriate executive seminars, developmental counseling, job enrichment, and sabbaticals. With regard to impairment issues, implementation includes assessing, confronting, and referring the impaired executive for treatment, followed by monitoring treatment, assisting the reintegration of the recovering executive into the corporation and periodically reviewing the impact of this policy.

The issue of confidentiality also must be spelled out in the policy. The policy must specify that every effort will be made to maintain the executive's privacy. This means that the impaired executive's records will not be incorporated into the executive's regular personnel file but rather will be held in a separate file by the clinician-consultant. Furthermore, professional ethics dictate that the clinician-consultant hold information obtained from the executive in the course of the evaluation and treatment in strict confidence.

Finally, the clinician-consultant should strongly encourage client corporations to adopt this formal corporate mental health policy for executives. Besides clarifying treatment issues, roles, and procedures, this policy serves as an important preventive psychological intervention. A prototype of a corporate policy for impaired executives is provided by Speller (1989, pp. 112–117).

Recommended Readings

Speller, Jeffrey. (1988). *Executives in Crisis: Recognizing and Managing the Alcoholic, Drug-Addicted, or Mentally Ill Executive.* San Francisco: Jossey-Bass.

Violence Prevention Consultation

As corporations have perceived that workplace violence is increasing, they have sought out consultants to help establish violence prevention programs. However, because few psychologically trained consultants have had experience or interest in this area, corporations have turned to security consultants instead even though violence issues require much more than the technical expertise that security consultants can offer. Clinician-consultants, on the other hand, can provide both technical and psychological expertise, making the area of violence prevention a unique practice niche for clinician-consultants. This section briefly overviews the components of a violence response plan, which should be part of the mental health and safety policies of the organization and should include the use of prescreening for potential new hires, the creation of a humane working environment, safe and legal discipline and termination procedures, and the offer of counseling for workers who request it. The plan should be filed in the CEO's office, the personnel office, the human resources office, the EAP office, and the security office.

The clinician-consultant assists top management, the human resources director, and the safety director in meeting to assess the corporation's unique needs and circumstances regarding violence issues and then assists the group in preparing a written plan, which should contain the following specifications: (1) Designation of who is to contact and how to contact the specified clinician-consultant immediately, no later than 24 hours after the incident. (2) An arrangement for the clinician-consultant to meet first at the top levels of the organization for executive debriefings and then to schedule meetings with anyone in the firm who wants to talk about what happened. (3) A postincident plan for returning the organization back on track and back to business as efficiently, safely, and humanely as possible. (4) A critical incident debriefing area for the responding clinician-consultant. (5) The designation of a representative to work with local law enforcement. (6) The designation of a staff member to notify the victims' families of the incident and the provision of immediate support, counseling, and debriefing services for them. (7) The designation of a media spokesperson to brief the media and to keep them away from grieving employees, family members, or eyewitnesses. (8) The offer to provide "debriefing" services for all potential workplace violence victims outside of the immediate survivors or employees. (9) Notification of in-house legal counsel or outside counsel about the incident, with the understanding that counsel will respond to the scene. (10) Notification of personnel managers to arrange for time off for grieving employees, as appropriate. (11) Designation of someone to immediately check, protect, or restore the integrity of data systems, computers, and files. (12) Provision for a crew to clean up the site of the attack. (13) Provision for a service to memorialize the victims. (14) Establishment of a clinician-consultant to return at intervals for further debriefings.

Recommended Readings

Mantell, Michael. (1994). *Ticking Bombs: Defusing Violence in the Workplace*. Burr Ridge, IL: Irwin.

7

Executive Dynamics

This chapter overviews basic information about the personality dynamics, job demands, and lifestyle of the senior executive for the clinician-consultant who does corporate therapy and consultation. It begins by describing the job expectations and demands of executives, the differences between male and female executives, and the motivational and leadership styles of executives. The work-personality styles of healthy and effective executives are then elaborated. Finally, the healthy executive is contrasted with the distressed and impaired executive. This chapter provides background for the discussion of coaching, consultation, and psychotherapy with executives in Chapter 8.

PROFILE AND LIFESTYLE OF EXECUTIVES

What are executives like, and what do they do in a typical day? This section briefly describes the functions, roles, and skills of executives; their typical day and demands on their time; female executives vs. male executives; executives' work-personality styles, and leadership styles and values; organizational barriers and the predictable career crises that they face; and executive–corporate fit.

Functions, Roles, and Skills

Executives and managers exist at all levels of an organization. *Senior executives,* or top managers, are those at the upper levels of an organization. Usually this upper level includes the chief executive officer (CEO), the chief operating officer (COO), and the vice presidents of various divisions or subsidiaries or of specific areas, like human resources/personnel, operations, marketing, and finance. These are *line positions,* and persons in these positions have actual decision-making responsibilities for subordinates. They are in contrast to *staff positions* since people who hold staff positions primarily have supportive rather than decision-making functions. Often the president of the organization is the CEO, although sometimes the chairman of the corporation's board of directors may serve as CEO, with the president functioning as COO. Top management's primary role is to set broad organizational policies, goals, and strategies.

The following three types of executives make up the corporation's middle management. *Junior executive* is an imprecise designation for the persons in staff positions supporting senior executives. *Middle managers* have titles like plant manager, general manager, operations manager, or department manager. They function to implement the strategies and policies set by top management. They also coordinate the work of first-line managers.

First-line managers have titles like section manager, foreman, or supervisor, and their function is to supervise employees. Over the past decade, the ranks of middle management have been greatly diminished through mergers and downsizing to make corporations "leaner and meaner."

Generally, managers at all levels perform five general functions: leadership, planning, decision making, organizing, and controlling. Recently, leadership function has been emphasized over the other four more "administrative" functions. Essentially, *leadership* refers to the ability to envision and to empower employees, which is accomplished by innovative thinking and galvanizing and motivating others to fulfill the corporate vision. The emphasis of each of these five functions varies with the different levels of management. Specifically, the organizing and controlling functions are emphasized by supervisors, with the leadership, decision making, and planning functions emphasized at the senior executive level (Kelly, 1980).

All managers fulfill three roles—interpersonal, decisional, and informational. *Interpersonal roles* include those of leader, figurehead, and liaison. *Decisional roles* include negotiator, resource allocator, entrepreneur, and conflict manager. *Informational roles* include monitor, disseminator, and spokesperson.

In order to function effectively in these roles, competent managers must be proficient in four skills—technical, interpersonal, conceptual, and diagnostic—but at various degrees at different levels of management. *Technical skills* and expertise related to the corporation's product or service are of greatest importance for first-line managers but are less important for top managers. *Interpersonal skills* reflect the manager's ability to understand, communicate, compromise, and resolve conflict. These interpersonal skills are most critical for first-line managers and are moderately important for middle and top managers.

Conceptual skills include the ability to think abstractly, appreciate interrelationships, and consider a global perspective. *Diagnostic skills* include the ability to understand, clarify, and define problematic situations and specify solutions. Conceptual and diagnostic skills are of critical importance for top managers but are less essential for first-line managers. In general, middle managers need an equal mix of all four skills, first-line managers need primarily technical and interpersonal skills, and top managers need conceptual and diagnostic skills (Van Fleet, 1988).

A Typical Day and the Demand on Time for Executives

Senior executives work 55- to 60-hour weeks. A classic study by Mintzberg (1973) shows that effective executives work at a relatively relentless pace, with few, if any, breaks during their workday. Approximately 60 percent of their time is occupied with formal, scheduled meetings. The rest of their time is filled with less formal face-to-face encounters, which tend to be brief, lasting less than nine minutes per encounter and are often focused on managing crises. Approximately one-third of their time is spent with subordinates, whereas only 10 percent involves time spent with their superior. Between 22 percent and 33 percent of their time is spent outside their office, primarily in contact with clients, colleagues, or peers. These executives were noted by Mintzberg to be preoccupied with scheduling, to show disdain for written communications such as their mail, and to skim professional articles at a rate of two per minute.

The Female Executive versus the Male Executive

Studies have noted that male and female executives lead and manage differently. Mintzberg's (1973) study, discussed in the preceding section, observed daily work and leadership patterns among successful male managers and executives. And as just noted in the previous discussion, the male executives in Mintzberg's study worked at an unrelenting pace and rarely took breaks, as they went from meeting to meeting and task to task. Their days were characterized by interruptions, discontinuities, and fragmentations. They spared little time for activities not directly related to their work, such as family concerns and involvement. They exhibited a preference for live encounters, such as face-to-face meetings and telephone calls, rather than for mail, memos, and the like. They spent roughly one-third to one-half of their contact time with subordinates planning strategy and "putting out fires," and about 10 percent of their time with their superior. They identified themselves closely with their job, believing that their identity was indistinguishable from their position or role. Finally, they lacked little time for personal reflection as they immersed themselves in the immediate experiences of their jobs.

Because of the intensity of their work style and minimal time for personal reflection, they had considerable difficulty with detachment. Mintzberg believes, though, that such detachment is desirable, in that the executive needs to perform various functions, which require a reflective, detached stance, such as figurehead, decision maker, coach, or negotiator. In short, the male style of leading reflects an attitude and sense of conflicting demands, time pressures, interruptions, task achievement, and work as a means to an end. Yet, despite their fast-paced schedule, these male executives took pleasure in the success of their accomplishments.

In contrast to Mintzberg's study, Helgesen (1990) observed the following leadership patterns in successful female executives: These women worked at a steady pace but took small breaks scheduled throughout their day. They did not view unscheduled encounters or tasks as interruptions. They made time for activities not directly related to their work, particularly family concerns. They preferred "live," direct encounters but also scheduled time to review and respond to their mail. They focused on the big picture and the long term, rather than being immersed in the day-to-day tasks of management. They saw their identities as complex and multifaceted and well beyond their job position or title. Finally, they scheduled time for sharing information. In short, the female leadership style reflects an attitude and sense of flow, interaction, access, networking, nurturance, creativity, and involvement.

As the complexion of business rapidly changes—driven by ever-changing technology, shortages of skilled labor, global competition, and a multifaceted workforce—corporations must be able to accommodate a wider focus; foster creativity; and nurture new ideas, products, and services, in order to survive. Given the changing nature of work and the workforce, a need is emerging for leaders who manifest many of the patterns and characteristics noted in successful female executives.

Specific Issues Facing Female Executives

Because it has been barely 20 years since a critical number of women entered the executive suites of corporations, relatively little research has been reported on women executives. Although the corporate career patterns of men have been articulated by writers such as Levinson, in *The Seasons of a Man's Life* (1978) and Maccoby, in *The Gamesman* (1976), these life cycles or stage patterns do not reflect the experiences of most women executives.

Hardesty and Jacobs (1986) describe six stages of the corporate career paths of the women executives they studied in detail. They provocatively titled these stages as follows: 1) "Wooed and won" describes how women choose and experience corporate culture; 2) "Proving up" describes how women executives experience the early stages of their career; 3) "Seeds of disenchantment" refers to the initial doubts of these women about the value of their corporate contribution and rewards; 4) "Success and self-betrayal" refers to the stage of conflictual thoughts and feelings these women experience about remaining within the system; 5) "The pivot point" refers to the decision process of staying or leaving the corporate culture; and 6) "Reconcilable differences" describes the way in which women who stay in the corporation adjust emotionally and professionally to its barriers.

The "glass ceiling" phenomenon—that is, the barriers that women experience when attaining top executive positions—remains a prevalent reality today (Morrison, White, & Velsen, 1987). Only 4.5 percent of the highest-ranking corporate jobs belong to women. At the "pivot point" of Hardesty and Jacobs's scheme, women must decide whether to break away from corporate barriers and start their own companies or to stay and keep trying. But even if they break down the initial barriers, they may unexpectedly encounter a second barrier—a wall of tradition and stereotype that separates them from top executive positions.

It is usually assumed that women are held back from executive positions, particularly CEO positions, by men. Often this assumption is true. However, Madden's (1987) nationwide survey reports that women also can block the advancement of other women. Madden refers to this as the "uncivil business war," wherein conflicts among women of different socioeconomic classes or generations directly or inadvertently thwart the upward mobility of women in corporations.

Some believe that top management is now becoming more sensitive to gender differences, particularly with regard to participative management. Similarly, fears about women executives being "too soft and giving away the store" are starting to subside. Male executives who have worked side by side with female executives note that leadership that combines firm direction with genuine empowerment—the ability to make decisions on things that affect one's job— creates an organization that stirs individuals to produce their best work because they feel good about where they work and about themselves. This kind of leadership requires a high level of communication and a high level of teamwork, which women have a propensity for (Rizzo & Mendez, 1990). However, the question has been and still remains: Will top management encourage and allow such a "feminine" approach to leadership?

Of the many issues with which contemporary women executives grapple, three relational issues stand out: effects of parental employment on the children's emotional development, child care, and dual-career marriages.

Interestingly, there are notable similarities and differences between male and female organizational consultants as well. A national survey of 416 organizational consultants—150 women and 266 men—from three professional consulting organizations showed considerable similarity about the focus of consultation and the intervention strategies utilized. The main difference, however, was that female consultants placed more importance on humanistic values in consultation work for the future than men (Waclawski, Church, & Burke, 1995). Whether these findings reflect the values and practice style of male and female clinician-consultants remains to be studied.

Motivational Styles of Executives

Anyone who regularly interacts with executives has noted their need for *power* and *influence*. McClelland (1975) reports that the power need is twice as high in managers as in the general populace. Those with a high need for power feel most fulfilled when they believe they are controlling or strongly influencing the behavior of others. Status, position, and reputation are valued as befitting adjuncts by "power needy" people. Three other important needs for executives, in various lesser degrees, are the need for: achievement, affiliation, and autonomy.

Individuals with a high need for *achievement* derive considerable satisfaction from personal accomplishment. They feel best when meeting their self-imposed standards of excellence and making a unique contribution. They are not motivated primarily by power, wealth, or prestige but rather regard these things as signs that others recognize and value their accomplishments (McClelland, 1975).

Individuals with a high need for *affiliation* like to be with other people and enjoy being a team member. They are most content when they are liked and accepted by others, and they make concentrated efforts to please. They tend to avoid conflict whenever possible and to resolve it as amicably as possible (McClelland, 1975).

Those with a high need for *autonomy* are most content when they feel self-directed and can avoid the interference of others. They prefer to be alone and are "reluctant" team members (McClelland, 1975). Most individual executives have some mix of each of these four needs, although one need—usually power—tends to predominate.

Because most executive positions require leadership reflective of power and dominance, individuals with relatively high and healthy power needs tend to feel comfortable and are effective in such roles. Thus, a good "fit" results between a position requiring high power and an executive with high power needs. On the other hand, corporations that support a friendly, "family" atmosphere or a team focus tend to favor individuals who have higher affiliation needs to match their power needs. Thus, individuals with high affiliation needs are highly likely to find a better "fit" in a family-like corporation than those with high autonomy needs. Also at first glance, hard-driving, high production-oriented firms might seem a great "fit" for individuals with high achievement needs. However, unless the individual also has relatively high power needs, he or she may quickly burn out.

Work-Personality Styles of Executives

Recently, there has been a growing interest in the personality dynamics of executives. Kets de Vries (1989; Kets de Vries & Miller, 1987) has written widely about personality styles among top executives. He believes that individuals with narcissistic, controlling, paranoid, and aggressive styles, or combinations of these styles, tend to gravitate toward top leadership positions, whereas individuals with histrionic, dependent, passive-aggressive, and masochistic styles do not. He also notes that a combination of healthy narcissism and control creates a complementarity that is quite effective and successful in business, whereas the paranoid and detached styles are a poor combination for effective leadership.

While such characterizations of executive personality styles are immensely valuable, many executives and consultants are uncomfortable with the use of such clinical designations to describe healthy, adaptive workplace functioning. Therefore, the following descriptions of the various work-personality styles utilize the nonclinical designations suggested by Millon and Everly (1985) and Oldham and Morris (1990). These descriptions elaborate the work-personality styles from the Taxonomy of Organizational and Work Dysfunction noted in the Appendix to Chapter 4.

Devoted Work-Personality Style

Individuals with a devoted work-personality style tend to gravitate toward nonprofessional job classifications. They are least likely to be found in sole proprietorships or in positions requiring entrepreneurial talent or energy. Rather, they thrive in work settings in which they take direct orders or fulfill the needs of others. This includes secretarial work, secure positions in family-owned businesses, assembly line work, or staff—rather than line—positions in corporate settings. These individuals also are likely to be hard workers and team players, to abhor competitiveness and shrink from it, and to avoid job situations that require them to make decisions independently. In addition, they take orders well, cooperate with coworkers, and aim to please their superiors. They seem also to have little need to take credit for outcomes or even to share glory. Instead, they seek to be liked and appreciated.

Furthermore, these individuals avoid conflict or the circumstances that might lead to it and can work well with a variety of other personality styles. They are particularly well suited to working with conscientious superiors, especially if their boss will direct their efforts. Because they are loyal and noncompetitive, they can also tolerate self-confident superiors, especially those who do not expect much initiative or independence from them.

Since this personality style shrinks from autonomy, devoted individuals generally avoid the managerial track. If in managerial or professional ranks, they tend to be followers rather than leaders, and functionaries rather than visionaries. However, because of their cooperativeness and competence, they may be promoted to a supervisory or management position. Not surprisingly, such jobs may prove their undoing.

For devoted personality individuals with additional traits, such as self-confidence and conscientiousness, though, certain leadership positions may be tolerable. Such individuals can be friendly, encouraging, and sensitive toward their subordinates. They may easily accept and even seek staff initiative and decision making, and they are drawn to concepts like team leadership and quality circles. However, because they tend to be preoccupied with what their staff thinks of them and have difficulty asserting authority in difficult conflictual situations, their effectiveness is likely to suffer. The DSM-IV clinical counterpart to the devoted work-personality style is the Dependent Personality Disorder.

Dramatic Work-Personality Style

Individuals with this personality style tend to avoid repetitive, routine jobs and technical careers. Instead they are attracted to exciting and creative work settings and careers. These individuals tend to be "broad stroke," idea people who operate on hunches and intuition rather than on reasoned, deductive thinking and details. They tend also to be creative, emotional, persuasive, and energetic and are often fun to be around. Not surprisingly, they are able to promote, sell, and wheel and deal, when it comes to a product line or service. They may have difficulty, however, following strategic plans, instructions, and protocols, and staying on budget and keeping accurate records is alien to their free-spirited approach to life. Thus, they look for others to take care of administrative details. They seem to be happy and content in job settings that can accommodate their creative flair, in terms of work habits, dress code, and working hours. Accordingly, these individuals often choose careers in teaching, sales, marketing, and in the various entertainment industries.

As executives, dramatic personality individuals tend to be strong managers. They can be inspiring bosses to work with and for and are usually appreciative and generous in rewarding the efforts of their subordinates. Likewise, they can show their anger and displeasure at a subordinate's shortcomings. They may be gruff, make threats, and be uncommunicative one day, only to forget it all and be enthusiastic and cheerful the next day. Successful managers with this personality style may be able to assemble a strong organization to complement their creative flair. Usually this means hiring assistants and staff members who are more compulsive to handle finances, legal issues, regulation, and paperwork. The DSM-IV clinical counterpart to the dramatic work-personality style is the Histrionic Personality Disorder.

Self-Confident Work-Personality Style

Individuals with this personality style are energetic, outgoing, and competitive as well as visionary, hardworking, and decisive. In addition, they can set priorities, plan, delegate, and galvanize the commitment of their subordinates. They present themselves as interested, interesting, and impassioned, and they possess considerable political savvy that enables them to size up the power structure and informal networks within a group or organization and proceed to establish personally advantageous power alliances. Generally, they can work comfortably and productively with others. Nevertheless, they view others as the means to the successful ends they constantly seek. While they may be deferential and cooperative to those in authority or from whom they seek gain, they can be generous in their financial and persistent support to loyal subordinates. In short, they can be extraordinarily effective and efficient workers and make excellent leaders.

As managers and executives, they will allow subordinates sufficient autonomy and leeway to get the job done or accomplish a shared vision. They are quite skilled at team building of which they must be clearly the source and center, and they demand loyalty to the job and team goals, as well as to themselves. Furthermore, they can be jealous of those in power and can be quite skillful in unseating an "opponent." They are innately competitive and relish staying one step ahead of their nearest competitor.

While they are the acknowledged leader and things are going as planned, they seldom insist on a hierarchical structure. And, as long as no one criticizes, competes, or attempts to share their glory, they can be encouraging, supportive, and fun to work with and for. However, if this unwritten agreement is breached, they can react with vengefulness. Finally, they can function effectively in the mentor role, provided that those under their tutelage are perceived as loyal and noncompetitive. The DSM-IV clinical counterpart to this work-personality style is the Narcissistic Personality Disorder.

Adventurous Work-Personality Style

Individuals with an adventurous work-personality style reflexively seek out challenges. When they perceive work to be a challenge, they are likely to approach it with excitement and anticipation. They will then function in a disciplined, focused, and responsible manner, and their efforts will be not only energetic but also resourceful and innovative. In time, however, they may become bored with the task, and if they no longer find it stimulating and challenging, are likely to drop it and move on to another project, or even another job. On the other hand, if this style is combined with sufficient compulsivity, these individuals are more likely to persevere and see the task through to completion.

These individuals do not particularly like authority figures and may resist those who attempt to control them. Not surprisingly, they tend to gravitate to occupations that combine risk and challenge with skill. They tend to see themselves as "top guns," whether they are fighter pilots, ski instructors, heart surgeons, trial attorneys, salespeople, or venture capitalists, and they energize themselves by thinking of ways to outwit the conventional wisdom and standards. Being inner-directed, they may bend rules for expediency, if they don't believe the rules make sense or apply to them.

As managers and executives they may build corporate empires through wheeling and dealing. They can function exceedingly well as entrepreneurs, but when it comes to professionalizing an organization, they often have neither the skills nor the desire to attend to such managerial functions as initiating strategic planning and management systems, budgeting, control systems, and the like. Generally, they prefer to operate on ingenuity and instinct rather than on the basis of rational thinking and long-range planning. Because of their tendency to resist authority and external constraints and regulations, they may run aground of state and federal regulating agencies or even their board of directors. The DSM-IV clinical counterpart to this work-personality style is the Antisocial Personality Disorder.

Solitary Work-Personality Style

Individuals with a solitary work-personality style can function relatively well in certain workplace settings and job classifications, despite their overall isolative mode of functioning. On the one hand, they can be hardworking, diligent, focused and no-nonsense employees. They are not easily bored or distracted, and once given a task, they neither need nor want oversight or feedback. Yet, surprisingly, they take criticism well. On the other hand, they don't relate well to others, particularly those who are unknown to them. They tend not to be sensitive to others' needs and subtleties of meaning and are not diplomatic. In addition, they find it difficult to engage in small talk and feel awkward around those who do. Thus, they are not good team players. Instead, they gravitate toward more solitary occupations, such as a security guard, maintenance worker, forest ranger, lighthouse tender, laboratory scientist, technician, accountant, or bookkeeper.

Occasionally, an individual with this personality style will have managerial responsibilities. Although they can be particularly useful with the technical and task-oriented side of management, they may have considerable difficulty with the people-oriented side. Besides having little patience with office politics, they find it difficult to understand the needs and concerns of their subordinates, and handling personnel problems is perplexing to them. Needless to say, management is not a good match for individuals with this personality style. The DSM-IV clinical counterpart to this work-personality style is the Schizoid Personality Disorder.

Sensitive Work-Personality Style

Individuals with a sensitive work-personality style can be quite at ease with jobs or careers that involve routine, repetition, and concentration. They tend to be safe and comfortable with familiar coworkers and are likely to avoid those who are unfamiliar, whether they be new coworkers or customers. As such, they are attracted to technical specialties and jobs in predictable work environments, such as accounting and data processing, in which they can feel safe and secure. They are reliable, steady and effective employees who work best with a few colleagues with whom they feel trust. Their workplace becomes like a nurturing family, a safe haven. They have more need for safety than variety, and if they are comfortable, would stay with the same corporation indefinitely.

Unlike individuals with other work-personality styles, who find routines pure drudgery, sensitive individuals are actually attracted to routine because it structures their day. Similarly, they prefer defined roles that provide consistent, unchanging expectations. They are also thorough workers who can easily focus their attention and concentration to the task at hand. Interpersonally, they tend to be slow to warm up to coworkers, but once they establish relationships, they are friendly and loyal.

Because they care about what others think of them, they attempt to perform their best. Not surprisingly, though, dealing with superiors, performance appraisal, and other situations in which they or their work is evaluated can be quite stressful. Consequently, they gravitate toward workplaces with lower stress, family-like atmospheres.

Essentially, these individuals can be extremely competent, committed, and loyal workers. Even though they may be attracted to the challenges of management, they often resist promotions, particularly if it might increase exposure to other levels of feedback and potential criticism. Not surprisingly, when sensitive individuals are in a management position, they tend to avoid contact with individuals outside their immediate unit and instead may appoint subordinates to act as their liaison. Within their immediate unit, these managers are likely to promote a family atmosphere among their subordinates. They also tend to work toward building commitment and loyalty among their staff. In part, this is because they dread turnover. The prospect of newcomers joining their unit is difficult for them, and they may initially appear cold and aloof until they are reasonably assured that these new individuals are safe and solid performers. The DSM-IV counterpart to this work-personality style is the Avoidant Personality Disorder.

Leisurely Work-Personality Style

Individuals with a leisurely work-personality style approach work for purely financial reasons, such as paying bills, insuring a pension, or financing their hobbies and recreation. Rather than being attracted by the possibilities of fame or success, they are attracted by security. These individuals can be good workers and adequate team players, but they are quick to draw the line between work time and personal time. They won't take work home with them, they don't worry about job matters in off-hours, and they'll refuse to do more than is required of them. When their job demands efforts beyond their stated responsibilities, they balk. They have little need to please their boss or coworkers or to feel better about themselves by being altruistic and dedicated. Rather, they will meet their stated job requirements but not allow themselves to be exploited by anyone. Generally they don't seek meaning or fulfillment in their jobs or in the workplace; rather they look for fulfillment in their personal lives.

Not surprisingly, these individuals are not driven or achievement oriented. While they work slowly and comfortably, they tend to chafe when deadlines are imposed. In reaction to authority figures, they are likely to be mildly suspicious and wary. When asked to work faster or to do more, they are likely to feel they are being treated unfairly. These individuals are also keenly aware of their rights and of avenues of redress for perceived wrongs or exploitation. Consequently, if their supervisor insists and demands, they are likely to threaten to file a grievance. Furthermore, they can tolerate a considerable amount of routine and tedium. Individuals with leisurely work-personality style are likely to be found in a wide range of job classifications and careers, but because of their need for security, they gravitate toward jobs in union shops, the military, civil service, and other bureaucracies. They may achieve promotions but are unlikely to achieve the top slots.

Because they are not inherently ambitious in their careers, these individuals are unlikely to be found above the middle management level. Their reluctance to sacrifice personal time, energy, and effort tends to keep these individuals from advancing to top management. As managers, they have no higher expectations of their subordinates' performance than they have for themselves. Consequently, they expect their staff to follow protocol and meet quotas, but they don't make unreasonable demands. At best, they are average and competent managers but not leaders per se: they don't, or can't, develop and hold up a vision of how things could be, don't galvanize motivation and support for it, and don't muster the dedication and energy to achieve it. But, they are able to keep the wheels of industry turning. The DSM-IV clinical counterpart to this work-personality style is the Passive-Aggressive Personality Disorder.

Conscientious Work-Personality Style

Individuals with a conscientious work-personality style like to do things the right way, as compared to individuals with Obsessive-Compulsive Personality Disorder, who must do things perfectly. The need of those with the conscientious style to do things right is likely to result in uncompleted or delayed projects because the finished product may not be good enough. They gravitate toward jobs involving bookkeeping, copyediting, or auditing functions. Thus, the consientious individual who is writing a report will edit and reedit sentences, laboring under the belief that there must be a better way to say it. These individuals figuratively drown themselves in a sea of never-ending possibilities and details, doubts that cannot be stilled, and decisions that seldom seem to get made. They can become so obsessed with minor details that they can leave the most important tasks to the end, when time is at a premium. Essentially all their sense of priority is lost.

Having misplaced a list of things to be done, they spend an inordinate amount of time looking for the list rather than taking a moment or two to reconstruct it. Or, they may spend too much time and energy filling out reminders and schedules that could have been used toward completing the scheduled task. In addition, these individuals avoid opportunities to relax. They invest the vast majority of their energy in their work, but over time lose most of their enthusiasm for it. They are tense, anxious, and overwhelmed by the amount of work before them, whether it involves their job or profession, or their hobbies and vacations.

Conscientious managers and executives tend to be critical, demanding, and even tyrannical in the face of small errors made by subordinates. They demand more attention to small detail, neatness, and perfection than executives with other work-personality styles. A conscientious executive cannot recognize that her staff admirably completed a rush job because she keeps spotting minor imperfections—a few minor typographical errors or a computer terminal that was not turned off. Furthermore, these individuals tend to equate overtime with job commitment and loyalty. Thus, they are likely to believe that subordinates or colleagues that leave the office at the regular quitting time are leaving early.

Although these executives may be rigid and lack interpersonal skills and political savvy, they tend to be extremely competent. They expect tasks to be accomplished thoroughly and to follow standard protocol, while they frown upon creative and innovative approaches. They also expect loyalty and consistent performances but may find it difficult to offer reassurance and praise. They are likely as well to form quick judgments of others that are long lasting and difficult to change, and they may hold grudges. In addition they tend to dress conservatively and conventionally. As mentors they may be quite talented and knowledgeable, but they tend to be emotionally distant, proper, nonspontaneous, and only minimally encouraging. The DSM-IV clinical counterpart to this work-personality style is the Obsessive-Compulsive Personality Disorder.

Idiosyncratic Work-Personality Style

It is more likely that individuals with an idiosyncratic work-personality style can sustain long-term employment than those with a Schizotypal Personality Disorder. Nevertheless, sustained employment depends largely on whether these individuals can find work settings that tolerate their eccentricities and how well they can adapt to specific job expectations. Obviously, those individuals who can contain most or all of their idiosyncratic thinking and behaviors do the best. Since these individuals tend not to be overly competitive, ambitious, or concerned with office politics, they tend to gravitate toward routine occupations involving repetitive tasks. They seem to do particularly well in jobs in which they can "tune out" while accomplishing a task. Jobs such as typist, word processor, file clerk, postal carrier, baggage handler, and librarian permit a good deal of self-preoccupation while adequately performing a work task. Despite adequate job performance, the extent to which idiosyncratic behavior distracts or offends coworkers often determines longevity in a particular job. Thus, finding the best "fit" job in the most accepting work environment is critical for idiosyncratic individuals who want or need ongoing employment.

Needless to say, these individuals are unlikely to achieve management positions in which the supervision of a subordinate is required. On the other hand, other types of management are possible. For instance, individuals with this work-personality style and an entrepreneurial bent have been successful in managing or even owning one-person businesses. These include bookkeeping firms, mail-order businesses, and the like. The DSM-IV clinical counterpart to this work-personality style is the Schizotypal Personality Disorder.

Mercurial Work-Personality Style

In the psychodynamic literature the prototypic description of a higher functioning individual with the mercurial or borderline personality style is that of a 29-year-old unmarried nurse who has worked in a hospital or clinic for a half a dozen years, whereas a lower functioning individual with a Borderline Personality Disorder may be unable to hold a job. Individuals with the mercurial work-personality style, such as the aforementioned nurse, tend to be quite successful in the workplace. These individuals can be quite bright, energetic, creative, and outgoing and gravitate to several occupations and careers ranging from entertainment, to teaching, to the helping and health care professions. They seem to function best in creative fields where their emotive capability can be operative.

On the other hand, they seem to do less well in technical and quantitive fields, where they work alone, or have little structure in their workplace. They can focus their energy and work diligently when they are appreciated and rewarded for their efforts. However, should their efforts be unnoticed or spurned, they will quickly lose interest in working hard and may possibly react with strong emotion. Typically, they become intensely involved in the lives of their coworkers and idealize them, particularly their supervisor, whom they may try to impress and develop a special relationship with.

These individuals are not well suited to management, particularly those that require the dispassionate evaluation and handling of performance appraisals and interpersonal conflict among coworkers.

Since they have a tendency to become intensely involved with others and to develop idealizing relationships, they find it difficult to remain objective. They tend to unreasonably expect a level of dedication and effort that few subordinates can attain or maintain. When subordinates fail to meet such expectations, these managers take this as a personal affront. They are likely to be moody and possibly utilize the defense mechanism of splitting.

Individuals with this work-personality style who likewise have conscientious and adventurous stylistic traits, though, might have a chance for success in the executive suite. But often, they will need a loyal, structured, detail-oriented person as their assistant. The DSM-IV clinical counterpart to this work-personality style is the Borderline Personality Disorder.

Vigilant Work-Personality Style

Individuals with this work-personality style tend to gravitate to work settings and careers where there is a good "fit" with their talents and style. They tend to be perceptive, alert, sensitive to subtle cues, and not easily misled. Their ability to attend to a variety of cues and multiple levels of meaning and communication suggest an exquisite sensitivity to people and situations. They tend also to be ambitious and hardworking. But the degree to which they are successful in their work is often a function of their relationship with bosses and coworkers since they are likely to be sensitive to an organization's power structure. Furthermore, they dislike and are uncomfortable with subordination to and dependence on others. And because of their belief that power can be used against them, they can find it hard to trust authority figures and to feel comfortable within particular organizations. Accordingly, they may work best in careers and occupations in which they can operate with considerable leeway and independence or with limited oversight from a superior.

While many individuals with this style are able to tolerate their boss and peers, they are quite aware of inequities in corporate policies and practices and may be quick to point these out. It shouldn't be surprising that corporate watchdogs and whistle-blowers tend to have this personality style. These individuals may be excellent investigative reporters, diagnosticians, critics, and researchers. Others may prefer to work with technologies rather than people, being well served by their unique ability to concentrate. Although some individuals with this personality covet the rise through the ranks, others choose to function more independently and gravitate to roles in which they can perform their duties without worrying about managing subordinates.

As managers and executives, these individuals require the assurance of loyalty from their subordinates. When suspecting disloyalty, they can be angry, unforgiving, and grudging. In some instances they may mistake a subordinate's ambition for disloyalty and subsequently thwart that subordinate's movement within the company. Generally, however, these managers tend to take particularly good care of their staff. In certain situations, these managers may even protect their subordinates against corporate policies or actions they perceive as demeaning or unfair. Yet, since they need to feel in complete charge of their unit, they may find delegating important—especially politically sensitive—responsibilities most difficult. They don't mind though, putting in longer hours or being out "among the troops" as this provides them an opportunity to closely monitor people and the particular situation. The DSM-IV clinical counterpart to this work-personality style is the Paranoid Personality Disorder.

Leadership Styles and Values of Executives

Based on extensive research with executives, Maccoby (1988) articulates five leadership styles that reflect changing societal values: the expert, the helper, the defender, the innovator, and the self-developer. He believes the self-developer is the leadership style most congruent with the changing organizational scene. He also notes that work has various meanings for individuals, and that individuals are most strongly motivated to work when the work demands made on them fit their dominant values.

Experts represent specialized technical excellence and professional knowledge and reflect the dominant value of mastery. Approximately 50 percent of the managers studied by Maccoby reflected this style. *Helpers* are service focused and seek to make the workplace a family atmosphere. They made up about 22 percent of Maccoby's leaders and reflect the value of relatedness. *Defenders* are most concerned with policies, survival, protection, and defending human dignity. They comprised only 1 percent of Maccoby's sample. *Innovators* are enterprising, creative executives who made up about 8 percent of the sample. They have made a significant impact on the complexion of business and the economy. *Self-developers* focus on facilitating problem solving with customers and clients and emphasize dominant values, such as personal growth and participatory management. They demand that work be balanced with personal and family needs. Self-developers represented 20 percent of the executives and up to 90 percent of business students and interns studied.

Organizational Barriers and Crises Facing Executives

Based on extensive consultation with executives, Bramson (1989) notes a number of barriers or predictable hazards that executives face as they move up the corporate ladder. These include job overload, a nonsupportive work environment, competition for the small number of top executive positions, power pathologies manifested in the executive suite, and unethical or illegal organizational practices.

Blotnick (1985), based on 25 years of research with 5,000 male and female executives, delineates five predictable crises in an executive's career. Interestingly, these inevitable obstacles correspond to the decades of a person's life. For individuals in their 20s, the crisis involves finding the right corporate stance, that is, managing an appropriate and balanced impression of themselves and avoiding destructive behavior patterns. For individuals in their 30s, the crisis involves developing the ability to work with others and to function maturely as a team member. When in their 40s, the challenge is to become indispensable rather than obsolete. Reluctance to keep current about new technical demands and advances in methodology is an ever-present danger for executives in their fourth decade.

When in their 50s, a major temptation for executives is to stagnate and become self-absorbed, rather than to impart wisdom to subordinates. Erikson (1980) uses the term "generativity" to describe this mentoring task for late-middle adulthood. Mentoring comes naturally to executives during this period, if they do not succumb to replaying negative authority transference. Finally, the crisis of executives in their 60s involves the question of executive succession or choosing the right heir.

These predictable crises seem commonsensical, at least to individuals with some basic understanding of human development. However, this is apparently not the case among most individuals in business; Blotnick (1985) reports that few business people—only 3 percent of the 5,000 persons studied—had an accurate idea of the kinds of developments and crises that could make or break their career.

Executive–Corporate Fit

The concept of "person–organization fit" (Levinson, 1981) was described in Chapter 3 where it was noted that essentially, the better the fit between the person and the organization, the greater the likelihood of better job performance, commitment, satisfaction, and personal self-esteem, with little stress. On the other hand, the poorer the fit, the higher the likelihood of distress, burnout, role ambiguity, and role conflicts (Muchinsky, 1990). The preceding section of this chapter suggests that other factors influence fit—namely, the correspondence of motivational needs or styles, work-personality styles, leadership styles and values between executives and the corporation. Likewise, the impact of predictable barriers and crises can influence the degree of fit.

EXECUTIVE HEALTH, DISTRESS, AND IMPAIRMENT

A basic assumption of this book is that the level of health, distress, or impairment observed in an executive is influenced by a number of personal as well as organizational deficits. The discussion now turns to healthy, distressed, and impaired executives.

Healthy, Effective Executives

What characterizes the executive who has achieved sustained professional success and personal well-being? A recent study of male and female chief executives offers an initial answer to this question (Quick, Nelson, & Quick, 1990). These researchers report four noteworthy dimensions of executive personality and behavior. Healthy, successful executives were characterized by: *active leadership, high needs for power and control,* and *high levels of stress, and risk-oriented behavior,* as compared with unsuccessful executives, who were characterized as passive followers with a low need for power, who experienced little stress, and avoided risk.

Effective executives also tend to be active, both physically and psychologically. James Rippe, M.D., a cardiologist and exercise physiologist, surveyed 1,139 successful CEOs and found they were characterized by stamina and energy (Rippe, 1989a). Rippe also found that 64 percent of these CEOs—with an average age of 50 years—exercised regularly, 90 percent watched their diets, and most believed there was a clear connection between a healthy lifestyle of diet and exercise and executive performance. These CEOs were significantly healthier than male and female executives who did not make it to the top and as a result succumbed to "achiever suicide" (Rippe, 1989b).

As noted earlier, a high need for power and control is basic to the executive role. Although executives regularly experience high degrees of stress with their work, their high level of control over their job offers considerable protection against the harmful effects of stress. Furthermore, risk taking is a key feature of executive life. Rather than avoiding risk, effective executives "attempt to control the risks by placing their best bet and then changing the odds even more in their favor" (Quick et al., 1990, p. 19).

Stressors for executives are both external and internal. One of the internal sources of stress is their ego ideal, which activates their personality and impels them to positions of leadership, wherein they exercise their need for power and influence. The ego ideal of the executive actively shapes the organization's ideal, which energizes the organization.

Healthy executives tend to be relatively stress resistant, owing in large part to their self-reliance while embedded in a rich network of professional and personal relationships that sustain and nurture them. In short, healthy executives are interdependent: able to be autonomous while at the same time investing in relationships in a healthy manner.

Distressed Executives

What characterizes distressed executives? How are they different from impaired executives, and what is the workplace psychiatrist's role with them?

Basically, distressed executives are active, functioning members of their corporation, family, and community. Yet their ability to function well on the job, at home, or in the community is at times inconsistent because of various stressors in their lives. Despite their distress and occasional crises, though, they are able to bounce back from setbacks, unlike the impaired executive, who often cannot bounce back.

Epidemiological data on distress in executive populations are difficult to come by. Nevertheless, Smith and Siwolop (1988) estimate that approximately 15 percent of executives would be considered distressed. Unrealistic deadlines, overly heavy workloads, and poor communication are cited by these authors as job-induced stressors for distressed executives, along with a host of competing personal, family, and social stressors.

Moss (1981) notes the more frequent reasons why distressed executives seek consultation: marital problems; personality clashes with peers and supervisors; suppressed emotional reactions to peers and superiors; problems with control of hostility; difficulty asserting or responding to authority; hidden conflicts about dependency and disappointed ambition; and unconscious fears of success, with an associated tendency toward self-defeat, often triggered by problems related to career choices or relations with superiors. In DSM-IV terms, these would constitute Axis V codes or be classified as adjustment reactions.

Kiechel (1988) reports that insomnia is another common form of distress for executives which appears to be a function of stress, evening socializing, heavy travel across time zones, and work compulsivity. Disproportionate numbers of individuals with aggressive type A personalities experience anxiety, which further exacerbates their insomnia.

The primary prevention strategies required for managing stress in executives include a balanced work–family perspective; effective use of leisure time; time management, planning, and goal setting; and an effective social support system. Secondary prevention strategies include exercise, relaxation, prayer, and faith (Quick et al., 1990). Prepackaged stress management programs and seminars, though, are usually not as effective as individual and group therapies that include coping skills training (Pelletier & Lutz, 1991).

What is the clinician-consultant's role in regard to the distressed executive? Initially, the clinician-consultant should assess levels of distress, evaluate the need for primary and secondary prevention-oriented stress programs, and advocate for such programs. Next referrals of overly distressed executives for focused individual or group therapy should be made. A third task involves developing and advocating a policy regarding the distressed executive, which would become part of an overall corporate mental health policy for executives.

Impaired Executives

How does impairment present itself in the executive suite? To begin, consider the term *impairment.* Nearly 20 years ago, the American Medical Association offered the following definition of impairment in physicians: The *impaired physician* is "one who is unable to practice medicine with reasonable skill and safety to patients because of physical or mental illness including deterioration through the aging process, or loss of motor skills, or excessive use of drugs including alcohol" (Logan, 1989, p. 33). The media typically portray both impaired physicians and impaired executives as substance-abusing middle-age men. However, among physicians who have been sanctioned by state licensure boards, the six most common presentations of impairment were Personality Disorders, substance abuse, suicidal tendencies, major mental disorders, elderly with dementia, and sexually acting out (Logan, 1989). In short, the range of impairment in physicians is much broader than that shown in media stereotypes.

Among the very few reported epidemiological data on impairment among executives, the Human Resources Group study of impairment in eight major United States corporations specified the following disorders as common among executives: drug and substance abuse disorders, stress-related disorders, and marital problems (Kiechel, 1988). Perhaps the most detailed epidemiological study of impairment in executives was reported by Bromet et al. (1990). They studied 1,870 executives from one major United States corporation and reported on DSM-III-R major depression and alcohol abuse/dependence. Among the male executives, the lifetime and one-year prevalence rates for depression were 23 percent and 9 percent, respectively, whereas the rates for the female executives were 36 percent and 17 percent, respectively. Lifetime and one-year prevalence rates for alcohol abuse/dependence were, respectively, 16 percent and 4 percent for the male executives and 9 percent and 4 percent for the female executives.

In *Executives in Crisis*, Speller (1989) does not offer incidence or prevalence data but lists alcoholism, drug abuse, depression, Bipolar Disorder, and Schizophrenia as the most common forms of impairment among executives. There is no indication, though, that sex differences were observed in this study. Pasick (1990) likewise notes that male executives who enter therapy most commonly present with depression, anxiety, and substance abuse or dependence disorders. However, further exploration of these presenting problems reveals underlying work-related issues, including workaholism, stress-related disorders, success addiction (similar to workaholism except that the craving is specifically for success rather than for increased work time), work dissatisfaction, and underemployment. Unlike Logan's (1989) data on physicians, there is little indication in either study that severe Personality Disorder and dementia are considered forms of impairment among executives.

It may be helpful to operationally define executive impairment as a dysfunctional pattern of behavior that reflects a lack of "fit" or negative interaction between a predisposed executive and his or her corporation that has clear precipitants and perpetuants and meets criteria for one or more DSM-III-R Axis I and/or Axis II diagnoses.

The *dysfunctional pattern* specified in this operational definition of impairment represents decompensated behaviors in which impaired executives lose touch with their surroundings and behave strangely, unpredictably, or inappropriately. They may become apathetic, pessimistic, indecisive, and confused or forgetful. Their insight and/or judgment may deteriorate, or they may lose their business sense and savor. They might get violent or overreact to relatively insignificant matters. Or, they may become overwhelmed in the face of intense and painful affects. Unlike the distressed executive who is able to bounce back from unexpected setbacks and master challenges, the impaired executive is not able to do this.

Predisposition in this definition of impairment refers to various biopsychosocial vulnerabilities in the executive, which might include biological loading for an affective or addictive disorder and might involve any number of intrapsychic representations, conflicts, or dysfunctional cognitions—for example, that self-worth is totally dependent on achievement. These vulnerabilities could also reflect deficiencies in coping skills, like assertiveness or decision making, or could represent reenactments of early parental authority issues with a CEO or a member of the board of directors. It could even reflect the absence of a caring social support system.

Corporations can be thought of as having vulnerabilities also. Each of the neurotic organizational styles described by Kets de Vries and Miller (1984, 1987) predisposes such organizations to characteristic corporate cultures, reward systems, leadership styles, and so on. For example, a paranoid organization would be more vulnerable to rumors about a takeover bid than a depressive organization.

The precipitants mentioned in the impairment definition can include an event of obvious importance, such as a spouse unexpectedly demanding separation or divorce, the death of a parent or sibling, job loss or unexpected reassignment, or a major investment that soured. Other precipitants may be less obvious, but nevertheless they represent a loss or an unfulfilled expectation, such as a minor traffic accident, or child's suspension from school.

Perpetuants in the impairment definition refer to any number of personal, family, or corporate reinforcements for the impaired pattern. It is exceedingly commonplace for coworkers to "cover" for the increasing absences, forgotten appointments, temper tantrums, and the like of a troubled executive. Such enabling behaviors, however, only delay treatment for the impaired executive and are indicative of the need for establishing a corporate mental health policy for executives.

A few words on "lack of fit" are in order in this description of impairment. A basic premise is that pathology and impairment do not reside solely in the executive or employee. An executive's vulnerabilities might well be expressed in symptomatic or even impaired behavior in one corporate setting but not in another, or at one point in time but not at another. The clinician is trained to search for just the patient's vulnerabilities and predisposition, but the clinician-consultant must search for pattern, precipitants, perpetuants, and vulnerabilities within the corporation as well as within the executive. The competent clinician-consultant will be able to articulate the protective as well as the distressing and impairment-provoking features of the corporate environment.

Finally, the requirement for one or more DSM-IV Axis I and/or Axis II diagnoses is included in the operational definition of impairment for two reasons. First, although severe depression, acute psychosis, and many manic episodes are considered bona fide types of executive impairment by organizational researchers, other Axis I and most Axis II disorders apparently are not. The executive with a Personality Disorder is probably as prevalent as the physician with a Personality Disorder—considered the most common type of impaired physician (Logan, 1989). Kets de Vries (1989) provides several case examples of executives with a Personality Disorder who wreaked corporate havoc. Second, research into the epidemiology of executive distress and impairment will not improve until data collection efforts are systematically undertaken and consistent criteria—that is, DSM-IV criteria—are utilized.

8

Executive Consulting, Psychotherapy, and Coaching

In our rapidly changing, increasingly complex society, and global economy, it has become more and more challenging and stressful to function as an executive. The loneliness, power, and sheer demands inherent in top management are such that many executives are now looking for someone they can trust to provide objectivity, support, and counsel. Because of their training, clinician-consultants can well serve this consultation function: They have already learned to respect confidences and personal loyalties to clients and are accustomed to retaining objectivity during ongoing intense relationships. And if they have training and experience in leadership and management, the combination is even more fruitful. This chapter describes how the clinician-consultant can respond to the executive's need for consulting, psychotherapy, and coaching, and it describes and illustrates three individually focused consultation interventions: executive consulting, executive psychotherapy, and executive coaching.

COMPARISON OF CONSULTATION, PSYCHOTHERAPY, AND COACHING

Comparing consulting and psychotherapy with executives clarifies the role and task difference between the clinical and consulting roles.

In most forms of psychotherapy, the clinician may function primarily in a process-oriented and nondirective role, whereas in executive consultation the consultant may utilize a more expert-oriented and directive role. Psychotherapy tends to occur on the clinician's turf, where the usual supports and rules of the clinician prevail. However, consultation tends to occur on the executive's turf with none of the clinician's usual supports, and thus the consultant must negotiate the "rules of the game" (Nevis, 1987). The agenda in psychotherapy is usually negotiated by both client and clinician, whereas in consultation the client sets the agenda, and the duration is often much longer than the 50-minute psychotherapy hour. While the focus of psychotherapy usually involves "working through" characterological issues and past events, executive consulting often "works around" characterological styles and emphasizes here-and-now concerns.

Beyond these differences, there are similarities between executive consultation and psychotherapy. First, is the matter of confidentiality. While confidentiality must be observed in both instances, maintaining confidentiality in consultation is much more complex than in psychotherapy (Tobias, 1990). Second, effective consultation, like effective psychotherapy, is not possible without the consultant engaging the executive in a close, collaborative relationship. And as noted earlier, the clinician and consultant must both establish a bond that is friendly without becoming a friendship. Table 8.1 summarizes these commonalities and differences.

Like executive consultation and psychotherapy, executive coaching can occur in one-to-one settings, but unlike consultation and psychotherapy, the need for a close personal bond and confidentiality is as not as great in coaching. The focus of coaching is primarily on helping executives learn or modify specific self-management and relational skills, such as active listening, assertive communication, negotiation, team leading, and handling difficult employees. In other words, coaching emphasizes skill development more than self-understanding—which is more the domain of psychotherapy—or problem solving—which is more the domain of consulting.

Figure 8.1 visually depicts the commonalities of skill and focus in executive consulting, coaching, and psychotherapy.

TABLE 8.1

Comparison of Psychotherapy with Executive Consultation

Psychotherapy	*Executive Consultation*
1. Client seeks out and chooses clinician; pays clinician; one-to-one relationship.	1. Executive seeks out and engages consultant who is paid by the organization; one-to-one relationship.
2. Work on clinician's turf; rules of clinician prevail.	2. Work on client's turf; rules are usually negotiated.
3. More process oriented and client centered.	3. More likely to involve advising and to be expert oriented.
4. Agenda negotiated by client and clinician.	4. Agenda usually set by client.
5. Sessions usually involve 50-minute hour and scheduled weekly.	5. Sessions of variable length.
6. Confidentiality issues are relatively straightforward.	6. Confidentiality issues may be more complex; "double agentry" is not uncommon.
7. Often involves "working through" characterological issues.	7. Usually involves "working around" defenses and characterological issues.

EXECUTIVE CONSULTATION

As noted previously, many senior executives—particularly CEOs—find it necessary to bounce their ideas and concerns off someone in order to clarify their impressions and validate the reasonableness of their conclusions. Often, the executive's concerns focus on problems with people, but they may also include uncertainty about a merger, personal health and fitness, or a family concern. Executive consultation serves as this "sounding board" as well as an advisory function. The consulting relationship is usually initiated by the executive because of prior positive experience with the consultant and if the chemistry is right, a close, trusting bond is likely to develop.

Executives tend to have certain expectations of the executive con-

FIGURE 8.1

Commonality of Skill and Focus Among Psychotherapy, Consultation, and Coaching

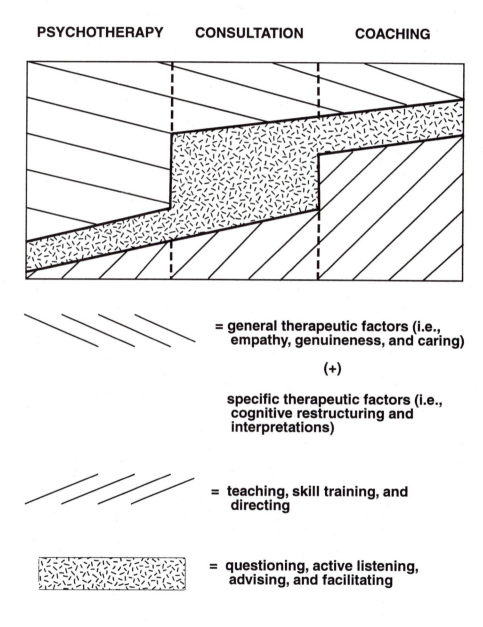

PSYCHOTHERAPY   CONSULTATION   COACHING

= general therapeutic factors (i.e., empathy, genuineness, and caring)

(+)

specific therapeutic factors (i.e., cognitive restructuring and interpretations)

= teaching, skill training, and directing

= questioning, active listening, advising, and facilitating

sultant. First, they believe the consultant will be able to increase their effectiveness as both a manager and a person. A second expectation is that the consultant will help them integrate information, providing not only perspectives and objectivity but also a keen insight into problems with people. Third, executives expect that it will be safe to share with the consultant their deepest concerns, and even immature thoughts, believing the consultant will help them grow personally and become more effective in meeting the scrutiny of more critical audiences.

As described in the previous section, typically, discussions between the executive and the consultant are initiated by the executive and are most likely to take place in the executive's office. The agenda is set by the executive and consists primarily of here-and-now professional and personal issues. Executive consultants often deal with individuals whose characterological style may preclude sensitivity and empathy to others. However unlike psychotherapy, the consultant needs to work obliquely around characterological issues, so the adaptive effort of the executive and the client organization may be supported (Levinson, 1991).

Also, unlike the 50-minute psychotherapy hour, the consultation may last ten minutes or ten hours straight. Extended consultations allow the consultant to directly observe a variety of encounters between the executive and others, which provide first-hand data as well as the opportunity for feedback to the executive. These extended time periods mean shared meals as well as involvement in the social life and activities of the executive and corporation. The consultant may be asked to play tennis, have dinner at a club, or spend a weekend at an executive's estate.

During the course of their meetings, the consultant guides the executive to think through the presenting concern by asking key questions, helping the executive formulate the problem, generating and considering various courses of action, as well as anticipating the consequences of these options. Thus, helping the executive formulate the right questions and make informed judgments is a critical task of the executive consultant.

Finally, the consultant must also be available to advise the executive, since the executive may not be able to act wisely without specific information that provides a reasonable rationale for appropriate action. In all this, relationships that develop with executives must remain on a professional level and not as the type of therapeutic relationship that would develop into executive psychotherapy. At this point it might be helpful to further differentiate the consultive and psychotherapy process.

Case Example: Consultation with an Executive

J.F. was a 45-year-old married chief financial officer (CFO) of a third generation family-owned machine products corporation. The corporation had 75 employees and $11 million in sales each of the past four years. J.F. sought consultation because of increasing job dissatisfaction, concern about his future with the corporation, and guilt feelings when he considered leaving it.

J.F.'s grandfather had started the company 75 years earlier, at a time when there was little competition. Increasingly, however, competition in this market had become intense. Leadership was passed to J.F.'s father, who served as CEO until his unexpected death in 1980. Succession went to J.F.'s older brother. Loyalty and family pride were basic values. When J.F. graduated from college, he at first refused his father's offer to join the family business as head of accounting, saying he wanted to be free to travel throughout Europe and the U.S. and to find his "own way." Besides, he explained, he was more excited with the prospect of meeting people than in poring over spreadsheets, and he wondered how he had ended up as an accounting and finance major in college, when he really liked sales and marketing. His father was quite saddened by this decision but in time was able to accept it. Eventually, however, J.F. returned home and took the position as head of accounting. The young CFO came to believe, though, that his guilt feelings about his job dissatisfaction were related to his father's expectation that the company would always be run by his loyal sons and their sons.

J.F's fascination with travel, nevertheless, continued unabated over the years. He was happy and energized in his off-hours, planning long, intricate trips to remote places in South America and Asia for his wife and himself. Yet, he felt uncomfortable and even guilty when he was away from the office on scheduled vacations. Often, he wondered what it would be like to own and manage a corporation geared to international business travel.

The consultation session with J.F. consisted of two half-day meetings and took place in his office. The meetings focused on his career issues as well as his guilt feelings. At the outset of the consultation, the consultant primarily listened to J.F.'s story concerning his ambivalence about the family business and his own hopes and dreams. Eventually, J.F. was able to admit that the company could survive, and even prosper, even if he was not in his office every day of the year.

The consultant reframed the CFO's job dissatisfaction and ambivalence as markers of his ambition to find his "own way," rather than as simply family and corporate disloyalty. J.F. then began to wonder if the company might do well to develop business in Eastern Europe and the former Soviet Union. If so, he could combine the interests of the family business with his personal interest in travel. J.F. decided he would develop such a business plan and present it to the executive committee and the board. He proposed that he would spend up to three months, twice a year, overseas selling and marketing the company's machine products. Needless to say, the plan was approved. As a result of the consultation, J.F. discovered how he could be loyal to the family business and to his own interests and ideals as well.

EXECUTIVE PSYCHOTHERAPY

Psychotherapy can be directed toward general treatment goals or more focused goals. Today, because of both economic and clinical advances, there is an increasing emphasis on focused treatment. Well-known examples include Klerman, Weissman, Rounsaville, et al.'s *Interpersonal Psychotherapy of Depression* (1984), and Beck, Freeman, & Associates' *Cognitive Therapy of Personality Disorders* (1990). Furthermore, because executives have a strong bias toward problem solving and the pragmatic, they tend to find long-term dynamically oriented psychotherapy foreign and tedious. Production of fantasy material and disclosure of affects also may be initially resisted. Similarly, the slow pace of progress and change in long-term therapy may be a significant source of frustration for them. Not surprisingly, executives tend to prefer time-limited and focused approaches, in line with the executive's natural inclination toward action and outcomes.

As noted in Chapter 6, Lowman (1993) advocates that psychotherapy should address work and work dysfunction. Lowman defines work dysfunction as any persistent difficulty or failure in the work site associated with psychological characteristics of the individual. These dysfunctions can be independent of or interactive with the nature of the worker's job or the organizational context in which the work takes place. The clinician's first task is to assess the presence of psychopathology and its relation, if any, to work functioning, while also assessing the presence of work dysfunction and its impact on psychopathology.

As therapeutic goals of treatment have become more delimited, work problems have emerged as one area in which clinicians can make important contributions to individual well-being. Furthermore, such therapeutic goals can often be accomplished without a major restructuring of personality and in a relatively time-efficient manner.

A central theme of Lowman's approach is that characteristics of individuals that combine to create work difficulties do not exist separately from those of organizations and occupations. In providing psychotherapy to executives who present with work-related concerns, the clinician must evaluate the executive's workplace, even if evaluation must occur outside the actual work context. In treating work-related issues, the clinician must caution against allowing a psychological view to mask from consideration other factors that may be germane. Ignoring features of the work itself, or the work context, that may be the primary source of the executive's difficulties is a common error of clinicians beginning to treat work-related issues.

Determining whether work difficulties exist independently of, in combination with, or secondarily to psychopathology is an important diagnostic consideration. The clinician, if not the executive, needs to be clear about the plan for addressing work-related difficulties and, when appropriate, psychological difficulties unrelated to work.

TABLE 8.2

Common Focal Issues in Psychotherapy with Executives

1. **Over-Undercommitment:** burnout, fear of success/failure, work addiction, procrastination
2. **Loss:** job, death, failed expectations, and anticipation of loss, as in succession and retirement
3. **Interpersonal Conflict:** employee, peers, board of directors, family, spouse
4. **Developmental Dysynchrony:** relational, children, and/or career
5. **Characterological Issues:** narcissism, compulsivity, paranoia, authority issues, stonewalling, and so on
6. **Life–Role Conflicts:** particulary work–family issues
7. **Symptoms:** performance anxiety, depression, psychosomatic issues, Bipolar Disorder, substance dependence, and the like

In cases in which both psychopathology and work difficulties are present, it is useful to have some sense of which is primary and how the one relates to the other.

For instance, an executive who is recently divorced, clinically depressed, and about to be laid off may need help in determining which is the most pressing issue and which will be the initial focus of the therapy. On the other hand, executives whose work difficulties are much broader and involve overarching conflictual life themes, such as procrastination or fear of success, may benefit from working on the central theme or focal issue, addressing both work and non-work concerns. Among executives, common themes and focal issues are particularly noted in the following seven areas: over-undercommitment, loss, interpersonal conflict, developmental dysynchrony, characterological issues, life–role conflicts, and symptoms. Table 8.2 futher specifies these issues.

The clinician should keep these central dynamics firmly in mind and then interpret or reframe behavior—whether work related or not—in light of the central theme. However, in manifesting resistance, the executive may attempt to shift the treatment focus among significant life concerns or may undermine genuine progress made in one area by lamenting lack of progress in another.

In work-focused psychotherapy (Sperry et al., 1996) the quality of the therapeutic relationship depends to some extent on the executive perceiving the clinician to be on his or her side, and in many treatment approaches, self-discovery is the goal. Thus, assuming the validity, or at least the perceived validity, of the executive's understanding of the work situation may be a better stance than unnecessarily or prematurely bringing in outside parties to explain the executive's work concern. However, the clinician can still raise questions or interpretations, particularly when there is reason to doubt the reality of the executive's presentation of a work concern, but should do so in the context of a private relationship between two parties attempting to understand and work through issues at hand. For example, if the executive's lifestyle dynamics are the source of his/her work-related problems, it is very likely that they will present themselves in the therapeutic relationship with the clinician or in a pattern of reactions that will become apparent with time.

Furthermore, the clinician needs to guard against overanalyzing and overinterpreting work issues except when there is clear and compelling evidence that such factors are the driving force behind the executive's work-related problem. For example, an executive presenting with depression and complaints of job burnout may be manifesting clinical depression or may simply be exhibiting common symptoms of burnout. The clinician could intervene with various strategies accordingly. Suggesting a job or career change, at least on a temporary basis, is one practical, perhaps well-founded way to proceed. Recommending physical exercise and vigorous non-work activities as antidotes to the emotional exhaustion associated with the job might also be appropriate. Or the clinician might assist the executive in exploring reasons for his or her career choice or his or her tendency to become overly involved with high-flown goals that result in his or her depression when personal efforts have been ineffective. These strategies might be pursued over the course of therapy, particularly when there are issues related to family-of-origin or family constellation dynamics.

Short-term, behaviorally focused interventions seem to be particularly effective in treating many work dysfunctions provided that more complicated psychopathology or severe personality disorders are not present or, at the least, that the broader, contextual issues are kept in mind (Sperry, 1995a). Lowman (1993) suggests that metaphorical approaches that encapsulate a central dynamic of the person through the presenting work concerns are also effective. Kopp (1995) describes a number of strategies for utilizing metaphor in the psychotherapeutic context that are particularly valuable in working with executives in short-term psychotherapy.

The clinician may need to "work around" lifelong characterological issues when working with individuals experiencing both Personality Disorders and work dysfunctions. Whether in executive consultation or in work-focused psychotherapy, it is quite useful to distinguish between "working through" and "working around." The process of "working through" usually involves extensive and repeated utilization of interpretation, confrontation, or cognitive restructuring to effect changes in personality structure. In contrast, the process of "working around" is not directed at the arduous task of modifying personality structure but rather at psychologically sidestepping the facet of the individual's personality structure that is operative in a given situation. Accordingly, the use of *reframing, redirection, distraction, minimization,* and *paradox* are the specified intervention strategies. (Sperry, 1995b). For example, the clinician-consultant working with an executive who reports experiencing a narcissistic injury could tell the executive: "I know you're upset. But when you look at the bigger picture, you really have a lot going for you, so why sweat the small stuff" (*minimization*); or, "Letting your colleague get to you like this is really giving him a lot of power over you. Do you want that?" (*redirection*).

Practical career counseling and career management can also be useful with some executives, particularly those with relatively pervasive Personality Disorders. For instance, stern warnings about the real-life work consequences of continued aberrant work behavior may be as instructive and influential in working with certain Personality Disorders as long-term psychotherapy. Such executives may be much more motivated to be compliant if they face job loss or restriction.

Finally, marital and family issues are common among hardworking, hard-driving executives who travel frequently and spend long hours away from home. Not surprisingly, communication difficulties, role conflicts, and sexual problems are common. Family therapy can provide more functional interaction and improved conflict resolution and communication. Similarly, couples therapy can be quite useful for relational and sexual issues, particularly when the executive is involved in a dual-career marriage. In short, adjunctive family or couples therapy might complement work-focused individual psychotherapy for the executive.

Case Example 1: Work-Focused Psychotherapy with a Male Executive

A vice president of corporate accounts pulled his clinician-consultant aside one day and mentioned that he was having some difficulty with concentration. After a brief discussion, the vice president agreed to an outside referral for an evaluation. In the course of the evaluation, the clinician-consultant learned that the executive was a well-regarded member of the corporation's management team. He oversaw a sales force of over 135 insurance agents and four regional sales managers, and he reported directly to the executive vice president of administration. Also this executive had been with the corporation for nearly 12 years and had held his current position for the past year and a half.

He presented with insomnia, depressed mood, low energy, and increased worry, and these symptoms had been present for nearly four months. Furthermore, he had little response to the antidepressant prescribed by his family physician.

The clinician-consultant also learned that, to remain competitive, the corporation had been going through a series of downsizings for the past year, and one of the most difficult parts of this executive's job had been laying off or discharging regional managers and insurance agents that he had befriended over the years. The vice president found this task increasingly difficult and painful and did not believe he could continue doing it. He described laying awake nights ruminating about his laid off friends, asking himself: Had they found jobs yet?; Were they angry with him?; and Could he face the prospect of discharging any more of the people who reported to him? He even imagined himself as "a 'hatchet man' doing the senior VP's dirty work and scorned by everyone who knows me." He reported as well that his personal life had never been better: He was happily married, and had just returned from a family reunion, which he attended with his wife and three grown children. Furthermore, the vice president could not identify any precipitants other than his job.

The clinician performing the evaluation decided that a brief, work-focused psychotherapeutic approach would be more appropriate than a traditional insight-oriented focus on the early life determinants of the executive's current problem and symptoms, which might require between 20 and 50 sessions, rather than the four sessions that the work-focused treatment utilized. The clinician's work-focused goal was considerably more focused than the traditional approach, achieving symptom reduction and assisting the executive in moving forward with his life, most notably on the job.

In particular, he worked together with the executive to come up with a detailed list of factors and circumstances that were and were not under the executive's immediate control. Not surprisingly, the list of work factors was relatively short. The clinician utilized *reframing* so that the executive could begin to visualize other options. One of these was that the executive could act more proactively, rather than continue acting reactively and passively, as he had during the past several months. The clinician framed the executive's stance of waiting for his boss, to announce the next round of layoffs, as one of no control. The executive was then helped to explore more proactive alternatives that were within his span of control.

A four-fold plan of proactive action was devised: the executive could engage in various cost-cutting measures in his office and in some of the "fatter" regions, revise sales territories, update the marketing plan, and consult with his regional managers about prospective layoffs. The executive was able to make progress in all of these areas. Perhaps, most heartening for him was that he could share responsibility for layoffs with his regional managers. This not only reduced his stress and guilt but also provided him considerable emotional support from his colleagues.

In addition to reframing, the clinician utilized the metaphors of controlling both the tempo of the game and the strokes used while playing tennis—the executive's favorite activity—in comparison to his job activities, in an interchangeable fashion, so that the executive could feel more empowered and in control. By the fourth session, the vice president was considerably less stressed, was sleeping better, and no longer viewed himself as the corporation's "hatchet man."

Case Example 2: Work-Focused Psychotherapy with a Female Executive

J.L. was a 34-year-old single white female who was manager of MIS services for a high-tech biomedical firm. She was referred by the vice president of personnel for increasing anxiety and "memory problems." The initial evaluation involved an assessment of J.L.'s current and past levels of functioning as well as her strengths, personality style, capacity to develop a therapeutic relationship, readiness for treatment, and her presenting concerns: memory lapses and anxiety. Although she indicated that "memory problems" were constant throughout her life, they had worsened in the past two months.

She also reported engaging in considerable fantasy and daydreaming, particularly when authority figures, like her boss, had given her a task with a deadline. These fantasies were largely about men and sex. She indicated a single incident of fondling by her older brother when she was ten years old about which she was frightened and confused, and reportedly, she had only recently recalled it. However, J.L. remembered instances of "memory lapse" that occurred much earlier in her life, and these instances usually involved her mother and father.

Furthermore, she had had considerable difficulty establishing and maintaining intimate relationships with eligible men over the past five years. Prior to that she indicated that she seldom dated, even though she was quite attractive, interesting, and available. The four men she had become intensely attracted to turned out to be "womanizers" who would flaunt the other women they were involved with in front of J.L. Her response was to become "insanely jealous" of these women and "promise to do anything" to hold onto these men. Occasional binge drinking—particularly on weekends—was also reported. And, she denied prior psychotherapy or psychiatric treatment.

J.L.'s family consisted of her parents, who still resided in the home where she was reared, and four older male siblings. Her mother was described as emotionally distant, demanding, and as having been "unconcerned" with J.L.'s feminine needs—J.L. seldom wore dresses, used makeup, or adopted "feminine manners" until she started college. Also her mother had a "breakdown" when J.L. left home for college, presumably a depressive episode.

She described her father as caring and concerned but who had made little effort to shield her from her mother's demands. He apparently was grieved over his wife's expectation that J.L. "dress and act like a boy" but did not voice his concern, at least publicly. Her four brothers were described as "jocks" who were extremely competitive, and J.L. described herself as a "tomboy" in grade school but as "boy-crazy with hormones," throughout high school.

An investigation of her current life functioning showed that she had a stable network of female friends, some difficulty relating to her parents, and an unsatisfying and distressing relationship with her current boyfriend. However, she described only moderate dysfunctioning at work, particularly a confusing and distressing relationship with her female boss—J.L. had received high evaluations for her job performance from her subordinates and from her superior's boss but not from her immediate supervisor. In addition, her mental status exam was unremarkable. Based on these findings, her DSM-IV diagnosis was V 62.2 Occupational Problem, Anxiety Disorder NOS, with Histrionic, Passive-Aggressive, and Self-Defeating traits.

Although quite anxious at the beginning of the initial session, she was easily calmed and showed other indications that she could and probably would be able to form an effective, collaborative therapeutic relationship. Because she had been quite successful in meeting personal goals she had set for herself, such as losing 15 pounds and maintaining the weight loss for three years and giving up smoking four years earlier, it seemed she had sufficient capacity and readiness for change in therapy. She agreed to a contract for five sessions, which were subsequently authorized by her HMO. The focus of the sessions was to be on reducing both her anxiety and "memory loss." Accordingly, these five weekly sessions were scheduled.

During these sessions, the discussion of "memory lapses" as a safeguard proved to be painful but freeing for J.L. She shared her feelings of hopelessness and rejection regarding her difficult relationship with her mother and current and past boyfriends as well as her inability to emancipate herself from abusive relationships. However, since systemic issues involving authority and power at home and in the workplace were very deeply intertwined with J.L.'s personal dynamics, and even though she had experienced some symptomatic relief, such as reductions in anxiety and binge drinking, it was agreed that she should seek authorization for additional sessions. The request was made, and the utilization reviewer authorized up to 20 additional sessions, with a review after the tenth additional session. The treatment focus was to be primarily on job functioning and career development and secondarily on her enmeshed relationship with her mother and her abusive relationships with male friends and lovers. According to Lowman, 1993, framing therapy primarily around work-related issues has been found to reduce therapeutic regression and complex transferences, while requiring fewer sessions when more global interpersonal and intrapersonal issues are the focus.

The next three sessions focused largely on examining J.L.'s relationship with her female boss. J.L. viewed her as essentially incompetent at the newly created position to which she had been promoted six months prior to J.L.'s being hired. Since the position was new and her boss's superior traveled frequently for the company, there was little oversight or accountability for her boss, who refused to meet regularly with J.L. to review her performance. Instead, she would delegate much of her work to J.L. and provide only vague feedback to her, such as: "Don't worry about things, I'll let you know when you screw up." Also some rather obvious similarities between J.L.'s boss and her mother were discussed in detail. For example, with both women, J.L. was nonassertive and essentially backed away from any conflict with them. Since she could not directly express her concern or anger, J.L. utilized indecision, underachievement, and "memory lapses." As a result J.L. was frustrated and dissatisfied, and she dealt with this anxiety by drinking and becoming increasingly attracted to and then jealous about the abusive men she dated. Assertive communication training accompanied these sessions as did cognitive restructuring.

In the twelfth session, J.L. reported that increasing assertiveness with her boss was having noticeable results. She had no more "memory lapses," and her boss was no longer dumping her work on J.L. She also indicated she would no longer allow her boyfriend to continue his emotional abusiveness by his unfaithfulness. She would now require that the relationship be exclusive, or she would leave. In the thirteenth session, she reported that she had ended her current relationship and would now look for men who would treat her with respect and concern.

In the fourteenth session, she felt more confident that she could control her anger and anxiety without drinking. Career issues dominated the next two sessions: In high school, she planned to be a literature major and become a college professor like her aunt, but she had been "talked out of it by her family." Instead she became an accounting and computer science major because "they told me I was assured of getting a job with that degree." Although her advisor adjudged her to be the most capable student in the accounting program, J.L. did not apply herself and underachieved, completing her degree with a C+ average. After the sessions focusing on career issues, she believed she could make her own decisions about how she would spend her life.

The final sessions focused largely on reorienting J.L.'s self-view and worldview, specifically as they related to her job. She was also able to accept that choosing to recognize and develop her strengths and interests were not only possible, but necessary, for her to grow and individuate herself from her family and that doing this would not have disastrous consequences for her parents—she had feared that becoming successful would dishonor and somehow annihilate her mother and emasculate her father or brothers.

As a result of the sessions, J.L. was able to "own" that the career track she had taken was indeed satisfying and that it fit her abilities and strengths, rather than just being based solely on family expectations. Interpersonally, she began choosing nonabusive friends and intimates and individuating herself from her family—particularly from her brother—to a considerable degree. In addition, presenting symptoms of anxiety and memory loss were resolved. Although additional sessions could help J.L. to further work through and reorient her interpersonal relationship with family members, J.L. was satisfied with her progress.

Nevertheless, if J.L.'s psychotherapy had not been focused primarily on work functioning, her treatment would likely have been more regressive in nature and much longer in duration, with no guarantee that her work-related issues would have been resolved.

EXECUTIVE COACHING

Coaching primarily involves the teaching of skills in the context of a personal relationship with a learner. Although executive coaching can focus on various corporate skills and values, it is the most useful means of teaching human relations skills to executives (Levinson, 1981). Typically, corporations expect that executives will provide coaching—also called mentoring—to subordinates. However, when it comes to coaching senior executives, the psychologically trained consultant may be called upon to provide executive coaching.

As noted earlier, unlike executive psychotherapy and consulting, where the executive engages in deep self-disclosure, the need for a close personal bond and confidentiality is not as great in executive coaching. Yet, like executive psychotherapy and consulting, coaching may occur in a one-to-one context. But it also may take place in any number of other contexts. Since providing feedback on the executive's interpersonal relations and skills is a principal focus of executive coaching, the consultant may observe the executive handling a grievance, interviewing a prospective hire, disciplining a subordinate, or discussing a sensitive matter with the corporate board (Sperry & Hess, 1974).

Recently, coaching has begun to emphasize team building. Whether the team involves the executive's staff, the top officers of the organization, or even the board of directors, building a cooperative spirit among individuals who must work together has become one of business' highest priorities. The clinician-consultant's task in the role of coach is to facilitate bonding among the team members who have difficulty working together. Furthermore, the executive is challenged to design work environments that foster rather than inhibit the worker's innate sense of belonging and sharing (Cox, 1990).

Case Example: Coaching an Executive

J.G. was the 38-year-old manager of the research and development (R&D) division of a recently merged pharmaceutical company. Her last performance review noted morale problems in her division. Fearful that she would be terminated, J.G. sought out the advice of a clinician-consultant whom she had met at her tennis club. The clinician-consultant reviewed J.G.'s concerns and concluded that the primary source of disharmony in the R&D division was an older secretary who was disgruntled with the recent merger and generally difficult to work with because of her almost incessant demands for special privileges. And J.G. felt intimidated by this older woman.

J.G.'s manager believed her problem in managing the division and the difficult employee stemmed from her passive nature and domineering mother and thought J.G. might need formal psychotherapy. The clinician-consultant suggested framing the problem as one of skill deficits in assertive communication and negotiation and offered to provide some time-limited coaching. If the coaching was not sufficiently helpful, the issue of psychotherapy would then be revisited.

In a one-to-one context, the clinician-consultant utilized role playing and role reversal to assess J.G.'s communication and negotiation skills. The consultant first took on the role of manager and then that of difficult employee. Throughout the remainder of the first two-hour session, the two worked on preparing J.G. for a forthcoming six-month performance review with the difficult secretary. Roles were practiced and reversed until J.G. was confident that she could handle the performance review.

When they met the second time, J.G. reported that the review had gone reasonably well, as compared to previous reviews. Specific expectations for the employee's "attitude" and productivity had been mutually negotiated. Nevertheless, J.G. was still somewhat intimidated by the employee. Skill building continued with role playing that focused on typical encounters between both women. The consultant also coached J.G. in replacing her denigratory self-talk with more positive self-talk, when she anticipated dealing with the secretary. By the third coaching session, morale in the division was better, and J.G. felt more confident as a manager.

In this example, coaching, rather than psychotherapy, was the initial intervention of choice, and it was effective. Had an adequate course of coaching been only partially successful, though, formal psychotherapy might then have been offered.

CONCLUDING NOTE

It is anticipated that executives will increasingly seek out executive consulting, psychotherapy, and coaching. Although there is some overlap among these three services, there are considerable differences among them, requiring specific competencies. Also even though the number of psychological and psychiatric consultants, who are attuned to the inner world and the process of executive consulting, counseling, and coaching are increasing, the demand for them seems greater. Therefore, the need for more predoctoral and postdoctoral training opportunities in executive consulting, psychotherapy, and coaching is clear. At the same time, the need for more published research and the further development of intervention strategies in these three areas are essential. Finally, networking among consulting professionals—especially in the Division of Consulting Psychology of the American Psychological Association and the Academy of Organizational and Occupational Psychiatry—must be encouraged.

9

Consultation with Health Care Organizations

Until recently, hospitals, clinics, and other health care organizations (HCOs) were considered so different from business or work organizations in mission, accountability, and productivity that many wondered if they really should be considered work organizations. Today, however, HCOs have changed so dramatically that many of them now proudly proclaim that they are "in the *business* of providing health care." HCOs have recently worked diligently to become more businesslike in their operation, particularly in an era when health care cost containment is a national priority. Nevertheless, unique differences between the worlds of for-profit corporations and HCOs still remain.

Comparing a high-tech manufacturing corporation with a high-tech academic medical center illustrates some of these differences. Typically, the high-tech manufacturing organization might have a structure that is lean and responsive and governed by leadership that is precise and predictable while the high-tech academic medical center typically will have a structure made up of loosely coupled units and divisions and leadership that may resemble the director's efforts at improvisational theater!

Yet, clearly whether an organization currently is a for-profit business corporation or an HCO, the waves of change are battering both, with little end in sight. Change requires adaptation and, in some cases, transformation in mission, structure, culture, and leadership style. Organizations don't change easily from their own doing and often need expert assistance. And while profit and not-for-profit corporations have dramatically increased their utilization of a full range of consultants in the past few years, there is growing awareness that HCOs will need to continue to increase their utilization of consultants in the coming years.

This chapter describes the need HCOs have for consultation, the components of the consultation process, differences between consultation and clinical services, and the consultation process operative in HCOs. It also suggests a unique role for the clinician-consultant—that of corporate culture change agent. Extensive case material illustrates the consultation process in common HCO situations and settings.

THE NEED FOR CONSULTATION IN HCOS

Following are some reasons why HCOs need the services of clinician-consultants:

1. The rate of change experienced by HCOs is faster than in any other kind of organization. The concept of managed care illustrates this point. In the past ten years, managed care has gone through three generations of changes and is ready to evolve further. The first generation of managed care was "managed access," wherein costs were managed by limiting access to treatment. Managed access was marked by precertification, high copayment rates, nonclinical reviewers, and a limit on the number of providers. The second generation of managed care was characterized by "managed benefits," which emphasized utilization review, discounted fee-for-services networks, and cost containment over clinical care. Currently, the third generation involves "utilization management" with quality-based networks of providers and hospitals. The focus here is on providing the most appropriate care in the most appropriate setting while emphasizing treatment planning and quality management. Although today most HCOs reflect this generation, the fourth generation, "managed outcomes," which is an integrated behavioral health care system, is already on the horizon (Geraty, 1996).

Essentially, each of the first three generations of managed care required that not only patients, but particularly clinicians, accommodate to these changes in a very short period of time. Clinicians were forced to relinquish or repress many values and beliefs about the nature and process of therapeutic change, as well as practice styles, that may have originally taken years to acquire and refine.

2. While mental health clinicians are asked to treat clients who are suffering from the effects of major changes in their organizations— including merger syndrome, downsizing or job loss—many mental health clinicians are experiencing these same stressors, perhaps more intensely than their clients. In fact, Ronald Fox, Ph.D., the former president of the American Psychological Association, states that some psychotherapists are experiencing posttraumatic stress disorder as a result of the strain of managed care (Martin, 1995). Similarly, Sussman (1995) edited a book entitled *A Perilous Calling: The Hazards of Psychotherapy Practice,* which details the emotional, relational, and legal hazards that clinicians now face.

3. Although mental health clinicians have the intrinsic capacity to function in the role of consultant to HCOs as well as to other organizations, their individually focused training is actually an impediment to functioning in this role. Though not as vehemently as in the past, some clinicians can harbor an antipathy and distrust of organizational processes. Functioning in the role of consultant, however, requires viewing behavior from a systems perspective and formulating and strategizing change in categories such as morale/ cohesion, roles/communications, and norms/standards rather than in terms of ego defense mechanisms or dysfunctional cognitions. Nevertheless, clinicians who are able to learn to think organization- ally and can translate some of their clinical skills to organizational settings could become highly effective change agents and consultants to organizations. Since clinician-consultants fit these qualifications and have first-hand experience in HCOs, they stand to be the consul- tants of choice as internal or external consultants to HCOs.

In short, HCOs are changing and evolving at a dizzying rate of speed. Such change is bound to wreak havoc within organizations that are not structured to accommodate the resultant changes. Personnel within organizations, as a result, can and do experience considerable distress and suffering. And, finally clinician-consultants have consid- erable potential to understand the change process in the organizations in which they work, and can, with further training, function effectively as internal and external consultants to HCOs and other organizations.

Case Example: The Need for HCO Consultation

A psychiatry practice group was contacted by a medium-sized managed care corporation, with 110,000 subscribers, about contracting its psychiatric services. (Apparently, the previously contracted psychiatry group had declined to renew its contract.) The managed care corporation already employed 23 full-time master-level clinicians, who were deployed at three sites, and held a contract with a nonprofit psychiatric hospital for inpatient treatment. However, although the new psychiatry group was well regarded in the community, its members had no formal training or experience working in a capitated Health Maintenance Organization (HMO), and none of its members had any training in organizational consultation. The managed care corporation had shown a modest profit in only one of the previous three years, and so it was receptive when the new psychiatry group stipulated in a 12-month contract agreement that it would evaluate and modify policies about psychotherapist–psychiatrist relations and practice patterns, should it be deemed advisable.

During the first two months of the contract, the psychiatry group kept moderately busy becoming acquainted with medication-monitored patients. The group noted that while psychotherapists were supposed to be seeing patients back-to-back at 20-minute intervals, some psychotherapists were standing around the coffee machine or had their office doors open, suggesting that they were not in session. A review of utilization data showed that psychotherapists were averaging only 12 billable hours per week while psychiatrists were averaging 31 hours. Further review of data indicated that 104 patients had been referred to other clinics outside the capitated programs. Presumably this was because those clients were deemed inappropriate for the type of therapy provided by the corporation's psychotherapists.

The corporation's three clinic sites advertised that they provided brief therapy to families and individuals. A social worker completed an evaluation on all new referrals at each clinic site, which noted that those clients not adjudged to be candidates for brief therapy were referred to a psychiatist for medication evaluation or to outside psychotherapists. A review of caseloads at the clinics revealed a bimodal distribution among the psychotherapist use load: 55 percent of clients being seen for five or fewer sessions and 45 percent adjudged to be "chronic patients," of whom 40 percent were being seen weekly for three or more years. Although there was a weekly case conference at each clinic, the previously contracted psychiatry group had only asked to be present for the last 20 minutes of the conference, during which medication patients were reviewed. There was no other formal contact between psychiatrists and psychotherapists.

Over the next three months the new psychiatry group became increasingly angry at and discontented with the apparent inequality of workloads between psychiatrists and psychotherapists, such as the referral of medication-only patients, all-night call, and responsibility for all emergencies, day or night for psychiatrists, while psychotherapists, on the other hand, had regular 40-hour workweeks, no after-hours responsibilities, and minimal billable hours. During the sixth month, the head of the psychiatry group confronted the clinics' director, a social worker, and the corporation's financial officer with data from the previous five months. A set of "demands" including the expectation of at least 28 billable hours per week from psychotherapists, a reduced number of patients referred outside the system, and a cap of 70 percent of medication-only patients referred to the psychiatry group.

The demands were accepted and implemented to some extent. For the next month and a half the work atmosphere seemed more efficient but less cordial between psychotherapists and the psychiatry group. In the ninth month the psychiatry group insisted that each psychotherapist share night call responsibility with the psychiatrists, which was met with considerable consternation by the psychotherapists. Finally, at the start of the eleventh month, things had settled down sufficiently enough for relations between both groups to be reasonably civil. In addition, utilization review data was encouraging for the financial officer and the psychiatry group. The psychiatry group was asked to renew its contract but waited until the middle of the twelfth month before signing it. Ultimately, the change efforts of the psychiatry group had been effective, but the time and emotional price paid was high for all parties involved.

This case illustrates some of the difficulties involved in effecting change in an organizational system, specifically an HCO. Had either the psychiatry group or the managed care corporation drawn on the expertise of an internal or external consultant, the change process might have been much less painful, and it would likely have been considerably shorter, lasting only a few months, rather than nearly a year. While the psychiatry group's efforts were ultimately success-ful, the risk it assumed in making "demands" was high and could have backfired. The expertise of a clinician-consultant would have greatly reduced the risk while increasing the probability that the expected changes would be realized.

In short, then, HCOs face the same degree and intensity of prob-lems that other work organizations face. Also consultants to HCOs can facilitate both the process of planned change and unplanned change. Given that HCOs are qualitatively different from other orga-nizations, though, the more consultants are familiar and respectful of these differences, outcomes are likely to be more efficacious and rewarding for all parties involved in the change process.

THE CONSULTANT AS CORPORATE CULTURE CHANGE AGENT

It is becoming increasingly clear that health care cost containment and managing health care disability in the workplace can only effec-tively be achieved when the culture of a work organization supports and encourages the value and goal that healthy workers are produc-tive and satisfied workers (Sperry, 1991b). Corporate culture is the loom on which health and productivity are woven together. Corpora-tions with cultures that convey shared values and emphasize active involvement of all workers tend to be more productive and healthy. On the other hand, corporations with dysfunctional cultures—such as a type A organizations that focus on "numbers," that is, producing more, faster, rather than on product quality and the value of workers—

are generally poor performers and exhibit the corporate precursors of worker illness and disability. A change in culture is often the fundamental factor in the improvement of a corporation's productivity, worker loyalty, and well-being (Farrier, 1993). Irrespective of whether the corporation is involved in manufacturing, service, or health care, corporate culture significantly affects worker health and productivity.

Previously, management has kept a low profile in health and disability matters, taking a passive oversight stance regarding employee, health provider, and insurer. Today's attention to regulating health care cost levels and the increasing complexity of health and disability issues in corporations now require a more proactive stance and involvement by management. Management's best strategy for containing health care costs is to specifically address the broader health system and the individualized needs of the covered population, instead of merely contracting with providers and case systems (Barge & Carlson, 1993).

Farrier (1993) cites a study that indicates that rising health care costs are threatening to eliminate all profits for the average Fortune 500 corporation if costs are not contained. He also cites a Washington Business Group on Health (WBGH) study that disability claims— including rising stress disability claims—are related to workplace factors. WBGH contends that management can control much of the disability linked to workplace conditions and that effective management can prevent much disability. Obviously, this is currently not happening at many corporations.

Because worker health and corporate productivity are so closely intertwined and because the core culture of an organization influences both health and productivity, worker health and productivity will be enhanced when the corporate culture reflects the values of health, rather than illness and disability. Clinician-consultants then have an important role to play in designing and implementing a coherent health and disability strategy that could not only improve work productivity but also worker health, well-being, and job satisfaction.

The function of managing health care involves developing an individualized health and disability strategy and implementing it within the corporation's health systems framework. The strategy would involve the entire spectrum of worker health from primary to tertiary prevention. It would also link the effective use of information and systems for measuring and rewarding job performance as well as positive health behavior and improved health status. Furthermore, it would involve reducing the fragmentation of health services delivery and internal conflict within the health and disability systems.

A second focus, developing and managing a corporate culture of health, involves the translation of the health and disability strategy into operational terms such that it can be executed by staff and line managers. This would include formal programs, including wellness, EAP, safety, and substance abuse, as well as informal management practices, such as worker involvement, supervisory behavior, and management of change. Worker health status would then be reflected in corporate financial health, as healthy, involved workers tend to be productive workers (Barge & Carlson, 1993).

Clinician-consultants with an interest and some experience in the process of corporate culture change and in the dynamics of health and wellness should be able to quickly and easily establish a niche for themselves in the consultation field since the need for corporate cultures to change from an illness and disability perspective to one of health and productivity is indeed great. For those contemplating this type of consultation, the book *The Executive's Guide to Controlling Health Care and Disability Costs* (Barge & Carlson, 1993) is highly recommended. In particular, it describes several strategies for changing corporate culture to control health care costs, workers' compensation, and disability costs, as well as to increase employee health and productivity.

COMMON CONSULTATION ISSUES IN HEALTH CARE ORGANIZATIONS

Case 1: Implementing a New Treatment Outcomes System

A social worker with previous program evaluation experience was asked to assist the medical director of a large outpatient psychiatry clinic, in the role of consultant, to implement a new provision in its capitation agreement: an accountability system for monitoring treatment outcomes. Previously, the clinic had only utilized a quarterly patient satisfaction survey as a measurement of outcomes, but neither the clinic staff nor the capitation manager felt this survey provided useful feedback.

The consultant arranged meetings with the capitation manager, the clinic director, and four clinicians to clarify the new system's purpose and the expected specifications and budget parameters. She then proceeded to evaluate the commercially available outcomes systems and chose one that most closely approximated the specifications the group wanted. Provisions for purchasing and implementing the system were arranged.

At the same time, the consultant scheduled a series of meetings to inform the clinic and support staff about the reasons for replacing the old system with the new one and how the outcome measures system worked. It was demonstrated using two actual cases from the clinic. Since the system provided regular feedback—every fourth session—from a case manager to the respective clinician, the consultant helped the staff to process their concerns about this "intrusion" on their previous "independent" practice style, which involved little oversight by clinic management. In a half-day meeting the consultant was able to allay clinicians' fears of breaching patient–therapist confidentiality, the "intrusion" of case management, and the inconvenience of a change in routine. After one year the consensus by staff was that the system was working effectively.

This consultation illustrates how an internal consultant was able to utilize technical expertise (clarification of clinic's need and evaluating different systems), training (demonstrating the system to staff), and process consultation (working through the staff's concerns about the impact of the system on their practice style). This consultation could also have been provided by an external consultant, but given that the internal consultant was well regarded by the clinic staff and that she would be utilizing the new system herself, in this case it was more likely that there would be greater acceptance of the system and less resistance with an internal consultant than if an external consultant had been retained.

Case 2: Bringing Harmony to a Deeply Divided Staff

Discontent and increasingly high turnover among the psychiatry staff of a large staff-model HMO led the Chief Operating Officer (COO) to retain the services of a health care consulting firm. The consultant proceeded to interview all of the remaining psychiatrists, some key administrators, and a cross section of other clinicians. Telephone survey data from former psychiatrists was also collected. The data was then analyzed and presented to the COO with a recommendation. Essentially, it was reported that the status and role of psychiatry staff had incrementally changed over the past four years from one in which psychiatrists served as team leaders with broad discretion to provide a full range of clinical services as well as to supervise the psychology and social work members of their team.

In the current situation, psychiatrists were relegated to functioning as medical and medication consultants, while a social worker or psychologist assumed the role of case manager/team leader. Some psychiatrists felt than nonmedical clinicians were insistent that psychiatrists "sign off" on their cases without the psychiatrist even seeing the patient and in some instances, to request the psychiatrist "sign off" on medication changes that these nonmedical therapists were advocating. Morale among the psychiatrists had plummeted, and the prospect of even more psychiatrists quitting was high.

The consultant formulated the problem as principally one of power/authority and role/communications, and secondarily, as one of morale/cohesion. Initially, the consultant met with the COO and presented the formulation along with recommendations to revise the reporting relationship among clinical personnel. The psychiatry staff's concerns about legal liability and ethical principles regarding the issues of medication and "signing off" and the liability and malpractice implications of these practices were emphasized. It was then agreed that the COO would meet with the entire staff to discuss these matters. The consultant would also be present at the meeting to provide input and support the COO.

At the meeting, the COO reviewed changes in the past five years of the HMO's history. He then proposed a new experiment regarding reporting relationships and included the rationale for it. In the experiment, which would begin immediately and be evaluated in six months, all clinical staff would have dual reporting relationships. They would report to their team's case manager for fiscal and administrative matters regarding their patients, but for clinical matters, they would report to the team's psychiatrist. Furthermore, role expectations for all clinicians were clarified and articulated, particularly regarding medical malpractice and ethical standards. Since the consultant had assessed that the staff had a high level of trust and respect for the COO, he predicted that the COO's recommendations would be accepted, not only because the rationale was reasonable but also because the change was an experiment that would be reviewed in six months. And the clinic staff did, indeed, successfully implement these changes.

This case illustrates a technical-expertise intervention (data collection and advisement of the COO) for power/authority and role/communication problems in an HCO. By advising the COO to conduct the meeting and to frame the proposed changes in terms of a legal and ethical necessity, instead of as a "turf war," unnecessary conflict was avoided. Finally, framing the changes as an experiment, which would be reviewed after a short time, further reduced the potential for splitting and negative catharsis, while also increasing morale and cohesion among staff, particularly the psychiatrists.

Case 3: Consultation Involving Staff Safety

An organizational psychology firm, specializing in workplace violence, was engaged by the director of human resources (HR) of a skilled nursing care facility, after both clinical and support staff raised concerns about their safety and that of their patients. Apparently, a former boyfriend of a nursing assistant had been stalking her for over a month. Recently, he had been seen waiting for her in the parking lot. But one day the man was seen roaming the halls of the facility, brandishing a pistol. Fortunately, the stalked employee had left earlier that day to keep a dental appointment, and the stalker left upon learning this. Nevertheless, staff and patients who had seen the man with the gun were extremely distressed.

The two attending consultants quickly ascertained that although the facility had a security department, it had no safety/violence policy or programming in place for the aftermath of a violent episode. Their consultation took two forms: immediate attention to the current crisis situation and a program to prevent violence in the future. The consultants met with the stalked nursing assistant to assess her need for protection and crisis counseling. They also met with the HR director, the director of nursing, and the director of security to formulate a strategy for dealing with the stalker. The goal was to insure that proper security measures were in place to protect the facility, its employees, and its patients.

Next, the consultants assisted the HR director in establishing a work safety committee made up of four employee representatives plus the security, nursing, and HR directors. Their task was to develop and implement a safety/violence policy. The consultants provided examples of policies used by other nursing facilities and assisted the group in tailoring a policy to their unique circumstances. In addition, education programs to teach staff to respond to threatening situations were planned and implemented as was a violence aftermath program involving a group stress debriefing intervention and individual crisis counseling. The consultants also were contracted to provide counseling services to staff and patients and their families for violence-related issues, beginning with the recent episode.

This consultation was quite straightforward and illustrates how the external consultants provided clinical, technical expertise and process consultation that converged on the problem of morale/cohesion—the high degree of fear and threat engendered by the stalker. Secondarily, this consultation focused on the goal/objectives domain—the safety policy and programs. While an external consultant provided these services, one or more knowledgeable staff clinicians could also have assumed the consulting role.

Case 4: Decreasing Dissatisfaction and Increasing Strategic Focus Among Clinicians

A social worker in a small behavioral health care network was asked to be an internal consultant to improve the network's effectiveness in service delivery. Dissatisfaction had been expressed by clients and referral sources about the increasing time lag between referral and initial appointment. Some also complained that certain clinicians were inflexible in their practice style and were committed only to longer-term psychotherapy. The consultant was charged with defining the network's problem areas and prescribing strategies for effectively managing them.

The consultant had previous experience consulting to community health centers, in addition to having considerable clinical experience. She began by informing all network providers of the nature of the consultation. Interviews and surveys were then utilized to gather data from administration, providers, and present and former clients. Information was collected, with the guarantee of confidentiality, on matters such as the network's mission, culture, practice styles, and staff relations. Based on analysis of the data, the consultant concluded that there was minimal consensus about the network's mission, which led to a lack of understanding of the functioning of the network and the roles of different clinical and administrative staff members. The result was overall dissatisfaction and the emergence of factions, particularly among clinicians.

The consultant prescribed a review and modification of the mission statement and practice styles. Furthermore, she recommended that a three-year strategic plan be developed and suggested that all staff be involved in this process. Subsequently, the consultant facilitated a mission statement review and strategic planning retreat. Out of this consultation came an updated mission statement and set of guidelines for caseloads, practice style, and indications/contraindications for longer-term versus time-limited psychotherapeutic services.

This case illustrates a situation in which the consulting focus was primarily on goals/objectives and secondarily on norms/standards. Specifically, this intervention established practice guidelines for caseloads and practice styles for the network's clinicians, and since the clinicians themselves were thoroughly involved in the process, they "owned" these guidelines. The case also illustrates how both technical expertise—data collection by survey and interviews—and process—mission and strategic planning meeting—consultation modes were utilized.

CONCLUDING NOTE

Today, all work organizations are being radically affected by the mounting changes occurring in our society. In some ways, HCOs are experiencing these demands for change, even more painfully than other organizations. Consequently, HCOs are in great need of assistance, and clinician-consultants can assist HCOs to adapt to these changes, either as internal or external consultants. In particular these services may be provided by in-house HCO psychologists, social workers, or psychiatrists who have sufficient training and confidence that they can shift from a clinical to a consulting role.

References

Adizes, I. (1988). *Corporate lifecycles.* Englewood Cliffs, NJ: Prentice-Hall.

American Psychiatric Association. (1994). *Diagnostic and statistical manual of mental disorders* (4th ed.). Washington, DC: Author.

Andreasen, N., & Black, D. (1991). *Introductory textbook of psychiatry.* Washington, DC: American Psychiatric Press.

Argyris, C. (1985). *Strategy, change and defensive routines.* Boston: Pitman.

Arthur, M., Hall, D., & Lawrence, B. (Eds.). (1989). *Handbook of career theory.* Cambridge, MA: Cambridge University Press.

Arthur, M., & Kram, K. (1989). Reciprocity at work: The separate, yet inseparable possibilities for individual and organizational development. In M. Arthur, D. Hall, & B. Lawrence (Eds.), *Handbook of career theory* (pp. 292–312). Cambridge, MA: Cambridge University Press.

Barge, B., & Carlson, J. (1993). *The executive's guide to controlling health care and disability costs: Strategy-based solutions.* New York: Wiley.

Beck, A. (1977). *Cognitive therapy and the emotional disorders.* New York: International Universities Press.

Beck, A. (1988). *Love is never enough.* New York: Harper & Row.

Beck, A., Freeman, A., & Associates. (1990). *Cognitive therapy of personality disorders.* New York: Guilford Press.

Beer, M. (1980). *Organization change and development: A systems view.* Glenview, IL: Scott, Foresman.

Bennis, W., & Nanus, B. (1986). *Leaders: The strategies for taking charge.* New York: Harper & Row.

Birnbaum, W. (1990). *If your strategy is so terrific, how come it doesn't work?* New York: AMACOM Books.

Bjorksten, O., & Steward, T. (1985). Marital status and health. In O. Bjorksten (Ed.), *New clinical concepts in marital therapy* (pp. 81–110). Washington, DC: American Psychiatric Press.

Blake, R., & Mouton, J. (1964). *The managerial grid.* Houston, TX: Gulf.

Blake, R., & Mouton, J. (1976). *Consultation.* Reading, MA: Addison-Wesley.

Blake, R., & Mouton, J. (1983). *Consultation* (2nd ed.). Reading, MA: Addison-Wesley.

Blake, R., & Mouton, J. (1985). *The managerial grid III.* Houston, TX: Gulf.

Blotnick, S. (1985). *The corporate steeplechase: Predictable crisis in a business career.* New York: Penguin Books.

Boustedt, A. (1990). Job-related mental stress claims expected to pass all others in '90s. *Psychiatric Times, 7* (11), 78.

Brammer, L., & Humberger, F. (1984). *Outplacement and inplacement.* Englewood Cliffs, NJ: Prentice-Hall.

Bramson, R. (1989). *Coping with the fast track blues.* New York: Doubleday.

Bromet, E., Parkinson, D., Curtis, C., et al. (1990). Epidemiology of depression and alcohol abuse dependence in a managerial and professional work force. *Journal of Occupational Medicine, 32*(10), 989–995.

Bronte, L. (1993). *The longevity factor.* New York: HarperCollins.

Busch, M. (1990). Linking strategic planning to the management of people. In J. Pfeiffer & J. Jones (Eds.), *The 1990 annual: Developing human resources* (pp. 265–270). San Diego, CA: University Associates.

Caplan, G. (1970). *The theory and practice of mental health consultation.* New York: Basic Books.

Chandler, A. (1962). *Strategy and structure.* Cambridge, MA: MIT Press.

Connor, D. (1993). *Managing at the speed of change.* New York: Villard Books.

Cowan, D. (1993). An executive map of organizational problems. In R. Golembiewski (Ed.), *Handbook of organizational consultation* (pp. 119–128). New York: Marcel Dekker.

Cox, A. (1974). *Work, love and friendship: Reflections on executive lifestyle.* New York: Simon & Schuster.

Cox, A. (1990). *Straight talk and practice of mental health consultation for Monday morning: Creating values, vision and vitality at work.* New York: Wiley.

Czander, W. (1993). *The psychodynamics of work and organizations.* New York: Guilford Press.

Dauer, C. (1989). Stress hits 25% of the workforce. *National Underwriter, 93*(44), 49–58.

Deal, J., & Kennedy, A. (1982). *Corporate cultures: The rites and rituals of corporate life.* Reading, MA: Addison-Wesley.

Deming, W. (1982). *Quality, productivity and competitive position.* Cambridge, MA: MIT Press.

Diamond, M. (1993). *The unconscious life of organizations.* Westport, CT: Quorum Books.

Dougherty, A. (1990). *Consultation: Practices and perspectives.* Pacific Grove, CA: Brooks/Cole.

Drucker, P. (1954). *The practice of management.* New York: Harper & Row.

Dumaine, B. (1991). The bureaucracy busters. *Fortune, 123*(13), 37–50.

Dychtwald, K., & Flower, J. (1990). *Age-wave.* New York: Bantam Books.

Dyer, W. (1977). *Team building.* Reading, MA: Addison-Wesley.

Egan, G. (1993). *Adding value: A systematic guide to business-driven management and leadership.* San Francisco: Jossey-Bass.

Ellis, A. (1972). *Executive leadership: A rational approach.* Secaucus, NJ: Citadel Press.

Enelow, A. (1991). Psychiatric disorders and work function. *Psychiatric Annals, 21* (1), 27–35.

Erikson, E. (1980). *Identity and the life cycle.* New York: Norton.

Farrier, M. (1993). Perspectives on intervening to improve employee health. In R. Golembiewski (Ed.), *Handbook of organizational consultation.* New York: Marcel Dekker.

Feldman, D. (1985). A taxonomy of intergroup conflict-resolution strategies. In J. Pfeiffer & L. Goodstein (Eds.), *The 1985 annual: Developing human resources* (pp. 169–175). San Diego, CA: University Associates.

Fiedler, F. (1967). *A theory of leadership effectiveness.* New York: McGraw-Hill.

Fine, R. (1990). *Love and work: The value system of psychoanalysis.* New York: Continuum.

Flambolz, E. (1990). *Growing pains: The transition from an entrepreneurship to a professionally managed firm.* San Francisco: Jossey-Bass.

Forisha-Kovach, B. (1984). *The flexible organization.* Englewood Cliffs, NJ: Prentice-Hall.

French, J., Rogers, W., & Cobb, S. (1974). A model of person–environment fit. In G. Goehlo, D. Harnburgh, & J. Adams (Eds.), *Coping and adaptation* (pp. 316–333). New York: Basic Books.

French, W., & Bell, C. (1995). *Organization development: Behavioral science interventions for organizational improvement* (5th ed.). Englewood Cliffs, NJ: Prentice-Hall.

Gallessich, J. (1982). *The profession and practice of consultation: A handbook for consultants, trainers, and consumers of consultation services.* San Francisco: Jossey-Bass.

Geraty, R. (1996). The use of outcomes assessment in managed care: Past, present and future. In L. Sederer & B. Dickey (Eds.), *Outcomes assessment in clinical practice* (pp. 129–138). Baltimore: Williams & Wilkins.

Gerber, M. (1986). *The e-myth: Why most businesses don't work and what to do about it.* San Francisco: Harper Business.

Glickhauf-Hughes, C., Hughes, G., & Wells, M. (1986). A developmental approach to treating dual-career couples. *American Journal of Family Therapy, 14* (3), 254–263.

Goodstein, L. (1978). *Consulting with human service systems.* Reading, MA: Addison-Wesley.

Gordon, R., & Gordon, K. (1991). Assessing the elements of biopsychosocial functioning. *Hospital and Community Psychiatry, 42* (5), 508–512.

Gordon, T. (1977). *LET: Leadership effectiveness training.* New York: Putnam.

Gottman, J. (1991). Predicting the longitudinal course of marriage. *Journal of Marital and Family Therapy, 17,* 3–7.

Gottman, J., & Levinson, R. (1988). The social psychology of marriage. In P. Noler & M. Fitzpatrick (Eds.), *Perspectives on marital interaction.* Philadelphia: Multilingual Matters.

Grant, B., & Robbins, D. (1993). Disability, workers' compensation and fitness for duty. In J. Kahn (Ed.), *Mental health in the workplace* (pp. 85–105). New York: Van Nostrand Reinhold.

Greenhaus, J. (1987). *Career management.* Chicago: Dryden Press.

Greiff, B., & Munter, P. (1980). *Tradeoffs: Executive, family and organizational life.* New York: New American Library.

Greiner, L. (1972). Evolution and revolution. *Harvard Business Review, 50,* 37–46.

Greiner, L., & Metzger, R. (1983). *Consulting to management.* Englewood Cliffs, NJ: Prentice-Hall.

Guerin, P., Fay, L., Burden, S., & Kautto, J. (1987). *The evaluation and treatment of marital conflict.* New York: Basic Books.

Hammer, M., & Champy, J. (1993). *Reengineering the corporation: A manifesto for business revolution.* New York: HarperCollins.

Hardesty, S., & Jacobs, N. (1986). *Success and betrayal: The crisis of women in corporate America.* New York: Simon & Schuster.

Harrison, M. (1987). *Diagnosing organizations: Methods, models and processes.* Newbury Park, CA: Sage.

Harrison, M. (1994). *Diagnosing organizations* (2nd ed.). Newbury Park, CA: Sage.

Helgesen, S. (1990). *The female advantage: Women's ways of leadership*. New York: Doubleday.

Hirschhorn, L. (1988). *The workplace within: Psychodynamics of organizational life*. Cambridge, MA: MIT Press.

Hirschhorn, L., & Gilmore, T. (1980). The application of family therapy concepts to influencing organizational behavior. *Administrative Science Quarterly, 25,* 18–37.

Howard, A. (1991). Industrial/organizational psychologists as practitioners. In D. Bray & Associates (Eds.), *Working with organizations and their people* (pp. 14–44). New York: Guilford Press.

Jamal, M., & Jamal, S. (1982). Work and non-work experiences of employees on fixed and rotating shifts: An empirical assessment. *Journal of Vocational Behavior, 20,* 282–293.

Jaques, E., & Clement, S. (1991). *Executive leadership: A practical guide to managing complexity*. Cambridge, MA: Blackwell Business.

Jenkins, S., & Calhoun, J. (1991). Teacher stress: Issues and interventions. *Psychology in the Schools, 28* (1), 60–70.

Karasek, R., & Theorell, T. (1990). *Health/work: Stress, productivity and the reconstruction of working life*. New York: Basic Books.

Kast, F., & Rosenzweig, J. (1973). *Contingency view of organizations and management*. Chicago: Science Research Associates.

Kates, N., Greiff, B., & Hagen, D. (1990). *The psychosocial impact of job loss*. Washington, DC: American Psychiatric Press.

Kaye, K. (1991). Penetrating the cycle of sustained conflict. *Family Business Review, 4* (1), 21–44.

Kelly, J. (1980). *How managers manage*. Englewood Cliffs, NJ: Prentice-Hall.

Kepner, E., & Tregoe, B. (1954). *The rational manager*. New York: Harper & Row.

Kets de Vries, M. (1989). *Prisoners of leadership*. New York: Wiley.

Kets de Vries, M. (1993). *Leaders, fools and imposters: Essays on the psychology of leadership*. San Francisco: Jossey-Bass.

Kets de Vries, M., & Miller, D. (1984). *The neurotic organization: Diagnosing and changing counterproductive styles of management*. San Francisco: Jossey-Bass.

Kets de Vries, M., & Miller, D. (1987). *Unstable at the top: Inside the troubled organization*. New York: New American Library.

Kiechel, W. (1988). Looking out for the executive alcoholic. In *Office hours: A guide to the managerial life* (pp. 216–233). Boston, MA: Little, Brown.

Klerman, G., Weissman, M., Rounsaville, B., et al. (1984). *Interpersonal psychotherapy of depression.* New York: Basic Books.

Kopp, R. (1995). *Metaphor therapy: Using client-generated metaphors in psychotherapy.* New York: Brunner/Mazel.

Kurpuis, S., Fuqua, D., Gibson, G., et al. (1995). An occupational analysis of consulting psychology: Results of a national survey. *Consulting Psychology Journal, 47* (2), 75–88.

Landon, L. (1990, May). Pump up your employees. *HR Magazine,* 34–37.

Larsen, R., & Felton, J. (Eds.). (1988). Psychiatric injury in the workplace (special issue). *Occupational Medicine: State of Art Reviews, 3* (4), 719–726.

Leavitt, H., & Bahrami, H. (1987). *Managerial psychology: Managing behavior in organizations* (5th ed.). Chicago: University of Chicago Press.

LeBoeuf, M. (1985). *The greatest management principle in the world.* New York: Putnam.

Levering, R. (1988). *A great place to work: What makes some employers so good and most so bad.* New York: Random House.

Levering, R., Moskowitz, M., & Katz, M. (1985). *The 100 best companies to work for in America.* New York: New American Library.

Levinson, D. (1978). *The seasons of a man's life.* New York: Knopf.

Levinson, H. (1972). *Organizational diagnosis.* Cambridge, MA: Harvard University Press.

Levinson, H. (1973). *The great jackass fallacy.* Boston: Harvard Graduate School of Business Administration.

Levinson, H. (1981). *Executive.* Cambridge, MA: Harvard University Press.

Levinson, H. (1983). Clinical psychology in organizational practice. In J. Manuso (Ed.), *Occupational clinical psychology* (pp. 7–13). New York: Praeger.

Levinson, H. (1991). Counseling with top management. *Consulting Psychology Bulletin 43* (1), 10–15.

Lewis, J., & Lewis, M. (1986). *Counseling programs for employees in the workplace.* Pacific Grove, CA: Brooks/Cole.

Lippitt, G., & Lippitt, R. (1978). *The consulting process in action.* San Diego, CA: University Associates.

Logan, W. (1989). The evaluation of the impaired physician. In R. Miller (Ed.), *Legal implications of hospital policies and practices* (New Directions for Mental Health Services, No. 41) (pp. 33–53). San Francisco: Jossey-Bass.

London, D., Monana, H., & Loeb, R. (1988). Worker's compensation and psychiatric disability. *Occupational Medicine: State of the Art Reviews, 3* (4), 595–609.

Lowman, R. (1985). Ethical practice of psychological consultation: Not an impossible dream. *Counseling Psychologist, 13* (3), 466–472.

Lowman, R. (1991). *The clinical practice of career assessment.* Washington, DC: American Psychological Association.

Lowman, R. (1993). *Counseling and psychotherapy of work dysfunctions.* Washington, DC: American Psychological Association.

Maccoby, M. (1976). *The gamesman: The new corporate leader.* New York: Simon & Schuster.

Maccoby, M. (1988). *Why work: Leading the new generation.* New York: Simon & Schuster.

Madden, T. (1987). *Woman vs. woman: The uncivil business war.* New York: AMACOM Books.

Maddi, S., & Kobasa, S. (1984). *The hardy executive: Health under stress.* Chicago: Dorsey.

Mantell, M. (1994). *Ticking bombs: Defusing violence in the workplace.* Burr Ridge, IL: Irwin.

Manuso, J. (1983). *Preface.* In J. Manuso (Ed.), *Occupational clinical psychology* (pp. vii–ix). New York: Praeger.

Manzini, A. (1988). *Organizational diagnosis.* New York: AMACOM Books.

Marks, M., & Mirvis, H. (1986). The merger syndrome. *Psychology Today, 20* (10), 3–42.

Martin, S. (1995, March). Fox identifies top threats to professional psychology. *APA Monitor, 26* (3), 44.

Maslow, A. (1954). *Motivation and personality.* New York: Harper & Row.

Matteson, M., & Ivancevich, J. (1982). *Job stress and health.* New York: Free Press.

Matteson, M., & Ivancevich, J. (1987). *Controlling work stress.* San Francisco: Jossey-Bass.

Matteson, M., & Ivancevich, J. (1990). Merger and acquisition stress: Fear and uncertainty at mid-career. *Prevention in Human Services, 8* (1), 139–158.

Mayo, E. (1933). *The human problems of an industrial civilization.* New York: Macmillan.

McCall, M., Lombardo, M., & Morrison, A. (1988). *The lessons of experience: How successful executives develop on the job.* Lexington, MA: Lexington Books.

McCann, J., & Gilkey, R. (1988). *Joining forces: Creating and managing successful mergers and acquisitions.* Englewood Cliffs, NJ: Prentice-Hall.

McClelland, D. (1975). *Power: The inner experience.* New York: Irvington Press.

McCubbin, H., & Thompson, A. (1989). *Balancing work and family life on Wall Street.* Edina, MN: Burgess International Group.

McGregor, D. (1960). *The human side of enterprise.* New York: McGraw-Hill.

McGregor, D., Bennis, W., & McGregor, C. (Eds). (1967). *The Professional Manager.* New York: McGraw-Hill.

Merry, U., & Brown, G. (1987). *The neurotic behavior of organizations.* New York: Gardner.

Metzger, R. (1993). *Developing a consulting practice.* Newbury Park, CA: Sage.

Meyerson, A., & Fine, T. (1987). *Psychiatric disability: Clinical, legal, and administrative dimensions.* Washington, DC: American Psychological Association.

Miller, D. (1990). *The Icarus paradox: How exceptional companies bring about their own downfall.* San Francisco: Harper Business.

Miller, L. (1989). *Barbarians to bureaucrats: Corporate life cycle strategies.* New York: Fawcett Columbine.

Millon, T., & Everly, G. (1985). *Personality and its disorders.* New York: Wiley.

Mintzberg, H. (1973). *The nature of managerial work.* New York: Harper & Row.

Minuchin, S. (1974). *Families and family therapy.* Cambridge, MA: Harvard University Press.

Mirvis, P. (1991). *Managing the merger: Making it work.* Englewood Cliffs, NJ: Prentice-Hall.

Mitchell, J., & Bray, G. (1990). *Emergency services stress.* Englewood Cliffs, NJ: Prentice-Hall.

Morgan, G. (1986). *Images of organization.* Beverly Hills, CA: Sage.

Morrison, A., White, R., & Velsen, E. (1987). *Breaking the glass ceiling.* Reading, MA: Addison-Wesley.

Morrow, P. (1985). Retirement planning: Rounding out the career planning process. In D. Meyers (Ed.), *Employee problem prevention and counseling* (pp. 301–316). Westport, CT: Quorum Books.

Moss, L. (1981). *Management stress.* Reading, MA: Addison-Wesley.

Muchinsky, P. (1990). *Psychology applied to work* (3rd ed.). Pacific Grove, CA: Brooks/Cole.

Muchinsky, P. (1993). *Psychology applied to work* (4th ed). Pacific Grove, CA: Brooks/Cole.

Murphy, L., & Sorenson, S. (1988). Employee behavior before and after stress management. *Journal of Organization Behavior, 9* (2), 173–182.

Naj, A. (1994, August 29). Corporate therapy: The latest addition to executive suite is psychologist's couch. *Wall Street Journal,* pp. A1, A5.

Nevis, E. (1987). *Consulting in organizations: A Gestalt approach.* Cleveland, OH: Gestalt Institute of Cleveland Press.

Noer, D. (1993). *Healing the wounds: Overcoming the trauma of layoffs and revitalizing downsized organizations.* San Francisco: Jossey-Bass.

Oldham, J., & Morris, L. (1990). *Personality self-portrait.* New York: Bantam Books.

Ouchi, W. (1981). *Theory Z: How American business can meet the Japanese challenge.* New York: Avon.

Page, C., & Selden, C. (1987). *Asking just the right business questions.* New York: Crown.

Pascale, R. (1990). *Managing on the edge: How the smartest companies use conflict to stay ahead.* New York: Simon & Schuster.

Pasick, R. (1990). Raised to work. In R. Meth & R. Pasick (Eds.), *Men in therapy: The challenge of change* (pp. 35–53). New York: Guilford Press.

Pelletier, K., & Lutz, R. (1991). Healthy people–healthy business: A critical review of stress management programs in the workplace. In S. Weiss, J. Fielding, & A. Baum (Eds.), *Health at Work* (pp.189–204). Hillsdale, NJ: Erlbaum.

Peters, T., & Austin, N. (1985). *A passion for excellence: The leadership difference.* New York: Random House.

Peters, T., & Waterman, R. (1982). *In search of excellence: Lessons from America's best-run companies.* New York: Harper & Row.

Pfeiffer, J., & Goodstein, L. (Eds.). (1985). *The 1985 annual: Developing human resources.* San Diego, CA: University Associates.

Pfeiffer, J., Goodstein, L., & Nolan, T. (1989). *Shaping strategic planning.* Glenview, IL. Scott, Foresman.

Potts, T., & Sykes, A. (1993). *Executive talent: How to identify and develop the best.* Homewood, IL: Business One Irwin.

Quick, J., Nelson, D., & Quick, J. (1990). *Stress and challenge at the top: The paradox of the successful executive.* New York: Wiley.

Reddy, W. (1994). *Intervention skills: Process consultation for small groups and terms.* San Diego, CA: Pfeiffer.

Rice, D. (1979). *Dual-career marriage: Conflict and treatment.* New York: Free Press.

Rigaud, M. (1989). A model of consultation in occupational psychiatry. *Hospital and Community Psychiatry, 40* (7), 745–747.

Rippe, J. (1989a). *Fit for success: Proven strategies for executive health.* Englewood Cliffs, NJ: Prentice-Hall.

Rippe, J. (1989b). CEO fitness: The performance plus. *Psychology Today, 23*(5), 49–53.

Rizzo, A., & Mendez, C. (1990). *The integration of women in management: A guide for human resources and management development specialists.* Westport, CT: Quorum Books.

Robbins, H., & Finley, M. (1995). *Why teams don't work.* Princeton, NJ: Peterson's/Pacesetter Books.

Roskies, E. (1987). *Stress management for the healthy type A: Theory and practice.* New York: Guilford Press.

Rudisill, J. R., Painter, A., & Pollock, S. (1992). Psychological consultation to outplacement firms. *Innovations in Clinical Practice, 11,* 425–430.

Schein, E. (1987). *Process consultation: Lessons for managers and consultants, Vol 2.* Reading, MA: Addison-Wesley.

Schneider, W. (1994). *The reengineering alternative: A plan for making your current culture work.* Burr Ridge, IL: Irwin.

Sekaran, U., & Hall, D. (1989). A synchronism in dual-career and family linkages. In M. Arthur, D. Hall, & B. Lawrence (Eds.), *Handbook of career theory* (pp. 159–180). Cambridge, MA: Cambridge University Press.

Seligman. M. (1989). Explanatory style: Predicting depression, achievement, and health. In M. Yapko (Ed.), *Brief therapy approaches to treating anxiety and depression* (pp. 5–32). New York: Brunner/Mazel.

Short, R. (1985). Structural family therapy and consultative practices in organizations. *Consultation, 4*(4), 207–219.

Smith, E., & Siwolop, S. (1988). Stress: The test Americans are failing. *Business Week, 30* (47), 74–78.

Sommerville, K. (1991). Corporate psychology and the soul of the CEO. *Consulting Psychology Bulletin, 43* (1), 22–24.

Speller, J. (1989). *Executives in crisis: Recognizing and managing the alcoholic, drug-addicted or mentally ill executive.* San Francisco: Jossey-Bass.

Sperry, L. (1990). Development of organizations. *Human Development, 10* (2), 26–31.

Sperry, L. (1991a). Blind leadership and stumbling organizations. *Human Development, 11*(4), 24–29.

Sperry, L. (1991b). Enhancing corporate health, mental health, and productivity. *Individual Psychology, 47*(2), 247–254.

Sperry, L. (1993). *Psychiatric consultation in the workplace.* Washington, DC: American Psychiatric Press.

Sperry, L. (1994a). Consultation skills: Individual and organizational diagnosis. *Individual Psychology, 50,* 231–244.

Sperry, L. (1994b), Organizational psychiatry and occupational psychology: A look at similarities and differences. *Academy of Organizational and Occupational Psychiatry Newsletter, 3* (2), 4–5.

Sperry, L. (1995a). *Handbook of diagnosis and treatment of the DSM-IV personality disorders.* New York: Brunner/Mazel.

Sperry, L. (1995b). The workplace psychiatrist's focus: Organizational, clinical–organizational, or clinical interventions? *Academy of Organizational and Occupational Psychiatry Newsletter, 4* (2), 5–7.

Sperry, L. (1996). Work-focused psychotherapy with executives. *Individual Psychology, 52* (1), 48–57.

Sperry, L., Brill, P., Howard, K., & Grissom, G. (1996). *Treatment outcomes in psychotherapy and psychiatric interventions.* New York: Brunner/Mazel.

Sperry, L., Gudeman, J., Blackwell, B., & Faulkner, L. (1992). *Psychiatric case formulations.* Washington, DC: American Psychiatric Press.

Sperry, L., & Hess, L. (1974). *Contact counseling: Techniques for developing people in organizations.* Reading, MA: Addison-Wesley.

Steele, F. (1982). *The role of the internal consultant.* Boston: CBI.

Steiner, G. (1979). *Strategic planning: What every manager must know.* New York: Free Press.

Stoltz-Loike, M. (1992). *Dual-career couples: New perspectives in counseling.* Alexandria, VA: American Counseling Association.

Stumpf, S., & Mullen, T. (1992). *Taking charge: Strategic leadership in the middle game.* Englewood Cliffs, NJ: Prentice-Hall.

Sussman, M. (Ed.). (1995). *A perilous calling: The hazards of psychotherapy practice.* New York: Wiley.

Tannenbaum, R., & Schmidt, W. (1958). How to choose a leadership pattern. *Harvard Business Review, 36* (2), 95–101.

Taylor, F. (1911/1967). *The principles of scientific management.* New York: Norton.

Tobias, L. (1990). *Psychological consulting to management: A clinician's perspective.* New York: Brunner/Mazel.

United States General Accounting Office. (1991, May). *Management practices: U.S. companies improving performance through quality efforts.* National Security and International Affairs Division.

Uris, A. (1964). *Techniques of leadership.* New York: McGraw-Hill.

Van Fleet, D. (1988). *Contemporary management.* Boston: Houghton Mifflin.

Waclawski, J., Church, A., & Burke, W. (1995). Women and men as organizational development practitioners: An analysis of differences and similarities. *Consulting Psychology Journal, 47* (2), 89–107.

Wall, B., Solum, R., & Sobol, M. (1992). *The visionary leader: How to build leadership, trust, and participation in your company.* Rocklin, CA: Prima.

Walton, R. (1969). *Interpersonal peacemaking: Confrontation and third-party consultation.* Reading, MA: Addison-Wesley.

Ward, J. (1987). *Keeping the family business healthy: How to plan for continuing growth, profitability, and family leadership.* San Francisco: Jossey-Bass.

Weber, M. (1947). *Theory of social and economic organization.* (T. Parsons, Trans.). New York: Free Press.

Weisbord, M. (1978). *Organizational diagnosis: A workbook of theory and practice.* Reading, MA: Addison-Wesley.

Whyman, A., & Underwood, R. (1991). The psychiatric examination in worker's compensation. *Psychiatric Annuals, 21* (1), 36–52.

Zaleznik, A. (1989). *The managerial mystique: Restoring leadership in business.* New York: Harper & Row.

Zaleznik, A. (1990). *Executive's guide to motivating people: How Freudian theory can turn good executives into better leaders.* Chicago: Bonus Books.

Zedeck, S. (Ed.). (1992). *Work, families and organization.* San Francisco: Jossey-Bass.

Name Index

Adizes, I., 45, 50
Anderson, R. M., 137
Andreasen, N., 70
Argyris, C., 141, 142
Arthur, M., 44, 98
Austin, N., 65

Bahrami, H., 31, 39
Barge, B., 208, 209
Baum, A., 118
Beck, A., 28, 188
Beer, M., 72
Bell, C., 7
Bennis, W., 38, 66
Birnbaum, W., 51, 52, 54
Bjorksten, O., 62
Black, D., 70
Blackwell, B., 11
Blake, R., 26, 38, 65, 80, 81, 82, 83
Blotnick, S., 174, 175
Boustedt, A., 128
Brammer, L. M., 126, 127
Bramson, R., 174
Bray, G., 138, 140
Brill, P., 148, 149
Bromet, E., 179
Bronte, L., 108
Brown, G., 65
Burden, S., 62
Burke, W., 160
Burr, D., 53, 55
Busch, M., 41

Calhoun, J., 117
Caplan, G., 24
Carlson, J., 208, 209
Champy, J., 115, 116
Chandler, A., 85
Chaplin, C., 58, 60
Church, A., 160
Clement, S., 38, 57, 67
Cobb, S., 44
Connor, D., 141, 142
Cowan, D., 83
Cox, A., 65, 200
Czander, W., 27, 28

Dauer, C., 22
de Mik, L., 137
Deal, J., 32
Deming, W., 66, 67
Diamond, M., 27
Dickey, B., 149
Dorton, A., 108
Dougherty, A., 10, 23
Drucker, P., 64
Dumaine, B., 43
Durcan, J., 105
Dychtwald, K., 107
Dyer, W. G., 108, 109

Egan, G., 119
Ellis, A., 28
Enelow, A., 128
Erikson, E., 78, 174
Everly, G., 161

Subject Index